DYNAMICS OF PROSTAR

A Powerful Technique
for Mastering MicroPro® Software

DYNAMICS OF PROSTAR

A Powerful Technique
for Mastering MicroPro® Software

Jane Davis

DOW JONES-IRWIN
Homewood, Illinois 60430

MicroPro, WordStar, MailMerge, and SuperSort are registered trademarks of
MicroPro International Corporation. CalcStar, DataStar, ReportStar, InfoStar,
and SpellStar are trademarks of MicroPro International Corporation, San
Rafael, California.
CP/M is a trademark of Digital Research of Pacific Grove, California.
MS-DOS is a trademark of the Microsoft Corporation.
IBM is a trademark of International Business Machines Corporation (as is IBM PC and PC
DOS).

ISBN 0-87094-669-2

Library of Congress Catalog Card No. 85-70981

Printed in the United States of America

1 2 3 4 5 6 7 8 9 0 ML 3 2 1 0 9 8 7 6

Acknowledgments

No technical book of this nature is ever the product of one person entirely. I must thank those who have helped with the production of the book—my agent, Bill Gladstone, of Waterside Associates, and especially Barry Rubin (the other half of Davis Rubin Associates Ltd. and, incidentally, my husband) who has performed the sterling task of checking the examples for accuracy and did much of the development of the exercises for the transaction processing chapter.

Various companies have kindly loaned equipment for the testing of the MicroPro software under MS-DOS and IBM DOS. I must thank Derrick Maddern of Sanyo, U.K., for the MBC-555 (DOS 1); Chandru Idnani of the London Computer Centre for the IBM-compatible, multiuser, North Star Dimension system (IBM DOS version 2); and IBM United Kingdom Ltd. for the PC/AT (IBM DOS version 3). I used all these machines for checking the performance of the latest IBM versions of the MicroPro software (I used my own Kaypro 10 for the CP/M versions) and finally wrote the bulk of the text on the PC/AT.

Jane Davis

Introduction

My aim in this guide is to show you a clear path through the MicroPro software programs and to help you understand the way they work in concert with each other, yet enable you to achieve results within a very short time. This book describes the integrated method for mastering MicroPro software that I have developed over the past four years. Within only one or two days you will have gained a comprehensive overview of the main MicroPro programs, and you will learn to apply the integrated technique to your own particular problems from Day 1—even if you are a complete beginner to computing. By the end of Part Two, you will be very experienced in the day-to-day manipulation of the MicroPro software and will be ready to apply the techniques you have mastered to start building and developing your own customized business systems. Finally, you will be able to use this experience to start automating your daily office procedures with the transaction processing techniques described in detail in the advanced InfoStar tutorial.

Part One of the book starts off by familiarizing you with the computer, the handling of floppy disks (and the hard disk if you have one), and the basic workings of your computer operating system (covering both CP/M and MS-DOS).

In Chapter 2 you learn how to copy data from one disk drive to another and go on to create the tutorial disk (or hard disk user area) that you will use throughout the book for the exercises.

Chapter 3 covers the basics of WordStar—typing a standard letter, cursor controls, editing, and printing files; and, for those of you with WordStar and MailMerge only, there is a section on entering data files in WordStar.

In Chapter 4 you design a form for entry of customers' names and addresses using FormGen, then enter and edit data in DataStar, learn how to retrieve the data you have entered, sort the names and addresses into alphabetical order using FormSort, and produce a simple report with ReportStar.

In Chapter 5 you will see how all these programs link together to produce personalized letters and envelopes using MailMerge. These first five chapters that make up Part One can be worked through in one or two days—ideally split into several individual two- or three-hour sessions. By the end of this time you will have produced a merge printed mailing to a selected group of customers. By the end of the first week, with continued practice, you will be typing away happily in WordStar, designing your own forms in DataStar, producing reports in ReportStar, and confidently operating your computer and printer.

Part Two of the book takes you through each of the programs in more depth and introduces some new ones—the spelling checker and correction programs, CorrectStar/SpellStar; the spreadsheet program, CalcStar; and the separate sorting program, SuperSort. It starts with an in-depth tutorial on WordStar, followed in Chapter 7 by CorrectStar/SpellStar.

CalcStar follows next, showing you how to use the spreadsheet to produce sales projections, or to calculate your business expenses, for example.

Chapters 9, 10, and 11 are three full tutorials on InfoStar. The first covers advanced form design in great detail, showing you how to create a suite of linked forms. The second covers data entry and retrieval in DataStar and the generation of custom-designed reports using ReportStar. The third uncovers the hidden power of InfoStar, showing you how to automate your daily business activities with transaction processing; a detailed example shows you how you can run just one report to produce invoices from entered purchase orders, automatically debit your inventory with the items ordered, and give you the turnover for the day.

Chapter 12 covers SuperSort, the powerful and flexible sorting program.

Finally, Chapter 13 is a tutorial on advanced MailMerge techniques, which covers everything from merge printing letters, envelopes, and labels, through conditional printing of selected data, file insertion of boilerplate paragraphs, to restructuring your data files.

Examples are continued from chapter to chapter all the way through the book, emphasizing the importance of integrating the MicroPro packages. There are a glossary of computer terms, three appendixes containing listings of the DataStar and ReportStar forms, and a full index.

J.D.

Contents

tribute Definitions. Designing Your Own Forms: *Index Fields. Derived Fields.* Copying Forms. Conclusion.

1

General Preparations for Tutorials

The Computer Keyboard
The Disk Drives and Floppy Disks
The Computer Operating System
Preparation of New Disks

This manual is essentially a practical guide. It is designed for you to use at your side as you sit in front of your computer. At the head of each chapter are listed the key topics to be covered in the chapter. These may or may not represent subheadings as they appear in the text.

The aim of this chapter is to take you step by step through the essential procedures for preparing the floppy disks you will use for lessons and exercises in subsequent chapters. By the time you have completed the first two chapters, you will have gained confidence in your ability to operate your computer and will be ready to get the most out of your MicroPro software.

In this chapter I am going to assume that you have just received your new computer and that you know virtually nothing about computer operation, floppy disks, operating systems, or MicroPro software. You should have read through your computer's User's Guide and followed the instructions for connecting the power cable, the keyboard, and your printer. Throughout this guide I will avoid computer jargon as much as possible, and I will attempt to define any special terms as they appear in the text. When such words occur for the first time they will be printed in *italics* and, when appropriate, will be included in the Glossary of Terms at the back of the manual.

Although there is wide variation in the precise specifications of different microcomputer systems (the *hardware*), the MicroPro *software* is virtually independent of the computer that runs it. However, the *operating system* must be either CP/M or MS-DOS (or compatible with these). When you set up your new computer system, the software must be installed for your particular computer model—that is, each program must be "told" what system it is running on so that the hardware, software, and operating system will work together. If you bought your computer and software from a dealer, he or she normally will have done this for you. If you have to do it yourself, you will find software installation instructions in each MicroPro software reference manual. All the latest MS-DOS versions of MicroPro software except CorrectStar (see Chapter 7) are ready to run on IBM or truly IBM-compatible systems and will need minimal installation.

Before you start the tutorials on MicroPro software, you need to familiarize yourself with your particular computer system. I will take you on a brief tour of your keyboard, disk drives, and floppy disks. If you are new to MicroPro software but familiar with the operation of your computer, go straight to the section in Chapter 2 entitled Preparing Your Tutorial Disk.

THE COMPUTER KEYBOARD

Most microcomputer keyboards are similar to a typewriter keyboard, but they have some extra keys. These have specific functions that will be described as they are encountered in the lessons. If you are a touch typist it will probably take a little time to adjust to the new feel of the keyboard and to the positions of the extra keys. You will find the keys very light and responsive, and don't forget that (on most computers) the keys will *repeat* if you hold them down for more than a moment or two. When the computer is switched on, a highlighted square or bar, called the *cursor*, indicates your position on the line.

RETURN
ENTER
Pressing the **Return** key—marked **Enter** on the IBM and some other computer keyboards—will either move the cursor to the beginning of the next line (like a carriage return on a typewriter) or enter the command you have typed on the screen. Note that if you have a *numeric keypad* (a set of keys usually to the right of the main

keyboard and laid out like the numbers on a calculator) the key with this same function is always labeled **Enter**.

CONTROL

The **Control** key, which may be labeled **Ctl** or **Ctrl** on your keyboard, is used in conjunction with other keys—rather like a **Shift** key—to perform specific functions both in the operating system and within programs such as WordStar.

ESCAPE

Pressing this key, usually marked **Esc**, will usually allow you to escape from a mistake you have made within a program. For example, after you type an illegal or unintended command, pressing **Esc** takes you back to a position where you can try again.

DELETE

The **Delete** key, marked **Del**, has two modes of operation according to whether you are inside a program (such as WordStar) or in the operating system (that is, typing commands on the screen next to the A> prompt). In WordStar, pressing the **Del** key causes the cursor to move backward over the text, deleting it a character at a time. In the operating system it deletes text typed in, but it causes the characters to "echo" on the screen as they are deleted. Some manufacturers have disabled this function of the **Del** key in the operating system, since it can be confusing.

BACK SPACE

The **Back Space** key, sometimes labeled **BS** (or, on the IBM, with an arrow pointing left) again has two modes of operation. In the operating system, it moves the cursor backward over text already entered, deleting it a character at a time; in WordStar it moves the cursor backward without deleting text.

CAPS LOCK

This is equivalent to a **Shift Lock** key on a typewriter but, as the abbreviation suggests, it produces capital *letters* only and does *not* shift the number or symbol keys. **Caps Lock** is very useful for typing mixtures of uppercase letters and numerals.

CURSOR CONTROL KEYS

The keys that are labeled with **Arrows** move the cursor in the direction of the arrow (**Up, Down, Left**, or **Right**). These are often linked to WordStar functions and will be described at the appropriate point in the lessons. The arrow keys usually are in the numeric keypad.

NUMERIC KEYPAD

Most microcomputers have a calculator-style set of keys on the right of the keyboard, called the numeric keypad. It has the numbers 0 to 9, and probably a decimal point, plus and minus signs, a comma, and an **Enter** key. The keypad is very useful if you have many numbers to enter (in CalcStar, for example). You may find its keys have a second function—they can also be used to move the cursor in WordStar and other programs. To select the numeric function, you use a key labeled **Num Lock** or something similar (look in your own computer's User's Guide for details).

FUNCTION KEYS

Most microcomputers have a set of function keys, either in a row at the top of the keyboard or in a block on the left side; they may be a different color than the main keys and are usually labeled **F1** to **F10** (or whatever number of keys there are). They are programmed to perform various *functions* in the operating system or within specific programs using only a single keystroke; hence, function keys save the need for pressing the Control key and one or more additional keys at the same time.

THE DISK DRIVES AND FLOPPY DISKS

Your computer system will have at least one *floppy disk drive* that accommodates *floppy disks* (also called *diskettes*) of 3.5, 5.25, or 8 inches in size. To run MicroPro software efficiently, you need two floppy disk drives, though you can manage with one drive if you are running only WordStar and CalcStar, for example. Many business computers have just one floppy disk drive and a built-in *hard disk*. A hard disk has a considerably greater *capacity* than a floppy disk and this makes it very much easier to run the whole suite of MicroPro programs. Before you start using your microcomputer, you need to understand some terminology associated with disks and disk drives.

FORMAT Before a floppy disk can be used in any computer, it must be *formatted*—that is, its surface must be organized electronically to accept and store information in a way that is usually specific to each model of computer. The disk surface is divided into a set number of concentric *tracks*, which are further subdivided into *sectors* (like slices of pie). Any piece of information (*data*) stored on a disk can be found by a combination of its track and sector number.

According to your system, data may be stored on one side of the floppy disk only (*single-sided*), and either *single-* or *double-density* (the tracks and sectors are packed closer together on double-density disks). With *double-sided* floppy disks, data is stored on both sides of the disk, giving twice the *capacity*, and may be either single- or double-density. Double-sided, double-density disks are sometimes referred to as *quad-density*.

CAPACITY The capacity of floppy disks, hard disks, and computer memory is measured in *bytes*: one character (i.e., a letter, a number or a space) occupies at least 1 byte. A measurement of 1,024 bytes is called 1 kilobyte (usually abbreviated to 1K—the K implies 1,000), so if your disks have a capacity of 360K, you can store more than 360,000 characters on each disk. One million bytes is termed a *Megabyte* or 1MB: a hard disk can store between 5 and 20 million characters, or more (i.e., 5 to 20MB).

HARD DISK The hard disk in a single-user business microcomputer is usually built-in, and may be delivered to you preformatted and ready to load with software. You should check your User's Guide to see how the manufacturer or dealer has divided up the large capacity of the hard disk. If your disk has a 10MB capacity, you may find that you have, for example, two areas of 5MB each, giving you two "drives" labeled A and B (or C and D if the floppy disk drives are labeled A and B).

USER AREA The manufacturer may also have taken advantage of a built-in function in CP/M to divide each of the two hard disk "drives" into up to 15 *user areas* labeled, for example, A0 to 14 and B0 to B14, respectively. It is very convenient to set up the hard disk in this way so that you can use different user areas for different programs; if more than one person uses the same computer, you can allocate a different user area for each person's work.

PARTITIONS In multiuser MS-DOS systems with a built-in hard disk, it is often possible to divide the hard disk into drives and/or partitions. For example, the North Star Dimension multiuser system has a hard disk drive labeled C which is the *public partition*; the system manager can allocate one or more *shared partitions* (for storing shared programs, such as WordStar and InfoStar) and as many *personal partitions* to individual users as required.

The optional hard disk on the IBM PC/AT can be divided into one to four partitions, only one of which can be used at any time. Partitions can be made using MS-DOS or with "non-DOS" software, such as CP/M 86 or Concurrent CP/M, and then labeled accordingly.

THE COMPUTER OPERATING SYSTEM

Business computers do not generally have built-in software, so they will not perform any function until an operating system has been loaded into the internal memory of the computer. This operating system, either CP/M or MS-DOS, will have been supplied to you on the manufacturer's distribution disk and you should have a working copy of it labeled, for example, CP/M or MS-DOS WORKING DISK. The IBM PC family runs its own version of MS-DOS called PC DOS: in all the following tutorials, where MS-DOS is mentioned you can assume that PC DOS is included.

A computer operating system is simply a unique set of commands that drive the inner workings of the computer and its associated *devices* (keyboard, screen, disk drives, printer)—in other words, a special type of program. It controls all the internal and external functions of the machine. For example, the operating system ensures that: when you type on the keyboard, what you type appears on the screen; when you decide to print a letter from a file stored on your disk, the printer is activated correctly; and when you ask for a directory listing of all the files on a floppy disk, you see the list appear on your screen.

Booting Up the System

When you switch on (*power up*) the computer and load the operating system into memory, the process is called *booting up* the system, derived from the idea that the computer is "pulling itself up by its bootstraps" that is, starting up from scratch without built-in preprogramming. In everyday language, starting up the computer transfers a set of instructions from the floppy or hard disk into the computer's memory, thus preparing the computer to accept the commands you type on the keyboard and to act upon them in a logical way (assuming you get the instructions right!).

On some hard disk systems, booting is automatic when you power up the computer; you do not need a floppy disk in the disk drive in order to start up the computer. You should look in your User's Guide to check the startup procedure for your particular hard disk system.

On floppy disk systems, the computer can be started up from any floppy disk with an operating system on it—normally a CP/M or MS-DOS working disk, though any disk can be formatted to include the operating system. The startup procedure (described in detail later) is first to switch on the computer, then to insert the floppy disk into the disk drive labeled A or 1, and close the latch, and finally to press the **Return** key (or as instructed in your User's Guide) to activate the disk drive.

NOTE: *Never* turn the computer on or off with a floppy disk in the disk drive.

Having familiarized yourself with the computer hardware, you can now prepare the disks to use for the tutorials on MicroPro software.

PREPARATION OF NEW DISKS

You will start by formatting new disks (remember, this organizes the surface of the disk electronically, so that information is stored correctly) and then adding an operating system to them so that they can be used for starting up the computer.

If you have a hard disk system, you should read the sections in your User's Guide that tell you how to format and add an operating system to new floppy disks: prepare a box of 10 floppy disks following these instructions. Note the names of the drives—probably A and B for floppy disk drives and C for the hard disk (if the hard disk has been divided into more than one "drive," you may have other physical drive names as well, such as C, D, and E). It may be a good idea to pencil in any differences in drive names at the appropriate positions as you come to them, in the following lessons and tutorials.

Floppy disks are fairly delicate and should be handled with great care; when you take a disk out of its paper envelope, make sure you do not touch the parts that are exposed through the disk sleeve, since oil from your fingers may stop that area of disk from being correctly accessed and read. Never smoke or drink around your computer. Keep all disks away from magnetic fields—this includes ringing telephones and the casing of a hard disk drive, as well as more obvious sources of magnetism. Do not write on a disk label with a ball-point pen (you should write disk labels before you apply them or use a felt-tip pen), and do not bend or fold the disk. By the time you have formatted a box of disks and copied an operating system on to some of them, you should overcome any fear you may have had of handling the disks and getting them safely in and out of the disk drives. Let's go!

Step-by-Step Procedure

1. Power up your computer and insert your CP/M or MS-DOS system disk into drive A.
2. Insert a new disk into drive B and close the drive doors.
3. Boot up the system by pressing the **Return** key (or as instructed in your User's Guide).

You will see the "disk drive active" light glow red as the operating system is copied from the floppy disk into a section of the computer memory. A line or two of information about the version of operating system will appear on the screen and in CP/M systems, a *prompt*, A>, on the left. This symbol is called a prompt because it is "prompting" you to type an instruction. In MS-DOS systems, you will be asked to enter the date (usually in the format of month-day-year or month/day/year) and then the time in hours and minutes. Only when you have entered this information (or pressed **Return** to bypass them) will the A> prompt appear. On more sophisticated MS-DOS systems, there is a built-in clock microprocessor that always "knows" the time and date, so you don't need to enter it every time you power up or reset the computer. Whenever you see the A> prompt, you know you are *logged on* to drive A, and the computer is waiting for you to give it a command.

The term "logged on to drive A" means that you have the A> prompt on the screen, and thus you are currently working on drive A. If you now switch to drive B (by typing **B:** and pressing the **Return** key), you would be "logged on" to drive B, and you would see the B> prompt on the screen. On hard disk MS-DOS systems, you will normally boot up from the hard disk drive and will have a C> prompt on the screen, indicating that drive C is the logged drive, and drives A and B are your floppy disk drives.

To get back to drive A (or C if you have a hard disk), type **A:** or **C:**. Now the computer is ready to obey your every command!

Try your first instruction—next to the prompt type **DIR** and press **Return**. Your screen will display the directory listing all of the files on the logged drive.

If you have a CP/M system, two of those files are of interest: one, called FORMAT.COM, is used for formatting new disks; the other, SYSGEN.COM, is used to add the CP/M operating system to the new disk. If you have MS-DOS OR PC DOS, you will still use the **FORMAT** command, but by typing **FORMAT/S** you will format, *and add a system to*, the new disk in one operation.

Formatting New Disks

In general it is impossible to cause any damage to your computer, or to the data stored on disks, just by typing on the keyboard. When you are formatting disks *this is an exception to that rule.* Formatting a disk wipes off any data stored on it—what a pity if you do this to a MicroPro program disk! Always check before formatting that you have the disk to be formatted in drive B and your operating system disk in drive A.

The program you will use for formatting disks in either CP/M or MS-DOS is called called FORMAT.COM. At this point you should turn to the section in your computer User's Guide that explains disk formatting, since the commands vary from one type of computer to another. The following instructions list the general form of the commands. The correct disks should now be in place, so let's start formatting:

Step-by-step procedure

1. Next to the prompt, type **FORMAT** (if you are running CP/M) or **FORMAT B:/S** (if MS-DOS) and then press **Return**.
2. You may be offered several options—select the appropriate option to format the disk in drive B, then press the **Return** key if required.
3. The disk drive active light will come on and you may see a message on the screen reporting the formatting of the various tracks.
4. As soon as the disk is formatted most systems offer you the options again. It is quicker to format a whole box of disks in one session—so remove the disk from drive B, replace it in its protective envelope and then put another new disk in drive B. Select the option to format the disk in drive B and press **Return** if necessary, and the second disk will be formatted. Continue until all your new disks are formatted.
5. Finally, select the option that returns you to the operating system, and you will find yourself back at the A> prompt.

If you have an IBM PC/AT you should take particular note of the formatting of disks—especially if you have a combination of high capacity, standard IBM floppy, and hard disk drives. Read the **FORMAT** command section in your IBM DOS manual before formatting any disks, particularly if you may wish to move them around from the PC/AT to other IBM (or compatible) computer systems.

Returning to the operating system will usually perform a *warm boot* on your computer operating system (this distinguishes it from starting up the system from scratch, which is termed a *cold boot*). A warm boot resets the system without turning off the power or reloading the operating system; thus it retains what you have stored in the computer memory. It is important to remember that your computer memory is volatile, that is, it is erased when the power goes off; anything you wish to save for future use must be transferred from the memory to a floppy disk *before* you turn the computer off.

Adding CP/M to the Formatted Disks

As explained earlier, if you add an operating system to the formatted disks you will be able to boot (start up) your computer from them. The program for achieving this when you are running CP/M is called SYSGEN.COM (meaning system generator). Remember, if you have an MS-DOS system, you will have used the **/S** option of the **FORMAT** command, which adds the operating system as it formats your disks, so you can bypass this section.

Again, you must check in your User's Guide for the precise instructions for adding a system to your disks; the general form for entering commands follows.

Step-by-step procedure

Go ahead now and generate a system on one of your newly formatted disks.

1. At the prompt type **SYSGEN** and press the **Return** key. You may see a message on the screen giving the version number of the SYSGEN program and then you may be asked for the *source drive.* This is drive **A** (or **1**).

2. When you are asked for the *destination drive* you must type in **B** or **2** (if the disk you wish to have the system transferred to is in drive B) then you just press the **Return** key and wait for the message to display telling you that the operating system has been transferred.

3. Again, it is quicker to put systems on all your disks in one session—if you have a message on the screen asking for a destination name, take the current disk out of drive B, replace it in its protective envelope, and put the next formatted disk in drive B.

4. Repeat SYSGEN procedure for all your disks. When you have generated systems on as many of your newly formatted disks as you need, select the option that returns you to the operating system. Your computer will warm boot, and you will find yourself back at the prompt.

Care of Your Disks

Always handle floppy disks with care. Following is a list of procedures to protect your disks.

1. As soon as you remove a disk from the drive, put it back in the protective envelope.
2. Do not touch the recording surface (the sections of disk that are visible through the various cutouts in the disk sleeve).
3. Remember to keep disks away from sources of heat or magnetic fields (radiators, telephones, hard disk drives, and any other equipment or source of radiation that could harm the storage on disk).
4. Establish right from the beginning a labeling scheme that describes what type of programs are stored on the disk you are using—use the colored labels that usually come with a box of new disks. For example, you could use red for master disks (CP/M, MS-DOS, WordStar, and InfoStar), green for system utilities (FORMAT, and STAT), orange for backup copies of your own data, yellow for working copies of program disks, and blue for current data disks.

With a box of newly formatted disks at your side, you are ready to delve deeper into your computer operating system and to prepare the tutorial disk you will use for the remainder of Part One— so now, proceed to Chapter 2.

2

Preparing the Tutorial Disk

CP/M Utilities
MS-DOS Utilities
Copying Master Files and the Distribution Disks
Preparing Your Tutorial Disk
MS-DOS Sub-directories
Printing Files
Good Office Routines

Now that you have a box of newly formatted system disks, you are ready to prepare the disk you will use for the tutorials and lessons that follow. If you have a hard disk system, you should check your User's Guide for any special instructions related to copying files from one drive to another, particularly if your manufacturer or dealer has implemented the user areas (in CP/M systems) or partitions (in MS-DOS systems).

First, familiarize yourself with the various *utilities* available in your CP/M or MS-DOS operating system. By the end of this chapter you will have become very familiar with handling disks and will have gained considerable confidence in the use of your microcomputer and its operating system. First the CP/M utilities are described, so if you have an MS-DOS system go straight to the section entitled MS-DOS Utilities.

CP/M UTILITIES

Your CP/M working disk should be in drive A and one of the newly formatted disks in drive B. Type **DIR** next to the A> prompt and press the **Return** key (in subsequent procedures you should assume you must press **Return** every time you type something, unless you are told otherwise). The screen will fill with a list of names known as the directory of files. A *file name* may be up to eight characters in length and is normally followed by a period and up to three characters that make up the *file name extension* (the period does not appear on the screen in the directory listing).

Where the label **A**> prompt appears you can substitute the appropriate label for your own system. For example, **C**> is the prompt in many hard disk systems, where A and B are the floppy disk drives.

CP/M DIR and STAT Commands

Built-in directory

Look at the display of files on the screen. The extension .COM signifies that the file is a *command file*, that is, a file containing a program of instructions. Among these you will see STAT.COM and PIP.COM (there will be a space instead of a period between the file name and the file name extension on the screen); these are utilities. Notice that there is no DIR.COM—the directory function is built in. There are other built-in commands that you will learn later. **STAT** is short for statistics. **PIP** stands for Peripheral Interchange Program; it allows you to make copies of files (described in detail later).

Checking the statistics of your CP/M system

Type **STAT** next to the prompt. The screen will show you how much space remains unused on the disk (in some systems you will get a lot more information about the statistics of your system). If you make a typing error, typing for example, SATT instead of **STAT**, and then press the **Return** key, you will simply get a message saying SATT? followed by the system prompt. Just type **STAT**, press **Return** and all will be well.

If you enter **STAT *.*** you will see a listing of all the files on the disk in alphabetical order, with the number of K bytes of information stored under each file name listed alongside. The first asterisk stands for *any file name* and the second for *any file name extension*. If you type **STAT *.COM** you will see a list of all the files with the file name extension **.COM**. In computer terminology, the asterisk used to replace all or part of a file name or file name extension is called a *wild card*.

Copying Files from One Disk to Another in CP/M

The CP/M copying command is **PIP** (Peripheral Interchange Program). This allows you to copy files from one disk drive to another.

If you have a hard disk system, you should go through the exercises that follow and pencil in the disk drive labels (A, B, C, and so on) that are correct for your particular system. If you have two floppy disk drives in addition to the hard disk, you could practice copying files from one to the other, as detailed here. If you have only one floppy disk drive, you can transfer files backward and forward between the hard disk and the floppy disk drive, or between two hard disk drives, if your system is set up this way.

Step-by-step procedure

1. Type **PIP** next to the A> prompt. After pressing **Return** you will see a new prompt on the left of the screen—an asterisk (*). To get back to the A> prompt, just press the **Return** key. To start with you will type the **PIP** instruction lines in full. Later, when you are copying several files one after the other, it is quicker to type the abbreviated commands next to the asterisk prompt.
2. To signify that you are referring to drive A and drive B you must type them as **A:** and **B:**. For example, a typical CP/M copying instruction is:

   PIP B:STAT.COM=A:STAT.COM

3. Note that in the **PIP** instruction you must give the *destination drive first* (the drive you want to copy *to*) and the *source drive second* (the drive you are copying *from*). If your manual says you should list the source drive first, check to see if you have a different operating system, since that is the convention in MS-DOS.

   Now examine the parts of the typical CP/M copying instruction:

   PIP B:STAT.COM=A:STAT.COM

PIP means copy the file; in this case the file is called STAT.COM. It is copied to the disk in drive B from a file called STAT.COM on the disk in drive A. There is a convention that you do not need to type the file name for the destination drive, as long as you wish to keep the same name.

4. Therefore, if you only typed:

   PIP B:=A:STAT.COM

   the effect would be identical to the first command—you would end up with a file on the disk in drive B called STAT.COM.

5. If, on the other hand, you wish to *change* the file name on the disk in drive B you would type, for example:

   PIP B:STATS.COM=A:STAT.COM

   Then the copy of the file on drive B is named STATS.COM while the original file on drive A would still be STAT.COM.

6. If you typed this last instruction, you now have a file on drive B called STATS.COM. To avoid confusion later, erase this file. You can use another utility for this: **ERA** (for erase). Type:

   ERA B:STATS.COM

   and press **Return**.

7. Now if you check the directory of files on drive B (by entering **DIR B:**), you will see that the file is no longer listed.

Note that you can copy the file STAT.COM from drive A to drive B (or between any other two drives) as often as you like; all that happens, when you keep the file names the same, is that each new copy from drive A overwrites the previous copy on drive B. That is, each file erases the previous file of the same name on that disk.

That is why it is so important to get the instructions about source and destination drives right when you make backup copies of your own files. Otherwise, you may inadvertently copy an old version of a file from drive B and overwrite the new version in drive A. Get into the habit of checking the **PIP** command line before pressing **Return** to be absolutely certain that you are over-writing the old copy with the new, and not vice versa.

Copying CP/M Utilities

Now that you are ready to copy the utilities, there is one further addition you should make to the copying command line each time you use it—a V—which automatically verifies that the copy is correct by comparing it with the original. In CP/M it is entered **[V]**.

Step-by-step procedure

1. Make sure that you have your CP/M working disk in drive A and one of your newly formatted disks in drive B, and you are ready to copy the **PIP** and **STAT** utilities on to your new disk:

2. Next to the A> prompt type **PIP** and press **Return**. You will now see **PIP's** asterisk prompt. Next to the asterisk prompt type:

```
B:=A:STAT.COM[V]
```

3. You will see the drive lights activated alternately as data is transferred from one disk to the other. When the process is complete you will see the asterisk prompt again. Next to this type:

```
B:=A:PIP.COM[V]
```

When the copies are complete the asterisk prompt appears; CP/M is waiting for the next instruction. Simply press **Return** to exit from **PIP** and to return to the A> prompt.

4. To ensure that you have successfully transferred copies of the utilities to drive B, you can view the directory of drive B from drive A. Simply type **DIR B:** and you will see on the screen:

```
STAT    COM : PIP    COM
```

5. Now you can transfer control to drive B (that is, log onto

B) by typing **B:** next to the A> prompt. After pressing **Return** a B> prompt will display, meaning that this is now your *working drive* or the drive you are logged onto. In turn, type the titles of the utilities next to the B> prompt to check that they are functioning correctly. Return to drive A by typing **A:**, and the A> prompt will appear once more.

Next you need to copy these utilities onto each of your other newly formatted disks. You will remove the disk from drive B and insert it in drive A; whenever you change the disk in the logged or working drive you must press **Ctrl-C** (that is, hold down the **Ctrl** key while you press **C**). This will warm boot the system. Remember, when you see the instruction to press a **Ctrl** character, you must hold down the **Ctrl** key and the key mentioned simultaneously. If you forget to press **Ctrl-C** you may find that you lose or damage (*corrupt*) data on your disk.

6. Having removed the CP/M working disk from drive A, replace it with the disk from drive B that has the files STAT and PIP on it. Warm boot by pressing **Ctrl-C** and then put a newly formatted disk in drive B.

7. Now for your first shortcut. You can transfer both the files on drive A to drive B with one command; next to the A> prompt, type:

```
PIP B:=A:*.*[V]
```

In the above command, the first asterisk represents any file name and the second, any file name extension, so the command line means: copy all files from A to B. Since there are only two files on the disk, and you want them both, this command is correct.

After you press **Return**, the screen will display the appropriate information as each file is transferred, so you will know what is happening and when copying is completed.

To copy the utilities onto each of your other formatted disks, simply remove the disk from drive B, replace it with the next disk, and repeat the **PIP** command as described in the instruction.

Since the working drive is drive A, it is not absolutely essential to press a **Ctrl-C** between changes of disk in drive B; however, it is a good practice to adopt so that you never forget to do it when it really matters.

The next section explains MS-DOS commands, so you can go straight to the section entitled Copying Master Files and the Distribution Disks.

MS-DOS UTILITIES

Your MS-DOS working disk should be in drive A and one of the newly formatted disks in drive B. Type **DIR** next to the A> prompt and press the **Return** key (in subsequent procedures you should assume you must press **Return** every time you type something, unless you are told otherwise). The screen will fill with a list of names known as the directory of files. A file name may be up to eight characters in length and is normally followed by a period and up to three characters which make up the file name extension (the period does not appear on the screen in the directory listing).

Where the label A> prompt appears you can substitute the appropriate label for your own system. For example, **C**> is the prompt in many hard disk systems, where A and B are the floppy disk drives.

MS-DOS DIR and CHKDSK Commands

DIR to display file information

When you type **DIR** next to the A> prompt, you will see a listing of file names and other information in columns across the screen, with the file name in the first column, followed by the file name extension, then some details about the number of bytes occupied by each file, and finally, the date and time that each file was created or last updated. At the end of the listing MS-DOS lists the number of files and, possibly, how much space (in K) remains on that disk.

The file name extention shows the type of file. For example, .COM indicates a command file, which is a file containing program instructions for a particular function in your computer.

If you have DOS version 2 or higher, you can create subdirectories and copy files into them. A section later in this chapter describes the creation and use of subdirectories.

CHKDSK to display disk statistics

The MS-DOS command **CHKDSK** is short for CHECK DISK. If you look at the directory listing, you will see a command file called CHKDSK.COM.

If you type **CHKDSK** next to the A> prompt, MS-DOS displays some statistics about the capacity of your disk, the number of files, and sizes of files currently stored on the disk. In addition, the last two lines tell you how much of your computer memory is still available. If you type **CHKDSK B:** you will be given similar information about the disk in drive B.

The information is given in *bytes*: if you are more familiar with K (short for kilobytes) you will have to learn to divide the number on the screen by 1,000. For example, if you are told that your files occupy 148965 bytes, this is the equivalent (approximately) of 149K. If you have a hard disk, you may see that your files occupy 3879763 bytes, which is equivalent to more than 3.8MB—remember that 1 Kbyte is shorthand for one thousand (1,000) bytes and 1 megabyte (MB) for one million (1,000,000) bytes.

Copying Files from One Disk to Another in MS-DOS

COPY is the MS-DOS utility that allows you to copy files from one drive to another.

If you have a hard disk system, you should go through the exercises that follow and pencil in the disk drive labels (A, B, C, and so on) that are correct for your particular system. If you have two floppy disk drives in addition to the hard disk, you could practice copying files from one to the other, as detailed here. If you have only one floppy disk drive, you can transfer files backward and forward between the hard disk and the floppy disk drive, or between two hard disk drives, if your system is set up this way.

Step-by-step procedure

1. To signify that you are referring to drive A and drive B you must type them as **A:** and **B:**. For example, here is a typical **COPY** instruction:

   ```
   COPY A:CHKDSK.COM  B:CHKDSK.COM
   ```

2. Note that in the **COPY** instruction you must give the *source drive first* (the drive you want to copy *from*) and the *destination drive second* (the drive you are copying to). If your manual says you should list the destination drive first, check to see if you have a different operating system, since that

is the convention in CP/M. Note the space before the B: in the above instruction.

Now examine the parts of the typical MS-DOS copying instruction:

```
COPY A:CHKDSK.COM  B:CHKDSK.COM
```

The copy command will copy the file; in this case the file is called CHKDSK.COM. It is copied from the disk in drive A to a file called CHKDSK.COM on the disk in drive B.

There is a convention that you do not need to type the file name for the destination drive, as long as you wish to keep the same name. Nor do you need the disk drive identifier (for example, the A:) for the file you are copying *from*, if the file is on the disk in your logged drive (in this case, drive A).

3. Therefore, if you only typed:

```
COPY CHKDSK.COM  B:
```

the effect would be identical to the first command—you would end up with a file on the disk in drive B called CHKDSK.COM.

4. If, on the other hand, you wish to *change* the file name on the disk in drive B you would type, for example:

```
COPY CHKDSK.COM  B:CHEKDISK.COM
```

Then the copy of the file on drive B is named CHEK-DISK.COM while the original file on drive A would still be CHKDSK.COM.

5. If you typed in this last instruction, you now have a file on the disk in drive B called CHEKDISK.COM. To avoid confusion later, erase this file. You can use another utility for this: **DEL** (for delete). At the A> prompt type:

```
DEL  B:CHEKDISK.COM
```

and press **Return**.

6. Now if you check the directory of files on drive B (by entering **DIR B:**), you will see that CHEKDISK.COM is no longer listed.

Copying MS-DOS Utilities

Now that you are ready to copy the utilities, there is one further addition you should make to the copying command line each time you use it—a V—which automatically verifies that the copy is correct by comparing it with the original.

Step-by-step procedure

1. Try entering this now:

COPY CHKDSK B:/V

Note that every time you **COPY** a file from drive A to drive B, the drive A version overwrites any existing file of the same name on the disk in drive B. That is why it is important to ensure that you have the source and destination drives right when you make backup copies of your own files. Otherwise, you may inadvertently copy an old version of a file from drive B and overwrite the new version in drive A.

As CHKDSK is copied, you will see the drive lights activated alternately as data is transferred from one disk to the other. When the process is complete you will see the A> prompt again.

2. Now you need to copy the **COPY** utility. You may have noticed that there is no file called COPY.COM listed in the directory of your disk in drive A; however, a file called COMMAND.COM includes the copying commands, as well as other built-in functions you will use later. Next to the A> prompt type:

COPY A:COMMAND.COM B:/V

3. To ensure that you have successfully transferred copies of the utilities to drive B, you can view the directory of drive B from drive A. Simply type **DIR B:** and you will see the two files listed on the screen.

4. Now you can transfer control to drive B (that is, log onto B) by typing **B:** next to the A> prompt. After pressing **Return** a B> prompt will display, meaning that this is now your working drive or the drive you are logged onto.

5. Type **CHKDSK A:** next to the B> prompt to check that it is functioning correctly. Return to drive A by typing **A:**, and the A> prompt will appear once more.

Now you need to copy these utilities onto each of your other newly formatted disks. You will remove the disk from drive B and insert it in drive A; whenever you change the disk in the logged or working drive you must press **Ctrl-C** (that is, hold down the **Ctrl** key while you press **C**). This will warm boot the system. Remember, when you see the instruction to press a **Ctrl** character, you hold down the **Ctrl** key and the key mentioned simultaneously. If you forget to press **Ctrl-C** you may find that you lose or damage (corrupt) data on your disk.

6. Having removed the MS-DOS working disk from drive A, replace it with the disk from drive B that has the files CHKDSK and COMMAND on it. Warm boot by pressing **Ctrl-C** and then put a newly formatted disk in drive B.

Now for your first shortcut. You can transfer both the files on drive A to drive B with one command; next to the A> prompt, type:

```
COPY A:*.* B:/V
```

In the above command, the first asterisk represents any file name and the second, any file name extension, so the command line means: copy all files from A to B. Since there are only two files on the disk, and you want them both, this command is correct.

After you press **Return**, the screen will display the appropriate information as each file is transferred, so you will know what is happening and when copying is completed.

To copy the utilities onto each of your other formatted disks, simply remove the disk from drive B, replace it with the next disk, and repeat the **COPY** command as described in the instruction.

Since the working drive is drive A, it is not absolutely essential to press a **Ctrl-C** between changes of disk in drive B; however, it is a good practice to adopt so that you never forget to do it when it really matters.

COPYING MASTER FILES AND THE DISTRIBUTION DISKS

Up to now you have been using your CP/M or MS-DOS distribution disk as your working disk. It is wise to create Master working disks, then to make one extra copy of each (a *backup copy*) that you keep in a safe place away from your immediate working environment. You should *never* use the distribution disk itself (the original disk supplied with your system) as a working copy.

Ideally, after you use them to make Master working disks, the distribution disks should be kept in a fireproof safe, or even in your bank vault. While this is not always possible, you should at least make sure that they are stored flat in a cool and clean environment that is removed from the location of your Master and backup disks.

Step-by-Step Procedure

1. Simply insert each of the distribution disks in turn into drive B.
2. Insert an appropriately labeled disk from your new stock of formatted disks into drive A.
3. Press **Ctrl-C** and when you get the A> prompt, type:

   CP/M users: `PIP A:=B:*.*[V]`

   MS-DOS users: `COPY B:*.* A:/V`

   Note that this time you are copying the files *from* drive B *to* drive A. What this means is that you can copy files on disks from any drive to any other drive.
4. Repeat this until you have backup copies of all your distribution disks. You should now have a pile of master working disks and a pile of your distribution disks.
5. Back up the distribution disks again, repeating steps 1–4. You will now have your distribution disks, a pile of backup copies, and a pile of master working copies.

Use only the master working disks. When these disks are full or become damaged or corrupted in some way, then make a new working disk from the backup copy of the distribution disk. It is very important to establish these routines right from the beginning so that they become second nature to you.

PREPARING YOUR TUTORIAL DISK

By now you should feel quite confident of your ability to handle disks, to insert and remove them from the drives, to know when you need to warm boot with **Ctrl-C**, to copy files from drive A to drive B (**PIP** or **COPY**), to see which files you have on a disk (**DIR**) and how much space remains for additional working files (**STAT** or **CHKDSK**). You are now ready to prepare the tutorial disk that you will use for the subsequent examples, exercises, and lessons in Part One.

If you are using a hard disk system, you can copy the files detailed here straight onto your hard disk. If you have separate drives or partitions on the hard disk, you should designate a particular drive or partition as the tutorial area. You will need to check carefully the instructions given here and pencil in any changes you have to make in the labels of your disk drives. (For example, the hard disk drive may be labeled drive C in your system).

MS-DOS version 2 (or higher) users may like to follow the instructions in the section entitled *MS-DOS Subdirectories*, and create a tutorial subdirectory for your files. This could be useful whether you are using floppy disks or a hard disk system.

If you have a CP/M hard disk system with User Areas (in which case your system prompt may be A0> or C0>) you can log on to a different User Area just by typing **USER 10**, for example, next to the prompt. Now you can copy all your tutorial files into User Area 10, by typing the appropriate commands next to the A10> or C10 prompt.

Step-by-Step Procedure

1. Put one of your newly formatted disks in drive A and the WordStar master working disk in drive B.
2. Press **Ctrl-C** and when you see the A> prompt, look at the directory of files on the WordStar disk. The files that you wish to transfer to your tutorial disk are WS.COM, WSMSGS.OVR, and WSOVLY1.OVR. Note that all these begin with the common characters WS.
3. As a second shortcut with the copying program, next to the A> prompt, type the appropriate copying command for your operating system:

   CP/M users: `PIP A:=B:WS*.*[V]`

   MS-DOS users: `COPY B:WS*.* A:/V`

You will see from the display on the screen that the three

files you need, all beginning with the characters WS, are copied one after the other. Again, the asterisks are acting as "wild cards."

Usually the dealer who supplied your MicroPro software has ensured that it already is installed for your particular system. If not, you should be able to install the program yourself without too much difficulty (there is a section on installation in the WordStar Reference Manual). *Installing software* fits it to your particular computer terminal and printer. If you have an IBM (or truly IBM-compatible) system, all the software should be ready to run, since MicroPro supplies IBM versions of its programs preinstalled. The only exception is CorrectStar (see Chapter 7).

4. Now remove the WordStar master working disk from drive B and replace it with the MailMerge master working disk. Press **Ctrl-C** and then look at the directory of files. You will need to copy only one file this time: MAILMRGE.OVR. Use **PIP** or **COPY** to copy this file.

If you have bought only WordStar and MailMerge, then this is your completed tutorial disk, and you should proceed straight to the next section, Printing Files. If you have InfoStar (DataStar and ReportStar) as well, continue here.

Tutorial Disk for DataStar and ReportStar

If your disks have a capacity of less than 270K, you will need to make two tutorial disks—one for WordStar and MailMerge and one for DataStar and ReportStar. Normally you will work with your program disk in drive A and your data disk in drive B, keeping your data files separate from the program disks. To get all the program files for WordStar, MailMerge, DataStar, and ReportStar, and the utilities on one tutorial disk you need a capacity of at least 270K.

Step-by-step procedure

1. If necessary, replace the disk in drive A with your second tutorial disk (remember to press **Ctrl-C**).
2. Remove the WordStar disk from drive B and replace with the InfoStar disk that contains the DataStar files.
3. Press **Ctrl-C** and after the A> prompt, use your copying command to copy three files to the disk in drive A: FORM-

GEN.COM, DATASTAR.COM, and BATCH.OVR. (If you have version 1.4 or later of DataStar, then the BATCH file has the extension .OVR (as above); in earlier versions the extension was .COM, so use this if appropriate.)

4. Remove the first InfoStar disk from drive B and replace it with the second, containing the ReportStar files.

5. Press **Ctrl-C**, and after the A> prompt, type **DIR** and look at the list of files. You are going to copy the files used for sorting and for Quick Reports only.

6. Use your copying routine to copy FORMSORT.EXE (or, if you have the 1.4 or earlier version, FORMSORT.OVR and FORMSORT.COM), REPORT.COM, RGEN.COM, and RSMSGS.OVR to your tutorial disk in drive A.

Your tutorial disk is now complete; you have everything you need to complete Part One of this book. If you have MS-DOS version 2 or higher, you may be interested in the technique for creating subdirectories, described next. If you have MS-DOS 1 or CP/M, proceed to the section entitled Printing Files.

MS-DOS SUBDIRECTORIES

The major difference between MS-DOS version 1 and later versions is the capability for creating *subdirectories* in the more recent versions.

When you first boot up your system, and the system prompt displays on the screen, you are automatically in the *root directory*. If you type **DIR** next to the system prompt, you will see a listing of the directory of files in the root directory. If you have already created some subdirectories, they will be included right at the end of the directory listing with <DIR> next to the chosen subdirectory name.

The use of subdirectories is especially convenient on a hard disk system, particularly if you have a large capacity hard disk on a single-user system, such as the IBM PC/AT with its 20MB hard disk. If you decide to keep the hard disk as a single partition, like a giant floppy disk, then you will want to create subdirectories so that you can organize your files and available space efficiently. Following are examples that apply equally well to a floppy disk system and are useful for keeping your various working areas separate from each other.

It is advisable for you to create a TUTORIAL subdirectory, the equivalent of a tutorial disk, then divide the files between a WORDTUTE sub-subdirectory (for the word processing programs and exercises) and a DATATUTE sub-subdirectory (for the data processing files). The structure of root directories, subdirectories, and sub-subdirectories, is often likened to an upside-down tree, where the trunk is the main (or root) directory, and the branches are the various levels of subdirectories.

The system I have just suggested for your tutorial area would be represented like this:

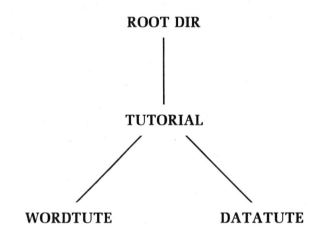

In Chapter 7 (the CorrectStar tutorial in Part Two of this guide) you will create another subdirectory for holding the files needed to run WordStar, MailMerge, and CorrectStar, called WORDPRO (for word processing). This will have sub-subdirectories for LETTERS, DOCS, and LABELS. If you have many users of WordStar on one system, you could each have named subdirectories to keep your own files separate.

Once you start to use the subdirectories, you have to keep their structure in your mind's eye. Moving from the root, down through the branches, and back again can get a little confusing, especially at the beginning. The main points to remember are:

- DON'T make your directory structure too large and complicated.

- DO use directories and subdirectories to organize your files efficiently, particularly if you have a large capacity hard disk.

Copying Files into Subdirectories

Starting with the TUTORIAL subdirectory, you will be copying the same files as in the previous instructions for creating a tutorial disk.

Step-by-step procedure

1. If you have a dual-floppy system, insert one of your newly formatted system disks in drive A (it must have the COM-MAND.COM files on it so that you have access to the copying and other commands you will need). The MicroPro program disks will go in drive B when you are instructed.

2. Boot up your system and type **DIR** next to the prompt: as mentioned before, this listing is the directory of files in your root directory.

3. You want to start by *making* the directories you need using the **MAKE DIR** command (which you can abbreviate to **MD**); next to the prompt type:

MD TUTORIAL

4. After you press **Return**, type **DIR** next to the prompt; now you will see **TUTORIAL** <DIR> at the end of the listing on the screen.

5. Next you want to copy some files into the directories. First you have to *change directories* by typing:

CD TUTORIAL

6. You are now *inside* the TUTORIAL subdirectory: if you type **DIR** you will see that there are no files yet (just two <DIR> files, with one period or dot that indicates the root directory and two dots, the subdirectory). However, if you type **DIR ** you will see the full list of files in the root directory. The backslash symbol (\) represents the root directory in MS-DOS version 2 or later.

7. Next you can create the two sub-subdirectories by entering two commands:

MD WORDTUTE

MD DATATUTE

8. If you type **DIR** you will see that you are in TUTORIAL subdirectory, and the two new directories are listed, with <**DIR**> next to the the names WordTute and DataTute.

9. Now you are ready to *change directory* to WordTute. Type:

CD WORDTUTE

10. If you type **DIR** you will see that you are in **\Tutorial\ WordTute**, and the directory files (dot and double dot) are the only files listed.

11. If you have been working for a while, and are not sure which directory you are working in, just type **CD** next to the prompt, and you will be given your current directory location—do so now. You will see \TUTORIAL\WORD-TUTE.

12. Now you must copy the WordStar files from your master working floppy disk into the WordTute directory. Put the working disk into drive B (or as appropriate for your system) and copy the three WS files all at once:

COPY B:WS*.*

You will see that the files are copied one after the other into your subdirectory—type **DIR** to see them listed.

13. Now you can replace the WordStar disk in drive B with the MailMerge master working disk and copy MAILMRGE.OVR in the same way.

14. To exit from WordTute back to the root directory, type **CD**. If you type **CD**, you will see the backslash symbol next to the prompt, indicating that you are currently in the root directory.

15. You are ready to change directories again—this time to the DataTute subdirectory. You can go straight into DataTute from the root directory by typing:

CD TUTORIAL\DATATUTE

16. Put your InfoStar master working disk into drive B (or as appropriate for your system) and copy the files you need

for the InfoStar tutorials:

```
DATASTAR.COM
RGEN.COM
FORMGEN.COM
REPORT.COM
BATCH.OVR
RSMSGS.OVR
```
FORMSORT.EXE (or FORMSORT.OVR & FORMSORT.COM)

17. That completes creation of the TUTORIAL subdirectories. To get from the DataTute sub-subdirectory into the Tutorial subdirectory, just type **CD..** (CD followed by two periods). Now type **CD** next to the prompt and you will see **\TUTORIAL**, which shows that you are in the Tutorial subdirectory. To get back to the root directory, you must type **CD** as before.

If you have not used subdirectories before, this has been a brief introduction for you. You should read the sections of your MS-DOS manual dealing with **MKDIR** (Make Directory), **CHDIR** (Change Directory), **RMDIR** (Remove Directory) and **PATH** (Set Search Directory) commands. We will look at these in detail in Chapter 7.

PRINTING FILES

Now that you are familiar with your CP/M or DOS utilities, and you have created your tutorial disk, user area, partition, or subdirectory (as appropriate for your particular system), you are ready to do some printing.

Once you have your printer working, you can list the directory of your disks on printer paper and keep that hard copy inside the paper envelope with the disk.

Step-by-Step Procedure

1. Make sure the cable is connected between the appropriate port at the back of your computer and the printer.
2. Switch on the printer and make sure it is *online*—there should be a light on the printer control panel that lights up when the printer is online or ready.

3. Type **DIR** and press **Return**. You will see the directory list-ing on the screen. To make this list appear on the printer, type **DIR** again but this time press **Ctrl-P** before you press **Return**.

4. Now the directory listing will be output to the printer. The **Ctrl-P** you pressed "switched on" the **PRINT** command and activated the printer.

5. You can get a listing of drive B by typing **DIR B:** and pressing **Return**. You will find that as you type, the printer is printing whatever is on the screen. It will continue to do so until you press **Ctrl-P** again; **Ctrl-P** is acting as a *toggle switch* to turn printing on and off.

6. Press the switch on the printer that turns it *offline* and then press **Form Feed**. The printer paper will scroll through to the next page. Tear off the section with the directory listing you want and put it away in the envelope with the corre-sponding disk. You will have to remember to update the listing whenever you add new files to that disk.

7. If the output to to the printer is not satisfactory, check with your dealer about the proper installation procedure for your printer.

GOOD OFFICE ROUTINES

Remember the point made earlier: You should get into good habits from day 1. Have you thought of making a backup copy of your tutorial disk?

Make an appropriately labeled working copy of your tutorial disk. If you cannot do this without some help, look back over the instructions at the beginning of this chapter.

When you have made your copy disk, store it with your other backup copies. Remember to label the disk with a meaningful description of its contents, for example:

TUTORIAL WORKING DISK—OCTOBER 1985
PROGRAMS
(BACKUP COPY)

Also include a printout of the directory listing so that you know precisely which files are stored on your tutorial disk.

You can develop a color-coding system for labeling disks that shows at a glance whether they are distribution, working, data, or backup disk. Some disks are sold with a selection of different colored labels; but even if yours are not, you can achieve the same effect by adding stripes of color from felt-tip pens.

These two introductory chapters were intended to prepare you well for the MicroPro tutorials that follow. If you are unclear about the concepts or step-by-step procedures, review them now.

I suggest you take a break now—have a cup of coffee and review what you have learned to date. By the time you have completed Part One, you will have typed in a standard letter (using WordStar), designed a simple form for entering clients' names and addresses (FormGen), entered half a dozen names and addresses (DataStar), sorted them into alphabetical order (FormSort), prepared a simple report listing the names (ReportStar), and finally merge printed them with your standard letter (MailMerge)—ending up with six individually addressed letters and matching envelopes. If you have WordStar and MailMerge only, you will achieve all of this, except the sorting routine, using a different technique.

After your break, resume with Chapter 3, where you'll learn WordStar.

3

WordStar Tutorial

Starting the Tutorials
Calling Up WordStar
Entering Text
Editing Text
Saving Files
Printing WordStar Files
Entering Data in Non-document Files

This chapter will provide you with the simplest possible exercise in WordStar. Using the minimum of commands and editing procedures, you will type the text of a *form letter* that will be used later for the MailMerge tutorial. Do not worry too much at this early stage about the control characters; you will soon know the essential ones by heart.

Recent versions of WordStar are 3.3 in the United States and 3.4 in Europe. The 3.3 version is available in CP/M and MS-DOS; at the time of writing, version 3.4 is available only for the IBM PC and compatibles. The 3.4 WordStar Professional Pack includes the CorrectStar spelling checker with an English dictionary (as opposed to American English in 3.3) and some enhancements to the program, such as on-screen boldfacing and underlining, and additional function keys.

STARTING THE TUTORIALS

Allowance has been made in the latest MS-DOS versions of the software (DOS 2.0 or higher) for the use of subdirectories. If you set up a tutorial subdirectory using the directions in Chapter 2, you should change the directory (enter **CD TUTORIAL\WORD-TUTE**) before you start this WordStar tutorial. Other users should boot up from the tutorial disk as usual. From now on you will load the tutorial disk you have prepared in drive A and one of the formatted disks in drive B—this disk will be used at the end of each session for making a backup copy of the tutorials and exercises.

Using WINSTALL

WordStar expects to find its various associated programs on drive A. If you are using a hard disk system, and the working drive is normally drive C or D, you will need to tell WordStar where to look for its programs. To do this, you would have to run through the WordStar installation program:

Step-by-step procedure

1. Next to the prompt type **WINSTALL**; type **E** to select the menu of WordStar Features, then **R** to set the system drive.
2. Type **C** to indicate that you wish to make a change. Then enter **3** (for drive C) or **4** (for drive D), as appropriate.
3. To exit WINSTALL, type ^**X**, then ^**X** again. Finally, type **A** to accept the changes you have made, and the WS.COM file will be updated.
4. Copy this version of WS.COM to your tutorial area.

You may feel it would be easier in the first instance for you to keep your tutorials on the floppy disk you created, and to use your floppy disk drive for the exercises until you have had more experience with your computer system.

Start now as you would at the beginning of any new session: power on the computer (if you had turned it off at the end of the last session); load your tutorial working disk in drive A and a backup disk in drive B; then boot up.

CALLING UP WORDSTAR

Now you must call up the WordStar program—called WS.COM—so that you can type in the text of your letter. WordStar is an extremely versatile word processing package and there are many *control characters* to learn. However, you can type in this first letter by following the instructions carefully. Remember this unique feature of WordStar: When you must press both the **Ctrl** key and another key simultaneously it will be written thus:

^C (Ctrl-C)

To save space WordStar menus use a caret (^) to represent the **Ctrl** key.

　NOTE: Previously you have used **Ctrl-C** to warm boot your system—a CP/M command. In WordStar it has a different effect, which will be explained in the tutorial.

　Your computer may have *function keys* (F1 through F10) that serve as special WordStar keys. They may be labeled with their function in WordStar; for example, **^C** would be labeled Scroll Down Page or words to that effect. Some companies market plastic or paper templates that list the uses of the **Ctrl** keys in WordStar. If your version of WordStar uses the function keys for special tasks, you then need only press one key for some of the most commonly used control characters instead of the **Ctrl** key as well. The MS-DOS versions of WordStar display the functions at the bottom of the screen, next to the function key number, so you don't need to memorize them. For those of you who don't have this luxury, it is a good idea to label the front of the function keys with the control character they represent so that you learn them as you go along. These tutorials use the control characters, since not everyone has a keyboard with the same layout of function keys.

Step-by-Step Procedure

Now, to call up WordStar:

1. Next to the A> prompt (or as appropriate for the hard disk) type **WS**. After you press **Return** the screen will fill with details about WordStar—the version number, etc. After that you will see the OPENING MENU, which displays a number of items for you to choose among. Beneath the menu is a directory of files on the disk in drive A (or the logged drive).

2. Option D is to OPEN A DOCUMENT FILE. Press the **D** key now.

3. You will be asked for the NAME OF FILE TO EDIT. Type in **FORMLETT.TXT.** You are allowed up to eight characters before the period, which will be the file name, and up to three characters after the period, the file name extension (just as in CP/M and MS-DOS). It is a good idea to make the file name mean something to you, (e.g., FORMLETT for Form Letter), and to keep the extensions the same for all similar files (for example, **.TXT** for letter text, **.DOC** for documents, and **.LBL** for label files.)

4. When you press **Return** the screen display will change. First, it will say NEW FILE, since FORMLETT.TXT does not already exist; then you will see the WordStar MAIN MENU with the HELP SCREEN below it listing some of the more important editing commands. Below that will appear the *ruler line* showing the position of right and left margins. The positions of the *tab stops* are indicated by the exclamation marks (!).

   NOTE: These symbols and some others are different in WordStar version 3.4 and later.

5. Now you can treat the screen as a blank page and simply type in your form letter, without any name or address at the top and without signing off (with Yours Sincerely)— these details will be filled in when you use Chapter 5, MailMerge Tutorial.

   Look at the following example but try to choose some text for a letter that you can send out to six clients or customers. You could notify them of a new product or let them know that you now have a computer and would like them to check the address details you have used for mistakes. If you cannot think of an immediate example, simply copy the text from the example in the next section.

ENTERING TEXT

You can start typing immediately below the ruler line, exactly as you would on a blank sheet of paper in your typewriter. You will have to adjust to the presence of some extra keys—the **Ctrl** key and the **Caps Lock** in addition to the **Shift Key**. **Caps Lock** is very useful for typing mixed capital letters and numbers; it is rather like **Shift Lock** (which is usually absent on computer keyboards) except that it shifts only *letters* from lowercase to uppercase, leaving *numbers* unshifted.

The ruler line determines the left margin (L), the right margin (R) and the tab stops (!). All of these can be changed to suit your individual requirements; you will learn how to do this in a later chapter, but for this exercise you should just leave the settings as they are.

Remember that you do not have to press **Return** at the end of each line. In word processing, the computer knows where the end of each line is and performs what is known as *word wrap* for you. You have to press **Return** only when you reach the end of a paragraph. When you do press **Return** you will see a < in the far right column on the screen; this signifies that you have entered what is termed a *hard return* (to distinguish it from the *soft return* that the WordStar program inserts automatically at the end of word-wrapped lines). The column on the extreme right of the screen is called the *flag column*, and the symbols that appear there, for example the <, are called *flags*.

Now type in your letter. For example:

> I am sure you will be interested to know that we now have a microcomputer in our head office and that this letter was written using the word processing package, WordStar with Mail-Merge. Since we have been able to enter your company details and product interests into the DataStar database, we will be keeping in much closer touch with you over the coming months.

> Please be sure to let us know of any changes that should be made in your address or in the details your office personnel— we would like to keep our records correct and up to date now that it is so easy to do so.

> Many thanks for your cooperation.

EDITING TEXT

As you are typing you may make mistakes; however, it is very easy to make corrections as you go along. Listed in the MAIN MENU at the top of the screen are the *cursor control characters*. After you have typed two or three lines, try to use them.

Cursor Movements

Move the cursor up a line at a time with **^E**, then down again with **^X**; move it along the line a word at a time with **^F**, and back again a word at a time with **^A**; repeat the movements a character at a time with **^D** and **^S**.

Your keyboard may have a block of four keys (usually on the numeric keypad to the right of the main keyboard) marked with arrows that perform the same functions—the cursor will move in the direction of the arrow. Try them out now. If these arrow keys are located in the numeric keypad, you may have to press a key labeled **Num Lock** (or something similar) to "lock out" the numeric function. On IBM keyboards the arrow keys operate when **Num Lock** is off.

There are various control characters for deleting letters, words, or whole lines. To delete the character to the immediate *left* of the cursor use the **Delete** key (marked **DEL**); to delete the character *under* the cursor use ^**G**; ^**T** will delete the *whole word* (or part of a word) to the *right* of the cursor, and ^**Y** will delete the *whole line*.

In the top right-hand corner of the screen at the end of the *status line* you will see the words INSERT ON. If you press ^**V**, this will disappear: ^**V** is a toggle switch that turns INSERT on and off. Press ^**V** again and you will see the INSERT ON message reappear.

Try the INSERT function now. With INSERT on, position the cursor on the first letter of a word already typed. When you start entering some additional text, the new letters you type are automatically inserted and the rest of the text is shifted to the right.

If you turn INSERT off and then type in a few letters, you will find you overtype the existing text and replace it with your new text. You will find both of these techniques very useful. When you first call up WordStar, INSERT is always on by default. You must press ^**V** before you start typing if you prefer to work with INSERT off.

Once you become an experienced WordStar user, you may find you would prefer to change some of the *defaults* in the program. Using the WordStar WINSTALL program you can, for example, set a new default Help Level (when WordStar is loaded the first time the default level is 3), set INSERT to OFF, set the file directory to OFF, and so on. All of these are listed in the Menu of WordStar Features in the WINSTALL program, along with the system disk drive option that was discussed in relation to hard disk users. For the moment, you will probably prefer to leave everything as it is.

Paragraph Reforming

Do not worry if after you have corrected your mistakes the spacing looks uneven. Wait until you have finished the whole paragraph, satisfy yourself that the content is correct, and then you can "beautify" it with a ^B—also known as *paragraph reform*:

Step-by-step procedure

1. Place the cursor over the first letter of the paragraph you wish to reform.
2. Press ^B. You will notice that as a paragraph reforms the cursor may stop whenever it reaches a word that is too long for the length of line that is set. You may be given the option to hyphenate words (called *hyphen help*) or to keep pressing ^B to reform the paragraph without hyphens; this depends entirely on your personal preference. There will be more irregular spaces between words if you do not use hyphens.
3. If you think that you will not want to hyphenate words, you can turn off hyphen help by typing ^OH (this is another toggle switch, like ^V). Then, when you press ^B, the whole paragraph will be reformed without pausing. To type ^OH, you simply hold the **Ctrl** key down, press the **O** key, and then release the **Ctrl** key and press the **H**. If this process takes you more than one second, after typing ^O you will see the ONSCREEN MENU appear at the top of your screen. After you press the **H** you will get back to the normal WordStar MAIN MENU.
4. Also note that the reforming process stops wherever there is a hard return (a < in the far right column on the screen). If you want to continue and reform the next paragraph, simply move the cursor with the appropriate cursor **Ctrl** or arrow key until it is at the start of the next paragraph. Then press ^B again.

Justifying the Text

When you first use a new WordStar disk, *right justification* will be implemented by default. You are accustomed to seeing the text right justified in newspapers and books; it is a matter of personal taste whether you like to see it in typewritten letters.

Step-by-step procedure

Here's how it works:

1. If you prefer to have right justification switched off, you can use yet another toggle switch—this time ^OJ—giving you

what is known as *ragged right text*. This text has a "ragged" right-hand margin but no extra spaces between words that are added in right-justified text.

2. If you want to change a paragraph that has already been typed in with right justification switched ON, simply type **^OJ** to toggle right justification OFF and then move the cursor back to the beginning of the paragraph and type **^B**. You can see what this paragraph looks like with right justification toggled OFF (in paragraph 3 below).

3. If you want to change a paragraph that has already been typed in with right justification toggled ON, simply type **^OJ** to toggle right justification OFF. Then move the cursor back to the beginning of the paragraph and type **^B**. You can see what this paragraph looks like with right justification OFF.

   If you prefer right justification, do not forget to type **^OJ** again to toggle it back on.

SAVING FILES

Once you have edited the text to your complete satisfaction, you now must save your file. At this moment, the text you have typed appears on your computer screen and is temporarily stored in the computer memory. If you turned your computer off now, you would lose the file you have just created. In order to save a file you must transfer it from the computer memory to the surface of your floppy disk.

Step-by-Step Procedure

1. Different computer programs have different techniques and commands for saving files. In WordStar you use **^K**. If you press **^K**, release the **Ctrl** key, then immediately type a **D** (usually shown onscreen as: **^KD**): the screen will announce that it is:

   SAVING FILE A:FORMLETT.TXT.

   If you take longer than one second to type the **D**, then after you press **^K** the menu at the top of the screen will change and now you will see the **^K Menu**, which is entitled BLOCK MENU. Notice that there are several options for saving files.

As soon as you press **D**, the file will be saved and you will see the SAVING FILE message.

2. If at any time you wish to save your file and exit WordStar straight back to the A> prompt (the operating system), you can type ^**KX**. This entry assumes that you have no further work to do in WordStar.

3. Once your file has been saved (WRITTEN BACK TO THE DISK), you will find yourself again at the OPENING MENU and you will see the name of your new file on the directory of drive A listed on the screen. You can now open another file, exit WordStar, or print the file you just saved.

PRINTING WORDSTAR FILES

Now that you have typed in your letter and saved it on the disk, you should try printing it. To print a file in WordStar you have to select the PRINT A FILE option from the OPENING MENU.

Step-by-Step Procedure

1. Select **P** from the OPENING MENU.

2. Type **FORMLETT.TXT** when asked for NAME OF FILE TO PRINT.

3. When you press **Return**, you will be required to respond to a set of queries: you can simply press **Return** as each query is listed—this will select the default answer—until you reach the last, which reads: READY PRINTER—PRESS RETURN.

4. Check that your printer is ready—the ONLINE light should be active.

5. When you press **Return** the printer will be activated and your letter will print. Do not worry at this point about the appearance of the *print out*; this can easily be adjusted later. *Do* check the text for errors.

6. When printing is complete you will see the OPENING MENU again; exit from WordStar by typing **X**.

You have now entered, edited, and printed out your first WordStar file. You should get into the habit of using WordStar for all your routine typing—even though at first it may actually take you longer than using your electric typewriter. You will soon learn the control characters if you practice, and it is much more useful to practice on letters or documents that are *needed* than to work through a lot of sterile exercises.

You can look ahead at Chapter 6, WordStar in Depth, if you need to. Do work through the rest of Part One as well, though, so that you see the way the major MicroPro programs link together.

Next, in Chapter 4, you will learn DataStar. It will take about an hour to familiarize yourself with this new program and to design your form for entering names and addresses, so if you need a break, stop now.

Before you continue, though, you should make a backup copy of your new file. With your tutorial disk in drive A and the backup disk in drive B, you simply type:

CP/M users: `PIP B:=A:FORMLETT.TXT[V]`

MS-DOS users: `COPY A:FORMLETT.TXT B:/V`

and you will have an up-to-date copy of this file on the tutorial disk. You should make a backup copy of any new files at the end of each chapter.

For those of you with WordStar and MailMerge *only*, the next section shows you how to enter names and addresses in a non-document file in WordStar. When you have completed that, you should proceed to Chapter 5, MailMerge Tutorial.

Even if you do have DataStar and ReportStar as well, it would be useful for you to see how non-document files work in WordStar. If you ever need to send a form letter to a small number of people, you may find this technique quicker than using DataStar to create a special form.

ENTERING DATA IN NON–DOCUMENT FILES

Although it is undoubtedly easier to enter names and addresses or other similar data into a predesigned form in DataStar, it is possible to achieve the same result using WordStar to create your data file.

Each complete set of data, in this case a name and address, makes up one *record* and the individual items that make up each record are termed *fields*.

Non-document Files

A WordStar *non-document file* is similar to a *document file* (the type you have used so far by selecting **D** at the OPENING MENU), but it has no ruler line and does not automatically word wrap for you. You will use this type of file for entering the names and addresses of the six customers or clients to whom you wish to send the form letter you have just typed.

First you must decide what information you wish to enter in each customer or client record, for example, LAST NAME, FIRST NAME (or initials), TITLE (Mr/Ms/Dr, etc.), POSITION (Manager/Director/Secretary, etc.), COMPANY NAME, STREET, CITY, STATE, ZIP CODE, SIGN-OFF (Yours faithfully/Yours sincerely/Kind regards, etc.) and SALUTATION (Dear Sir, etc.). You will probably find it easier to jot these headings down by hand on a piece of paper so that you will not make any mistakes.

Each of these items within a record is a field, and the titles of the fields are termed *field names*. Each field is separated from the next by a comma. You may not be able to enter all the information for each client; for example, you may not know his or her position within the company, or you may have no record of his or her initials. However, you must take great care to put in a comma wherever a field is omitted, so that you have the same number of fields in each record, and all in identical order. The importance of this will become more obvious to you when you learn about MailMerge.

Creating a Data File in WordStar

You will now create a new file to contain the names and addresses you wish to enter. As usual, the file name may be up to eight characters long, but this time make the file name extension .DTA to indicate that this is a *data file*.

Step-by-step procedure

1. Make sure you have the tutorial disk in drive A and a backup disk in drive B. Next to the A> prompt type **WS**.
2. Select **N** from the OPENING MENU to open a non-document file and type in a name—for example, ADDRESS.DTA.
3. You will find a status line and the same WordStar MAIN MENU at the top of your screen, but no ruler line.

4. Type in your first record in the order you decided, separating the fields with commas as shown:

```
Hughes,J,Mr,,J Hughes & Sons,1 Main Street,Cornwall,CT,06753,Sincerely,Dear Mr Hughes
```

Notice that there is no space after the commas between fields, and because there is no entry for the POSITION field, an extra comma after Mr. indicates the blank field.

If your record is long, you will find that the line simply continues to the right; in a non-document file there is no WORD WRAP. The screen shifts automatically so that you can view what you are typing; then, when you press **Return** and the cursor goes to the beginning of the next line, you will see the first 79 characters of the line you typed and a + sign in the flag column to indicate that there is more text on the line. Another example would be:

```
Hughes,J,Mr,,J Hughes & Sons,1 Main Street,Cornwall,CT,06753,Sincerely,Dear Mr Hughes
Smith,B,Mr,Manager,''W Evans, Inc.'',10 Broad Street,New Haven,CT,06533,Kind regards,
Dear Brian
```

Notice that there are no blank fields, but since there has to be a comma between Evans and Inc. in the COMPANY NAME field (and so that MailMerge will not think that this is the usual comma *between two fields*) you must place this field in quotes, as shown above.

5. Continue entering records until you have six names and addresses of people to whom you would like to send the form letter you typed earlier. Check carefully that you have kept the format constant and that you have inserted commas wherever you have left blank fields. The easiest way to do this is to count the commas in each record—*they should all total the same.*

6. When you have finished entering data you must save your file by typing ^**KD**.

7. If you would like to print out the data list, make sure the printer is powered on and online, then select **P** from the opening menu and type **ADDRESS.DTA** when asked for the name of file to print. Now you can simply press the **ESC** key to indicate that you accept all the default answers, and the printer will be activated immediately.

8. When the listing is finished, turn the printer offline and press the FORM FEED button on the printer to scroll the paper up. While it is still fresh in your mind, write (by hand) on the computer listing of your file, the file name, AD-DRESS.DTA, and the titles, in order, of your field names. This will make it easier for you if you need to add more names and addresses at a later date.

You will also need the list of field names, in the correct order, for the MailMerge tutorial—but before you go on, make a backup copy of your tutorial disk.

Exit to the operating system by typing **X** and then, at the A> prompt, type:

CP/M users:	`PIP B:=A:*.*[V]`
MS-DOS users:	`COPY A:*.* B:/V`

and you will have a duplicate copy of all the files on the tutorial disk.

If you think you will ever need to enter a sizable (for example, more than 20) names and addresses into one file, you should seriously consider using DataStar. DataStar allows you to design a form showing all the field names; then you simply enter the information you have available. If you skip a field, a comma is automatically inserted for you. It makes the whole process simpler, quicker, and almost foolproof.

If you have DataStar, you should go on to Chapter 4; for those of you with WordStar and MailMerge only, proceed straight to Chapter 5 and prepare yourself for the excitement of MailMerge! Perhaps it would be interesting for you to glance through Chapter 4 to see how you would tackle the exercise you have just completed using DataStar.

4

InfoStar Tutorial

Simple Form Design with FORMGEN
Data Entry
Data Retrieval
Sorting with FormSort
Creating Quick Reports with ReportStar

DataStar is the electronic equivalent of your existing card filing system. Perhaps at the moment you keep one list of names and addresses in alphabetical order by surname, another in order of company name, and perhaps yet a third subdivided into particular types of businesses. Although for a while you will have to keep your manual system running alongside DataStar, you will soon begin to appreciate the power of the computer for this kind of routine chore.

Using data entered into the very simple form you will design in the first section of this chapter, and then using a combination of FormSort and WordStar, you will be able to sort the lists for such uses as sorting clients by surname or company name, or writing to all your customers in Connecticut, or sending Christmas cards to all managing directors.

SIMPLE FORM DESIGN WITH FORMGEN

The DataStar FORM GENeration program, FORMGEN, allows you to design a form to your own specifications—you can choose to make it look exactly like a form that you currently fill in by hand, or you can create a completely new design.

In this preliminary tutorial you will design a simple form for entry of names and addresses of clients, customers, or whatever is appropriate to your particular business. In a later chapter in Part Two of this guide, you will learn to create much more advanced forms where, for example, the entry of a customer name will cause the delivery address to be filled in automatically, or the product code entered in an invoice triggers the description of the product and totals the prices and adds sales tax at the current rate automatically.

Designing Your Form

Ideally, you should plan your form on paper first. It should have a name that describes its content, say ADDRESS for a simple list of names and addresses.

Each complete name and address is record, and the individual items within each record are fields. First you must decide on names for each of the fields you will include and determine how many spaces must be allowed in each field to accommodate the longest possible surname or street name you could encounter.

There are several important points to be considered in advance, remembering that your ultimate aim is to have names and addresses entered in such a way that you can *sort* them, for example, in alphabetical order of surname, or perhaps by state or by zip code. Make sure that the items you may wish to use for sorting are separate: for example, put the last name in one field and the initials in another; keep the zip code separate from the state.

Typing in the Form

Remember, if you had to make two tutorial disks, you should now put in drive A the disk containing the InfoStar programs (and don't forget to press **Ctrl-C**). If you are using a hard disk system, substitute the appropriate drive label where drive A is mentioned in this section. You will use FormGen to create the form in DataStar.

Step-by-step procedure

1. Boot up your system from the tutorial disk and at the prompt type:

FIGURE 4–1   Sample Address Form

```
LAST NAME: _____  FIRST NAME/INITS: _____ TITLE: _____

POSITION:      _____
COMPANY NAME: _____
STREET:       _____
CITY:         _____  STATE: __  ZIP CODE: _____

SIGN OFF: _____  SALUTATION:  _____
```

FORMGEN ADDRESS

and press **Return**.

2. Read help screen 4 and then type a ^J to rotate it to help screen 3, which reminds you of the common control characters. The sooner you know the cursor control characters, the easier you will find it to move around your form.

3. Now you are ready to type in your form design. Starting directly below help screen 3, type in the field names and then define the length of each field by typing ^Q repeatedly or inserting underline characters.

   Figure 4–1 is an example of a simple address form.

4. Type the first field name (LAST NAME) on the far left of the screen, then leave two spaces (i.e., press the Space Bar twice) and press ^Q for as many blanks as you have decided are required to define the length of this field.

5. Then allow two spaces before entering the next field name, FIRST NAME/INITS, and press ^Q for each blank shown here.

6. Insert another two spaces and type TITLE, followed by ^Q six times. Note that when the cursor reaches column 79 it will automatically wrap to the next line. If you need more space for these first three fields, you have the choice of reducing the number of spaces in each field (using ^G to delete them), or you can put the TITLE field on the next line.

7. Try to space out the form in a neat fashion—remember you will spend quite a lot of time looking at this form design as you enter your names and addresses, so you may as well

make it look good! Most of the editing commands are the same as those you have used in WordStar and are detailed on the help screen, so you should have no trouble actually typing the form and correcting any mistakes as you go along.

8. If you wish, you can leave a blank line between blocks of data, as shown in the sample between the personal details and the company address details, to make it easier to see where you are when you start entering the names and addresses. To create a blank line, just press **Return** after the last ^Q on a line (for example, after the TITLE field in the sample form).

Key Fields and Index Files

Before you go on to the data entry phase in DataStar to enter some names and addresses, there is one more essential step. The form is not complete until you have designated at least one field to be a *key field*.

The key field (or fields) will be stored in a separate file, called the *index file*, which makes possible the process of searching for individual records later on.

Step-by-step procedure

1. Decide which field(s) you would like to use as your key(s); usually in a name and address file key fields are the LAST NAME and the FIRST NAME/INITS, but you may feel for your purposes it would be more appropriate to use the COMPANY NAME.

2. When you have decided, move the cursor to the field (make sure that the cursor is on an underline character), press ^K, and the field will fill with asterisks looking like this:

LAST NAME: ******************** FIRST NAME/INITS: ********** TITLE: _____

3. If you are not in a field when you press ^K you will see an error message on the screen; just follow the instruction to press the **Esc** key, move the cursor into the field, and press ^K again. If you look at the status line at the top of your screen, you will see the field number next to NUM.

4. If you change your mind about which fields you wish to designate as key fields, simply move the cursor back into

the field filled with asterisks, press ^K again, and the asterisks will disappear. Then move to the new key field and press ^K. You can only do this *before* the entry of any names and addresses. Once you have data in a file, you have to go through a special ReportStar procedure in order to change keys—so *plan ahead!*

Exit to DataStar

Now the form design process is complete and you can enter some data. If you look at the help screen you will see that you must type a ^C to indicate that the form is done.

Step-by-step procedure

1. Type ^C now; you will see some options.
2. If you would like to stop now and review progress, choose option **B** which will:

SAVE FORM AND BOOT OPERATING SYSTEM

exiting to the A> prompt.
3. If you want to enter names and addresses, select **D** to

SAVE FORM AND CHAIN DATASTAR

4. You will be asked to enter the drive where you want your data file to be created. Enter **A:**. Then, to create the index file enter **A:** again. The DataStar screen will now display.

Backup Copies

Before you choose to exit from FormGen back to the A> prompt, make a backup copy of your form straight away. Then, just in case you have a disaster when you start entering data, you can use the backup. If you want to go straight on to Datastar now, don't forget to make backup copies later. Use the appropriate command (**PIP** or **COPY**) to copy ADDRESS.DEF from drive A to drive B or from hard disk to floppy.

DATA ENTRY

Entering data in DataStar is very easy once your form is designed. If you chose option D at the end of FormGen, then your form is already on the screen and the cursor is in the first field waiting for you to type in the LAST NAME of your first client.

Step-by-Step Procedure

1. If you chose option B, then after the A> prompt type:

   DATASTAR ADDRESS

   and then press **Return**.
2. You will be prompted to enter which disk drive you wish to use to store the data file. Type **A** (to indicate that AD-DRESS.DTA should be stored on drive A), then enter the same for the index file—**A** again. After a moment the screen will display your form.
3. Above your form is a help screen displaying the main control characters. You do not need to know the functions of all the control characters listed, but note the ones governing cursor control so that you can move around the form and correct any errors you may make. Note the control characters that perform different functions from those you have just learned in WordStar: **^E** will not move the cursor up a line—it will cause you to exit from the current mode. Fortunately, this is one of the exceptions; most of the controls are the same as in WordStar.
4. Prepare to enter your first name and address. Make sure that the cursor is at the beginning of the first field (that is, positioned on the first dash in the line next to the field name) and then type in the LAST NAME; press **Return** to go to the next field. Continue typing in the details for the first client, pressing **Return** after filling in each field, until you end up with something like Figure 4–2.
5. Note that not all fields contain entries; this does not matter in InfoStar. However, *do* be sure to enter the correct information in each field. Think ahead to the sorting of your data files, which, to be efficient, relies on the entry of correct and accurate data at this stage.

FIGURE 4-2 Address Form with Entries in Fields

LAST NAME: Hughes_____   FIRST NAME/INITS: J_____   TITLE: **Mr**____

POSITION: _____

COMPANY NAME: Hughes & Sons_____

STREET: 1 Main Street_____

CITY: Cornwall_____   STATE: **CT**   ZIP CODE: **06753**

SIGN OFF: **Sincerely**_____   SALUTATION: **Dear Mr Hughes**_____

---

6. When you press **Return** after you have entered data in the last field, a new message appears at the top of the screen. It gives you several options; just press **Return** again to store the record you have completed in the data file AD-DRESS.DTA. As soon as the record has been saved, the screen shows a new form ready to be filled in. Continue until you have entered six or so records.

There is one very important point to make about your data files now, while you are entering the data, which will affect the way the MailMerge program works. In order for data to be merged correctly with your form letters, you must enter data *in the last field* of each record. In the form just designed, Salutation is the last field; you must always fill in the data in this field. When you begin to design your own forms, remember to make the last field something you must fill in; the worst design of all would include a field that sometimes is filled and sometimes is not. When you learn advanced form design in Part Two you will see how to specify that this field must be filled before the record can be saved.

Index Files

Each time you store a record, an entry is also saved in the index file, ADDRESS.NDX. However, this file contains just the key fields you have designated, so it is always a much smaller file than the data file.

The index file is an essential and integral part of the DataStar system; without it your data file is worthless. The workings of the index file will be explained in greater depth in Part Two of this book. For the moment, just remember that it is essential to have an index file for the form; by the time you reach the end of this chapter, you will have seen some of the ways in which it is used in DataStar.

Remember that every time you save a record it is indexed; if you make changes in the data (change an address, for example), then the index file is automatically updated at the same time. Remember, also, that you must not, under any circumstances, make changes in the data file other than by using DataStar. If you edit the data file with WordStar, for example, the changes you make will not be made simultaneously in the index file (as they will if you make changes to data in DataStar), and once the data file and index file do not match precisely, your file will become unusable. Also, you should never try to examine the index file using WordStar; even if you do not attempt to edit it, you may still damage or corrupt it in some way and you run the risk of rendering it useless.

In Part Two you will learn how to create new index files using ReportStar.

DATA RETRIEVAL

There are various ways of selecting the particular record you wish to examine from the six or so names and addresses you have entered. First, you must exit from Add mode and then select one of the Scan modes available in DataStar.

This is where the index file demonstrates its usefulness.

Changing Modes

Now that you have some records in your data file, you can switch from Add mode and see how the other modes function. To exit the current mode just press **^E**; you will see the list of alternative modes at the top of the screen.

Scan in data file order

Start with **D—SCAN IN DATA FILE ORDER**. The current mode is always shown in the top left hand corner of the screen. You will notice that in Scan mode (D) you have yet another help screen. To look at your records one after the other, simply type **^N** (next).

Correcting errors

While you are scanning your records, you can check to make sure there are no mistakes. If you see something has been omitted or is wrong, you can make the corrections by moving the cursor to the mistake and overtyping it. You also can take this opportunity to ensure that you have entered data in the last field (SALUTA-TION) of each record. Then type ^B to indicate that this is the end of the entry and, when the message appears at the top of the screen, press **Return** to file the updated data.

Scan in index order

To change modes again, type ^E and this time choose I—SCAN IN INDEX ORDER. This will show you that the entries in the index file are in alphabetical order of the first key field you designated, (that is, LAST NAME).

Again, you can look at the next record with ^N or at the previous one with ^P.

Select by key

Now try ^E and K to SELECT BY KEY. This time the cursor will move to the first key field (LAST NAME). Type in the LAST NAME and press **Return** to move the cursor to the next key field and enter the FIRST NAME/INITS. Press **Return** to display the appropriate record.

If you made a mistake in typing, you will get the message:

```
Key not found. Hit ESC to re-enter key
```

Press Esc, check to see where you went wrong, and type the field entries again.

The index file makes data searching and retrieval quick and easy in DataStar. Instead of searching the whole data file for a complete record, the index file (which contains only the key fields and *pointers*) is scanned, the appropriate record is identified by the key, and the pointer indicates the position of the required record in the data file.

Edit scan mask

Finally, try ^ES—EDIT SCAN MASK (^EM in version 1.4 or earlier). All the fields will fill up with asterisks. Move the cursor to the TITLE field and type in Mr; then type a ^B and a record with Mr in the TITLE field will display.

When a record is found that matches the characters you have entered with EDIT SCAN MASK the mode automatically changes to Scan mode (D) and you can scan through all the records with Mr in the TITLE field, in turn, by typing ^N. Try some other fields in this mode—just type ^ES (or ^EM) again, delete with ^G the **Mr** in the TITLE field (notice that as you delete the characters you entered previously, the asterisks are restored), then type, for example, **CT** in the STATE field and press ^B.

Scan through the records that contain **CT** in the STATE field with ^N as before: note that you can use ^P to scan backward.

If you have a recent IBM version of InfoStar you will see in the menu at the top of the Scan mode that you can erase the contents of the mask with ^Y, instead of using ^G to do this one character at a time. It doesn't make much difference when you have to erase Mr from the TITLE field, but you could have entered data in several fields—say, the CITY, the STATE, a few characters in the LAST NAME, and so on. It is then very convenient if you can empty the whole mask with one keystroke.

Exit to operating system

To save your data file you should type ^E to change modes and then **E** to EXIT CURRENT FORM. In newer versions of the software, you will see the system prompt; in earlier versions, you will be asked if you wish to enter a different form name. You don't have another form yet, so just type ^C to return to the operating system and the A> prompt. You can type this all in one entry— ^EEC—by holding down **Ctrl** and pressing **EEC**, or ^EE in the recent version.

Now you can type **DIR** next to the A> prompt and see that you have the three files named ADDRESS (ADDRESS.DEF, ADDRESS.DTA, and ADDRESS.NDX). You may also have ADDRESS.BAK if you edited a file.

SORTING WITH FORMSORT

FormSort is a program within InfoStar that allows you to sort your data into almost any order you like. FormSort is very easy to operate and is described in detail in the InfoStar chapter in Part Two.

In this chapter you will learn how to sort your six names and addresses into alphabetical order by surname. Since LAST NAME is the key field in your ADDRESS file, this is very straightforward and quick:

Step-by-Step Procedure

1. Next to the system prompt type:

    ```
    FORMSORT ADDRESS
    ```

    and press **Return**. You will see a few lines displaying the version number of FormSort, and so on. Then a message states that SuperSort is sorting your data file. You will be told that since you gave only the name ADDRESS, this will be the name of your output file.

2. Next you will be told that SuperSort is sorting your index file, then that the sort is completed, and, finally, the sizes of the two output files.

3. To see that your data file is now in alphabetical order of the last name, you can use another built-in command, **TYPE**. Next to the prompt, type:

    ```
    TYPE ADDRESS.DTA
    ```

    and press **Return**.

4. The listing of your file will appear on the screen and you can see that the last names are indeed in alphabetical order.

5. If you would like to print the list, check that your printer is powered on and online. Type the above command again, but before you press **Return**, type ^P. You will now have a printout of your alphabetical list of names.

6. Finally, you must make a backup copy of your ADDRESS files. Type:

    CP/M users: `PIP B:=A:ADDRESS.*[V]`

    MS-DOS users: `COPY A:ADDRESS.* B:/V`

    and all four files will be copied.

CREATING QUICK REPORTS WITH REPORTSTAR

The final program for you to try in the InfoStar package is ReportStar, the report generator. You will learn how to make a list of names, states, and zip codes from the ADDRESS.DTA file.

First, you must call up the form definition file, ADDRESS.DEF, and give each of the fields a name. Recent CP/M versions of InfoStar ask for field names only; in the version for IBM users, field numbers must also be present, but these are entered automatically.

Step-by-Step Procedure

1. Next to the prompt type:

    FORMGEN ADDRESS

    and press **Return**.
2. Using **^D**, move the cursor onto the dashed line of the first field,LAST NAME. Look at the status line at the top of your screen; you will see that you are in field 001.
3. Press **^R** to use the Field Definition mode of FormGen. The first prompt (in 1.6) reads: FIELD NUMBER/ NAME. You will have to press **Return** to move the cursor past the 001/. Then type:

    LAST NAME

    and press **Return**. If you have the CP/M version, you will not see the 001/—simply enter the field name as prompted.
4. A whole list of prompts appear, which you could use to specify all sorts of attributes for the LAST NAME field. For this first exercise, you should ignore them.
5. Type **^C** to indicate that the field definition is complete, then **^F** to move to the next field, and **^R** to define the FIRST NAME field in the same way: type FIRST NAME next to the prompt FIELD NUMBER/ NAME 002/ and then press **Return**.
6. Press **^C** to end the field definition, **^F** to go to the TITLE field, and **^R** to define the field.
7. Continue in this way through all the fields, naming them in turn. These field names are used in ReportStar, as you

will see in the next exercise. When you design your own forms, you should always go through the definition process and name each field in this way.

8. When you have finished the field definition process, type **^CB** to exit from FORMGEN back to the prompt.

9. At the prompt type:

RGEN

10. Your screen will display the usual information about the program and then you will see the message:

Please enter report name here (or press RETURN):

11. You are allowed only eight letters for your report name and the name you choose will appear at the top of the report when it is printed out, like a title. For example, if you enter ADDRESS as the name, then your listing will be headed:

ADDRESS REPORT

The ReportStar screen is displayed with a menu at the top detailing the control characters.

12. Since you chose ADDRESS as the name for your report, the cursor will be flashing next to the name ADDRESS. Just press **Return** to select it.

13. Now you will see a list of the field names from the AD-DRESS file on the screen (these are the names you entered in FormGen). You must choose from this list the fields you wish to include as headings for your ADDRESS table.

14. If you press **TI** the cursor will move to TITLE and you can just press **Return** to accept it. Then press **LA** for LAST NAME, **STA** for STATE and **Z** for ZIP CODE.

15. Now press **^C** to indicate that you have finished the selection phase. The screen display will change, giving you some new options. For this first use you should choose the default **R** simply by pressing **Return**.

16. If you are asked if you want Standard Error Reporting, select the default **Y** by pressing **Return**.

17. You are asked if you wish the report to be *printed* or *written to a disk file*; you will accept the default answer, **N** (because you do not want the file written to disk, you want it printed).

18. Check that your printer is powered on and online, then press **Return** to accept the default **N**, and you will see the screen change again.

19. Finally, you are asked to enter the date (two digits each for the month, day, year). If you don't want to enter the date, just press **Return** to move through each of the three fields in turn.

20. After the last **Return** the printer will be activated and your report will be printed, giving the list of names from your data file in alphabetical order, under the headings:

ADDRESS REPORT
10/01/85

TITLE	LAST NAME	STATE	ZIP CODE
Mr	Hughes	CT	06753
Mr	Smith	CT	06533

Wasn't it easy to prepare that report?

The Quick Report can be further edited in WordStar, or you can produce custom reports using the REDIT program in InfoStar. More of this will be discussed in Part Two.

Now that you have worked through the introduction to InfoStar, you are ready at last to merge your address data with the form letter you typed in WordStar back in Chapter 3. In Chapter 5 you will go back into WordStar to edit the form letter and to add the details required for the MailMerge operation.

Proceed to Chapter 5.

5

MailMerge Tutorial

Principles of Merge Printing
Merge Printing Letters
Merge Printing Envelopes
Troubleshooting for Merge Printing

In this chapter, everything you have learned so far will be used to produce six "merge printed" letters, each one based on the text you typed in earlier, but personally addressed to each of the clients in your ADDRESS data file. You will also merge print the envelopes in the same way from the same data file.

PRINCIPLES OF MERGE PRINTING

Having created a form and entered data, you now have a store of names and addresses that must be linked to your basic letter to produce six successfully merged letters.

At the top of FORMLETT.TXT you will identify the data file containing the names and addresses you wish to print, in this case, ADDRESS.DTA. This file will have the fields sorted in alphabetical order by names if you have the InfoStar program, or in data order (the way you typed them in) if you have WordStar and MailMerge only.

Then you will list the *variables* (or field names) in the same order as they appear in your form. Finally you will create "empty boxes" in the appropriate places in the letter, identified by the same field names, which will be filled with data from the named data file, record by record, until the data is used up.

TABLE 5–1 Summary of Commonly Used Dot Commands

Command Function

.OP	Omit Page numbers
.MT	Margin Top (default is 3 lines)
.PO	Page Offset (the left margin default is 8 spaces)
.PA	Page Advance
.DF	Data File name
.RV	Read Variables
.MB	Margin Bottom (default is 8 lines)
.PL	Page Length (default is 66 lines)

This will be much clearer when you actually do it!

Creating the Matrix Letter

You will have to modify the original form letter that you created and stored in Chapter 3 using WordStar to create the matrix letter for merge printing.

Step-by-step procedure

1. Boot up as usual. Next to the A> prompt type:

   ```
   WS B:FORMLETT.TXT
   ```

   (assuming your letter is stored on the disk in drive B) and press **Return**. You will see your letter reappear on the screen with the WordStar help screen above.

2. You must now enter special *dot commands* at the top of the form that will link your letter to the appropriate data file for merge printing. These are called *dot commands* because they each begin with a period (or dot) that must appear in the first column on the screen. These dot commands are recognized by the software as special merge printing commands, and so they do not print out on your letter. See Table 5–1 for a summary list of the dot commands you will use. Enter them as listed in these instructions, not from the table.

3. Create a blank line at the top of the form by pressing ^N (insert line): make sure also that INSERT ON appears in the top right-hand corner of your screen (if not, type ^V and it will appear).

FIGURE 5-1 FORMLETT.TXT with Added Data File
and Variables

```
.DF ADDRESS.DTA
.RV LAST,FIRST,TITLE,POSN,COMP,STR,CITY,STATE,ZIP,SIGNO,SALUT
```

I am sure you will be interested to know that we now have a
microcomputer in our head office and that this letter was
written using the word processing package, WordStar with
MailMerge. Since we have been able to enter your company
details and product interests into the DataStar database, we
will be keeping in much closer touch with you over the coming
months.

Please be sure to let us know of any changes that should be
made in your address or in the details of your office
personnel--we would like to keep our records correct and up
to date now that it is so easy to do so.

Many thanks for your cooperation.

NOTES:
1. You may abbreviate the field names.
2. When you have a two-word field name you must run the
words together, so ZIP CODE must be written as ZIPCODE. In
fact, you could just abbreviate it to ZIP.
3. Each field name must be unique.

4. Now type in the first dot command, **.DF**, followed by the name of the file, **ADDRESS.DTA**. Press **Return**. Then on the next line type **.RV** (for Read Variables) and list the field names (or variables), exactly as shown in Figure 5–1, with commas between each variable.

5. You will notice that just after you type in the dot of **.DF** and **.RV**, a **?** appears in the flag column. When you add the **DF** an **M** replaces the **?**, indicating that these are merge printing commands. If a **?** does not appear when it should, check that you have the dot in column 1; otherwise, your dot commands will not be recognized by the program.

Marking Variables

Now that you have identified the data file to be used and listed the variable names, you are ready to create the "boxes" in the letter that will be filled with the appropriate data from the named data file during merge printing. The technique is to position the field names where you want them to print out and to enclose them between ampersands (& signs).

Step-by-step procedure

1. Mark fields now as shown here, but first insert some space by typing ^N a few times.

2. It is important for you to type the variables, or field names, exactly as you have listed them next to the **.RV** (be especially careful if you have used abbreviations).

3. When you know that data for a particular variable is present in some records and not in others, then follow the field name with a **/O** (this is a capital O, *not* a zero). When the data file contains data in that particular field it will be printed, but if not, it will be *omitted* (hence the O) without leaving a blank line. Examples are:

&POSN/O&

&COMP/O&

4. MailMerge allows for different length fields between ampersands, so whether the LAST NAME is "Smith" or "Forbes-Huntingdon-Smythe" the space between ampersands will accommodate it exactly. Take care with the spacing between variable names when you have more than one to a line; when you type **Mr J Hughes**, you leave *one space* between the **r** and the **J**, and between the **J** and the **H**. Do the same with the variable names, counting the ampersands in with the names, for example:

&TITLE& &FIRST& &LAST&

Dear &TITLE& &LAST&,

5. There is one last dot command to use. When you reach the bottom of a page in WordStar you will see a dotted line form across the screen—this is the *page break*, marked with a letter *P*. Because your letter does not end at the bottom of the page, you must *force* a page break at the very end of the text by typing **.PA**. This tells the printer that when it has finished printing out the first letter it must go automatically to the top of the next page to start the next letter. This is especially important in merge printing. Look over your letter for consistency and correct any errors.

FIGURE 5–2 Merge Printing Letter with
Dot Commands

```
.OP
.DF ADDRESS.DTA
.RV LAST,FIRST,TITLE,POSN,COMP,STR,CITY,STATE,ZIP,SIGNO,SALUT
&TITLE& &FIRST& &LAST&
&POSN/O&
&COMP/O&
&STR&
&CITY& &STATE& &ZIP/O&

October 1, 1985

&SALUT&,

I am sure you will be interested to know that we now have  a
microcomputer in  our  head  office and that this  letter  was
written  using  the  word processing  package,  WordStar  with
MailMerge.  Since  we  have been able to enter  your  company
details and product interests into the DataStar  database,  we
will be keeping in much closer touch with you over the  coming
months.

Please  be sure to let us know of any changes that  should  be
made  in  your  address  or  in  the  details  of  your  office
personnel--we  would like to keep our records correct  and  up
to date now that it is so easy to do so.

Many thanks for your cooperation.
&SIGNO&,

A Smith
Company Secretary
.PA
```

Most of the dot commands you used here are not merge printing commands (except for the .DF and .RV), but are normal WordStar print formatting dot commands.

In Chapter 3's tutorial for WordStar you did not use these commands; you simply accepted the default values for page length, bottom margin, top margin, and page offset, and you accepted numbering of the pages. If you would like to stop page numbers from printing on your letter, put the command **.OP** at the very top of your letter.

When you reach the more advanced WordStar and MailMerge chapters you will try out the effects of all these different dot commands.

Figure 5–2 shows the finished letter ready for merge printing. (Note that any excess blank lines have been deleted. Use ^Y to delete them in your file.)

It is especially important when preparing a letter for merge printing to ensure that there is no extra line (shown by the hard return symbol (<) in the flag column) after the page break (.PA). Otherwise, after each letter is printed a blank page will follow. Use ^Y to delete any extra lines, then move the cursor right next to the .PA and press ^T. You will notice that now there is no < sign in the flag column on the far right of your screen; it has been replaced by a dot.

You are now ready to try merge printing your form letter, but first you must save it. Type ^KD, and FORMLETT.TXT will be saved.

MERGE PRINTING LETTERS

Rather than waste paper and time by printing out the letters now, you will run a quick check to make sure that you have made no errors and that the file is merging correctly.

One possible problem is forgetting to insert a comma where a field was left blank. You might find that the first one or two letters print correctly, but then you see that instead of printing *"Dear Mr Hughes"* your next letter reads *"Dear 1 Main Street"*—not quite what you had intended!

Output to Disk

To check that all is well, you can write the merged letters to a test file *on your disk* and then look at them in a WordStar non-document file. Just follow the instructions given here.

Step-by-step procedure

1. In the WordStar OPENING MENU, note that the merge print command is M; type **M** now.
2. You will be asked for the name of file to merge print. Type:

```
FORMLETT.TXT
```

and press **Return**.

3. You will now be asked a series of questions (similar to those that appear when you select **P** from the OPENING MENU, but this time you will not accept the default answers). The first is:

OUTPUT TO DISK? Y/N

4. Type **Y**. This answer means that instead of printing the output (the letters) to a printer, the output will go to a named file on your disk.
5. When you press **Return**, the next question appears:

OUTPUT FILE NAME:

Type in **TEST** and press **Return**.
6. All the remaining questions are irrelevant for this test, so simply press **Return** after each (you will see default answers being typed in automatically) until there are none left. You will notice the disk output being written and on the screen it will say:

P = STOP PRINT

This means that if you wished to interrupt the process, you could type **P** and it would pause.
7. When the merging has finished and the OPENING MENU displays again, type **N** (to edit a non-document file) and, when asked for the filename, type **TEST**.
8. Now the first merge printed letter will display. If you got everything correct and in the right place, you will see the data from the first record in your ADDRESS.DTA file slotted into the appropriate places in your form letter. Now type ^C to scroll down the page and check that all the other letters are correctly printed. If so, CONGRATULATIONS!
9. If not, do not despair. At the end of this chapter you will find a section entitled Troubleshooting, that lists possible reasons it stopped working this time. You will need to work through them carefully until you find your mistake. Practice makes perfect—particularly in merge printing.

10. Once the output to disk is satisfactory, you can route the output to the printer and produce your final letters.

Output to the Printer

Now you are ready to merge print your letters.

Step-by-step procedure

1. Make sure that the printer is powered on and online or ready.
2. Type **M** again and press **Return**, then enter the name of file to merge print, **FORMLETT.TXT**, and keep pressing **Return** to accept default answers until you reach

    PAUSE FOR PAPER CHANGE BETWEEN PAGES ?

3. Respond with **Y** to this question, since you need the printer to pause after each letter for you to put in the next sheet of paper, assuming you are using single sheets. If you are using continuous-form paper, you can accept the default **N**o to this question as well by just pressing **Return**.
4. When you have entered your selection for paper, the screen reads:

    Ready printer, press RETURN:

    As soon as you press **Return**, the first letter should start to print.
5. When the first page is finished, printing is paused while you insert another sheet (if you are using single sheets). As soon as you are ready again, you type **P** and printing will begin again. Continue until all the letters have been printed. Check through them carefully and make sure there are no errors.

If you have successfully completed your first merge printing run, take a break now before preparing the envelopes.

MERGE PRINTING ENVELOPES

Now, while you are still flushed with success, you can go on to create the ENVELOPE file. This will extend your knowledge of WordStar and MailMerge commands still further.

Step-by-Step Procedure

1. Select **D** from the OPENING MENU and enter the name ADDRESS.ENV. This is a new file. Now, since you need the same information regarding the name of the data file and the list of variables as appeared at the top of your form letter, the easiest way to obtain these is to "read them in" from that file (i.e. copy the file contents). You can do this easily with WordStar.

2. Type **^KR** and press **Return**.

3. You will be asked for the name of file to read. Type **FORM-LETT.TXT** and press **Return**. The screen will display the letter: the other copy still exists, so you can use this new one as a basis for creating the kind of format you need for producing merge printed envelopes, editing it as necessary, without affecting your original file.

4. The main change you require is to force the name and address to start printing half way across the envelope. To achieve this you can use a new dot command, **.PO** (the Page Offset command, equivalent to adjusting the default left margin). For a standard business envelope try entering a new setting **.PO 33**. This means that during the merge printing the name and address will start printing from column 33 instead of column 8 (the default column for Page Offset).

5. You want the address to start printing precisely where you set the envelope in position. Normally, when you print a letter, WordStar automatically scrolls down three lines before printing starts; this is the default value for the top margin, **.MT**. You will now reset it to zero lines.

6. You can adjust your printer for envelopes using the Page Length command (previously you have accepted the default length of 66 lines). If you choose **.PL 30** you will ensure that the envelope rolls out of the printer when its address is printed. You do not want page numbers to print, so also include the dot command **.OP** (Omit Page numbers).

7. Now you should delete the text below the address. First, press **^X** repeatedly until the cursor is in position below your last line of address. Then, if you press **^Y** repeatedly, you will delete the text line by line until you reach the

---

FIGURE 5-3 Envelope File with Dot Commands
and Variables

```
.PO 33                                                          <
.MT 0                                                           <
.PL 30                                                          <
.OP                                                             <
.DF ADDRESS.DTA                                                 <
.RV LAST,FIRST,TITLE,POSN,COMP,STR,CITY,STATE,ZIP,SIGNO,SALUT   <
&TITLE& &FIRST& &LAST&                                          <
&POSN/O&                                                        <
&COMP/O&                                                        <
&STR&                                                           <
&CITY& &STATE& &ZIP&                                            <
.PA                                                             .
```

.PA, which you should keep. Your envelope file should now look like Figure 5–3.

8. The changes to the file are complete; this will print out the names and addresses on your six envelopes, exactly as they appeared at the head of your letters.

9. Now save the file by pressing **^KD**, then select **M** from the OPENING MENU and type **ADDRESS.ENV** as name of file to merge print: select default answers until you reach:

PAUSE FOR PAPER CHANGE BETWEEN PAGES ?

10. Again type **Y**, unless you have continuous envelopes. Then press **Return**.

11. Insert your first envelope ready in the printer and check that the printer is still online. Press **Return** again; your first envelope will print out. If positioning of the address is satisfactory, and the name and address has printed correctly, then insert the next envelope and press **P** to continue printing; repeat until all are done.

12. If you find the positioning of the address not quite right, stop printing by pressing **^P**, then **Y** to abandon printing. Reopen your file and try changing the value of the .PO. Make it smaller to move the address to the left on the envelope or larger to move it to the right. Try printing again until the alignment is correct.

So now you have six letters with matching envelopes, all ready to be signed! Aren't you impressed with your progress?

Remember the golden rule and make a backup copy of the new files on your tutorial disk. Using the appropriate command, copy A:*.TXT and A:*.ENV to your backup disk. Now you have a complete record, with a backup copy, of all the tutorials in Part One.

Part One is now finished. You have worked through the main MicroPro programs and have a feel for how they integrate with each other. You should try to follow up these tutorials by devising some exercises of your own—remember why you wanted a microcomputer in the first place. The best practice of all is to solve your own real problems.

I hope that you are inspired to press on to the more advanced tutorials in Part Two, although you should first make sure that you are really proficient in what you have learned so far. If you try to run before you can walk, you may make a lot of mistakes and lose heart.

In Part Two you will be introduced to two additional MicroPro packages, CalcStar and CorrectStar.

TROUBLESHOOTING FOR MERGE PRINTING

If you are unlucky enough to fail in your first attempt at merge printing, don't be too downcast. There are several places where you could have gone wrong, so here is a checklist for you to work through, point by point.

In parentheses are the possible symptoms you may observe that could be the reason for the failure.

Checklist

1. Have you named the correct data file in the **.DF** command? (Did you get a message such as Filename not found?)
2. Have you entered *all* the variables next to the **.RV** in exactly the same order as they appear in the data file—not the order you want them in your letter? (Did you find that the data was appearing in unexpected positions in the merge printed output?)
3. Is there a comma between each variable name in the list next to the **.RV**? Remember, *you must have data in the last field of each record for MailMerge to function correctly.* (Did you find you were addressing "1 Main Street" instead of

"Mr Hughes" or that you were printing out every other record?)

4. Are each of the variable names between ampersands *identical* in form to the way it is listed next to the **.RV**? (Did you find that instead of data printing out that you had the variable name between ampersands instead? Or, did you get a message on the screen saying you had used an Invalid variable name?)

5. Are you sure that you have typed **/O** (capital O) not **/0** (zero) for Omit after variable names that may or may not be filled with data during merge printing?

6. Did you insert **.PA** at the bottom of your letter or envelope file with no lines or spaces after it? (Check the flag column for the < sign and remove with **^T**.)

Hopefully, after you make all necessary adjustments your merge print will be successful. In the unlikely event that you still cannot make it work, call your friendly computer dealer.

PART TWO

6

WordStar in Depth

Preparing for the Tutorial

Basic WordStar Menus

Find and Replace Commands

More Menus

Ruler Lines and Tabs

Standard Dot Commands

Block Operations

File Operations

Other WordStar Commands

WordStar on a Color Monitor

Conclusions

So far you have only scratched the surface of WordStar, using it as little more than a text editor. By the end of this tutorial you will have learned much more about its true word processing capabilities.

You will start by looking at the various Help Menus, which will give you an overview of WordStar, and performing a few exercises as you go along. Then you will move on to the more rigorous formatting of your letters and documents with sections on ruler lines, tab settings, and dot commands. This is followed by detailed sections on moving blocks of text within a document and from one file to another. When you have worked through this Chapter you should immediately practice your new talents by tackling your own specific projects. You will find that you learn much more quickly when you really need to find an answer to your own problems.

PREPARING FOR THE TUTORIAL

Those of you with dual floppy disk computers can continue to use your tutorial disk in drive A as a program disk, but from now on you should get into the habit of using a separate data disk in drive B. So you will call up WordStar from the disk in drive A but you will actually write your letters and documents on the disk in drive B.

Those of you with hard disk computers with the hard disk divided into logical drives or partitions can follow a similar procedure. After booting up from the hard disk, call up WordStar; then change logged drive and store all your letters and documents on the second drive or partition. It makes for easier "housekeeping" if your data and programs are stored in separate areas on the hard disk.

If you have the MS-DOS or IBM DOS operating system, version 2.0 or later, you have the option of creating subdirectories (described in Chapter 2) for the two main groups of MicroPro programs. You may have followed the instructions in Chapter 2 and created a Tutorial subdirectory, in which case you would change the directory to TUTORIAL\WORDTUTE before commencing this word processing tutorial. You should read through the sections in your DOS manual on directories and subdirectories before going any further. In Chapter 7 you will practice creating and using subdirectories for CorrectStar.

Step-by-Step Procedure

Now let's get on with the WordStar tutorial.

1. Boot up your system and next to the prompt type **WS** and press **Return** (or change directories, and then call up WS).
2. Once you see the OPENING MENU on the screen, type **L** to change logged disk drive (if you have two drives, see the previous comments above for one- and two-drive systems).
3. In answer to the request for a new drive, enter **B:**.
4. Now, press **D** to open a new file and enter the name:

NEWLETT.TXT

5. You can either type in some text now to use for the exercises in this tutorial or, if you have already typed a suitable letter or document (preferably more than one page in length), then you can read that in to NEWLETT.TXT using the ^**KR** command (remember that if the file is on a different drive you must type in the drive identifier, for example, A:file name). If you haven't yet created any new WordStar files, use FORMLETT.TXT.

BASIC WORDSTAR MENUS

You are already familiar with the OPENING MENU, which displays when you first call up WordStar, and with the MAIN MENU, which displays when you create or edit a file. However, so far you have not been through the commands in these menus in any detail.

The OPENING MENU

You will see that this menu is divided into various sections. Here you will go through each in turn.

PRELIMINARY COMMANDS

Under PRELIMINARY COMMANDS you find the following:

```
L  Change logged disk drive
```

This allows you to change from the current logged drive (the default is drive A) to drive B, as you have just learned.

It is good practice to keep your data files separate from the WordStar disk or partition. You will find that you will only ever need three or four working program disks, but you may end up with a dozen or more data disks in a few months.

```
F  File directory    now ON
```

The default for the file directory listing is ON. If you want to turn it off you must use the toggle switch, **F**. If you type **F** you will see the ON change to OFF and the directory listing will disappear.

H Set help level

The default help level is **3**, which gives you the maximum amount of information in the help screen. If you type **H** you can select a level between 3 and 0. Try them all now. You will need level 3 until you know the commands by heart.

COMMANDS TO OPEN A FILE

You are already familiar with the commands to open document and non-document files (**D** and **N**).

FILE COMMANDS

Under FILE COMMANDS, you have so far used only the print command, **P**. To rename a file, you type **E** and when asked for:

NAME OF FILE TO RENAME?

type the name of a file you wish to rename. Then after the next query:

NEW NAME?

type in the new file name.

Similarly for copying a file, type **O** and follow the question and answer sequence just given.

To delete a file, simply type **Y** and then when asked, type the name of the file to be deleted.

If you should type one of these commands by mistake, you can cancel the command by pressing ^**U** and then the **Esc** key.

SYSTEM COMMANDS

Under SYSTEM COMMANDS, you have already used **X** to exit to the DOS A> prompt.

If you now type **R**, you will be asked for the name of program to run, for example, type **STAT** (or **A:STAT** if you are logged in to drive B) to check how much space you have left on your disk before you start editing files (another good habit to get into).

WORDSTAR OPTIONS

Finally, under WORDSTAR OPTIONS are the commands for running MailMerge (**M**), which you used in Part One, or **S** to run one of the MicroPro spelling checkers, CorrectStar or SpellStar. You will use a spelling checker in Chapter 7 if you have one of these programs.

The MAIN MENU

Again, this is divided into subsections. You have a reminder of the cursor control and scrolling commands, also of some common control characters for tabbing (^I), turning insert on and off (^V), and paragraph reforming (^B). You should be quite familiar with most of these by now.

Listed under the subheading OTHER MENUS on the right of the MAIN MENU are:

```
^J - Help        ^K - Block
^Q - Quick       ^P - Print
^O - Onscreen
```

Type each of the control characters in turn and read through the information available in these other menus. They will be described in more detail below.

Note that to return to the MAIN MENU you just press the Space Bar.

You can escape from any of these menus if you make a mistake while entering text. For example, you may press the **Ctrl** key (for example, ^K) instead of a **Shift** key (such as capital **K**), or you might choose some function by mistake. If so, press ^U to return to the MAIN MENU. In some cases after you press ^U a message appears

```
***INTERRUPTED***   ***PRESS ESCAPE KEY***
```

You then must press the **Esc** key to return to the MAIN MENU.

The HELP MENU (^J)

One of the functions of **^J** is to control the amount of information displayed in the help screen at the top of your screen.

^JH can be used inside WordStar as an alternative to selecting **H** from the OPENING MENU. It performs the same function, and you have the choice of changing help levels (from 0 to 3) at any time during editing. Type: **^JH 1**—press the keys one after the other. This will change the help level to 1. The default is help level 3 (i.e., every time you go into WordStar, the help level will be 3 until you change it). If you now type ^JH, you will get a list of the help levels from 3 down to 0, a message telling you that the CURRENT HELP LEVEL IS 1, and finally the options of remaining in level 1 simply by pressing the Space Bar, or of changing to 3, 2, or 0 by typing the appropriate number.

Try them all out, then return to level 3 (which gives you the most help) until you are really familiar with all the commands. When you are more experienced and know the commands by heart, you will appreciate the extra screen size you can achieve by turning the help screen off.

If you *do* select level 1 to get the larger screen area and then find that you need to be reminded of a command, you can quickly turn help screen 3 back on by typing ^JH3, even if you are in the middle of typing a document.

You have probably noticed that if you press the keys in quick succession, you go straight to the function you want; however, if you pause after entering the control character (^J), the MAIN MENU is replaced by the special HELP MENU, and this tends to slow you down. Get used to typing the characters one after the other, without a pause. This will be easier when you know them by heart.

You will find that in the HELP MENU (^J) there are many options in addition to setting the help levels (**H**). Try them all, entering the selections one by one, and read through the information that appears on your screen. You will not necessarily understand everything at this stage, but when you come to use some of the functions later, they will not seem totally unfamiliar to you.

The QUICK MENU (^Q)

The QUICK MENU shows you some extra CURSOR MOVEMENT commands. As the name implies, these commands enable you to move around the text more quickly. Try them now and see how useful it is to be able to go straight to the beginning or end of a line, screen, or file (try ^QS, ^QD, ^QE, ^QX, ^QR, and ^QC).

These CURSOR MOVEMENT controls are easy to remember if you notice the position of the keys in relation to each other on the keyboard: the **E S D X** keys form a diamond shape (see Figure 6–1) with the **E** at the top, the **X** at the bottom, the **S** to the left,

---

FIGURE 6–1 Cursor Control Characters

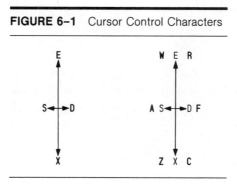

---

and the **D** to the right. These are also the directions in which they move the cursor, one character, or one line, at a time.

On either side of the **E** are the **W** and **R** keys, which move the screen display down, leaving the cursor in the same place— **W** a line at a time and **R** a screenful at a time. Similarly, on either side of the **X** key are the **Z** and **C** keys, which move the screen display in the opposite direction. To the left of the **S** key is the **A**, which moves the cursor left a word at a time and to the right of the D is the **F**, which moves the cursor to the right a word at a time.

Try all these out until you are completely familiar with the movements, and then try the additional ^**Q** versions again. The ability to find your way quickly around your screen and through your files is essential to efficient word processing.

FIND AND REPLACE COMMANDS

Other useful functions in the ^**Q** menu are the **FIND** command, ^**QF**, and **FIND AND REPLACE** command, ^**QA**. These commands will help you to find a particular word or phrase wherever it appears in the text and, if you wish, replace the word or phrase with an alternative each time it occurs. You could go through your whole letter, replacing all the lowercase *ing*'s with uppercase *ING*'s, for example.

Step-by-Step Procedure

1. Type ^**QA** and answer the first query FIND? with *ing* and the second, REPLACE WITH? with *ING*. Then, when you see:

OPTIONS?   (? FOR INFO)

press **?** (question mark).

2. You will be presented with all the various options available to you—select **N** and **G** (to replace the old characters with the new without asking in the entire file). Then watch the fun!

3. To change them back, type **^QA** again, but this time FIND *ING* and REPLACE WITH *ing* and choose options **BNG** (replace without asking in the entire file, and search backwards through file). You should be back where you started.

4. To simply FIND a word, letter, or phrase in your document, use the **^QF** command. When you are asked what you wish to find, just type something you know must be there, say **ARE**. When you press **Return** you are asked for OPTIONS—this time type **u** or **U** to say IGNORE CASE (that is, find all occurrences of ARE in either upper- or lowercase).

5. When you press **Return**, the cursor will stop next to the first *ARE* or *are* that it finds. Type **^L** and the cursor will find the next occurrence. Just keep typing **^L** and notice that you will find these three letters even when they are part of a longer word. If you should ever wish to find ARE only, you would have to choose the option **W** for whole word only.

6. When your search is complete, you may see your search term contained in the message:

***** Not found: Press ESCAPE key *****

Just press **Esc** and the message clears.

You have now tried all the options:

B = search backwards
U = ignore case
N = replace in entire file
G = replace without asking
W = whole words only

You can use any combination of these letters: the most useful ones are easy to remember as BUNG. Use these when you have typed the command ^**QA** and entered the characters you wish to FIND and REPLACE. Use them when you have the cursor positioned at the *end* of your file, you wish to search *backwards* through the file, ignoring the *case* of any occurrence, and you wish to replace each occurrence, *without asking*, in the *entire file*. If you typed BUNGW it would do all this, but only to *whole words*. Of course, when you are searching forward from the beginning of your file, the equivalent commands are UNG and UNGW.

There is one additional option for ^**QA**. You can enter a *number* to specify how many times the REPLACE should be repeated. For example:

FIND **ing**   REPLACE WITH **ING**   OPTIONS **5N**

This command would cause the first five occurrences of *ing* to be replaced with *ING*, without asking. Now, change them back.

When you start using the FIND AND REPLACE commands on your own files, especially if you are changing something throughout a long document, you can greatly enhance the speed at which the task is completed by pressing the Space Bar after entering the command line and pressing **Return**. However, you must be absolutely certain that your command is correctly entered; you will not see each replacement as it takes place.

Now you know that you can find any word, phrase, or specific group of characters anywhere in your text and, if you wish, replace them with other words or phrases. You will think of many valid uses for this function.

MORE MENUS

The BLOCK MENU (^K)

Type ^**K** and have a good look at the BLOCK MENU. It contains many essential functions; during the next few sessions you should try to familiarize yourself with them all. Notice that its functions are split under various subheadings; SAVING FILES, BLOCK OPERATIONS, FILE OPERATIONS, DISK OPERATIONS, and PLACE MARKERS.

SAVING FILES

You have already used the BLOCK MENU for saving your files at the end of editing (with ^**KD**, which saves the file and takes you back to the MAIN MENU).

You can also save files at any time during entering or editing text. You should get into the habit of doing so, especially when you are typing in long or complex documents, using ^KS. This saves your file but does not exit to the menu; after typing a ^QP, you are returned to the position you were at before you saved your file, and you can continue typing in text or editing. It is a good idea to type ^KS at the end of every page, or after any section that you would particularly not like to type in again if you lost it.

Try this now: type ^KS, and you will see that your file is being saved; then type ^QP when you see the instruction to do so. The cursor will return to its position prior to the save. Now, if by any mischance your file should not be saved at the end of editing, or if you lost it for any reason, you would have a .BAK file containing everything stored up to your last ^KS.

To convert the .BAK file to a .TXT or .DOC file, you must rename the file, selecting **E** from the OPENING MENU. (You cannot edit a .BAK file as such.) For example, rename NEWLETT.BAK to NEWLETT.TXT; now you can treat it as a regular file. This is one of the built-in safeguards in WordStar.

If you wish to save your file and exit from WordStar straight back to the operating system (that is, you have no further editing or printing to do), simply type ^KX. Your file will be saved and you will find yourself back at the system prompt. Otherwise, use ^KD as you have done previously to save your file but remain in WordStar.

ABANDON FILE

If you open a file and find that you do not need to edit it, or you have opened the wrong file, you can use the ABANDON FILE option by typing ^KQ. This function is useful, also, if you find while editing that you have done something really silly—like erasing 10 lines by mistake—you can type ^KQ. WordStar asks if you wish to:

```
ABANDON EDITED VERSION OF FILENAME.TXT?
```

You type **Y** to save your file in its *original* form with the 10 deleted lines safely in place. Of course, you will have lost any other editing you had done since the last save, but it's probably worth it to save the 10 deleted lines.

You will explore the rest of the BLOCK MENU—BLOCK OP-ERATIONS, FILE OPERATIONS, DISK OPERATIONS, and PLACE MARKERS—in a later part of this WordStar tutorial.

The ONSCREEN MENU (^O)

If you type **^O** you will see that the ONSCREEN MENU offers many different formatting commands to control margins, tabs, line spacing, and so on. You have used this menu already in Part One for the toggle switches that turn justification and hyphen help on and off (**^OJ** and **^OH**).

You will see that there are more toggle switches, too, controlling such features as word wrap and ruler line display.

MARGINS

NOTE: if you are using a recent European version of WordStar, the symbols for tab settings and flags have changed; you now have the option of creating your own, if you wish.

Try changing your left and right margins now.

Type **^OL** and respond with an appropriate number when asked for LEFT MARGIN COLUMN NUMBER (such as 9).

Now type **^OR** and give a column number for the right margin (such as 56). You will notice the changes in the ruler line at the top of your screen.

Now move the cursor to the beginning of the first paragraph of your letter and press **^B**—the paragraph will reform to the narrower margins.

You can easily restore the margins to normal—the left margin should be column 1 and the right, column 65. So go ahead and repeat the **^OL** and **^OR** commands and then type **^B** to restore your text.

You may feel that you would prefer different tab settings than those on the WordStar default ruler line (remember, the default tab settings are marked by exclamation points). It is very easy to change these.

First, get rid of *all* the tab stops by typing **^ON**. A message will appear at the top of the screen that reads:

CLEAR TAB AT COL (ESCAPE for cursor col; A for all)

You wish to clear all the tabs, so type **A** and press **Return**. To clear any particular tab stop, simply type in the column number of that tab position.

You will see that all the tab settings have disappeared, leaving just the left and right margin settings and the ruler line.

Now, to set your own tabs, decide on the positions and enter these one after another by typing ^OI and then the column number next to the query:

```
SET TAB AT COL (ESCAPE for cursor col)? 6
```

When you type **6** and press **Return**, you see the ! sign appear at column 6 on the ruler line. Continue entering ^OI and numbers until you are satisfied with the tab settings. If you make a mistake, remember that you can remove any tab with the ^ON command and the tab column number.

Another technique is to move the cursor by pressing the **Space Bar** until you reach the desired tab position on the screen and then press ^OI and **Esc**; the ! will appear on the ruler line at the column number of the cursor position (which you can check by looking at the column number in the status line). This technique is very useful when you are entering columns of data, since you can decide as you enter the first line of data precisely where you need to place a tab stop.

Later you will learn how to create your own ruler line, which can be saved with your document file and recalled every time you edit the file. This is especially useful if you must set up complicated tab settings for a table so that you do not have to recalculate the ruler line from scratch each time you need to edit it. Also, you will learn how to make decimal tabs for entering dollars and cents.

The PRINT MENU (^P)

You will find that you use the special print control characters listed in the PRINT MENU frequently.

There are controls that enable you to specify as you type in your text which words you would like, for example, to be under-lined (^PS), typed boldface (^PB), or both (^PB^PS).

If you ever type scientific or mathematical text, the subscript (^PV) and superscript (^PT) characters will be invaluable. Another special character (^PH) allows you to place an accent over certain letters in foreign language text.

You can also specify a point in the text where you would like the printer to pause (^**PC**) while you change to a different daisy wheel (for italicizing, for example), and yet another that can select the red portion of your printer ribbon (^**PY**) if you have a red and black ribbon.

The only way to see how these control characters work is to put some into your letter and then print it out.

Step-by-step procedure

1. Make sure that INSERT is ON; if not press ^**V** to turn it on. Select a word that you would like to underline. Move the cursor to the first letter of the word and then press ^**PS**. It will appear in front of the word you want to underline as ^**S**.

2. Move the cursor to the space after the end of the word and press ^**PS** again. The word is now contained *between* the first ^**S** and the second.

3. Notice that the line containing the special print control characters appears longer than the rest of your right-justified text. But if you put the cursor on the last letter in the line, you will see from the status line that the cursor is still in column 65 (or at the right margin column)—the control characters do not actually count as space in your file and do not respond to paragraph reforming.

4. Now select another word or phrase and enclose it in the same way with ^**PB** (appearing as ^**B** on the screen) and if you like, choose yet another and make it bold *and* underlined by enclosing it with ^**PS**^**PB** (which appears as ^**S**^**B**).

   If you make a mistake when typing in the control characters, don't worry—you can delete them with a ^**G** or **Del** key, just like any other text.

5. To see how these features appear when your document is printed out, first save your file with a ^**KD**. Turn on the printer, check that it is online, select **P** from the OPENING MENU, and print out NEWLETT.TXT. Don't the underlining and boldface look very effective?

Sometimes the extra length lines with the print control characters can be very confusing, particularly if you are entering columns of figures or information and have decided to boldface and underline the headings. In order to see your lines *without* the print control characters, type ^OD; they will not Display. Then it is easy to make sure that your columns of figures, for example, are correctly aligned with the column headings. Display the characters by typing ^OD again.

RULER LINES AND TABS

Up to now you have used the default ruler line that appears every time you call up WordStar. This may have proved quite satisfactory so far, but you should learn to type in your own ruler lines according to the requirements of your particular business.

You will save yourself a lot of time in the future if you spend a little time now setting up some standard files containing the left and right margins and tabs that you most commonly need. You could have files called, for example, RULER-1.TXT for letters, RULER-2.DOC for documents (such as minutes of meetings or whatever is appropriate to your particular office requirements), and RULER-3.TBL for a table. Devise your own system for numbering and naming files and their extensions (the three characters after the period), but do be consistent.

Setting Up Ruler Lines

In setting up the ruler lines you will learn two new functions. First, typing two periods or dots at the beginning of a line tells the printer *not to print* whatever follows on the rest of that line. Second, pressing **^P** and then **Return** puts a new flag (symbol) in the flag column of your screen. A — (minus sign) appears; this causes the printer to return to the beginning of the same line and to print the text, that appears on the screen to be on the line below, on the same line. This is called a "carriage return without a line feed." As usual, it is easier to do it than to read about it.

Step-by-step procedure

1. Select **D** from the menu and type **RULER-1.TXT**, which is a new file.
2. Directly below the normal WordStar ruler line, type in two dots starting in column 1. (Notice after the first dot you will see a **?** in the flag column, asking for a dot command; this disappears when you type in the second dot.)

3. You can now enter a comment to remind yourself when you use this new ruler line, for example:

`..THIS IS MY RULER LINE FOR STANDARD LETTERS`

safe in the knowledge that this will not print out with your document.

4. Now type two dots on the next line, and then type **^P** and press **Return**. Notice the minus sign in the flag column.

5. With the cursor in column 1, type **L** for the left margin. Follow the **L** with minus signs until you reach a column where you need a tab, then type in a !. Continue with minus signs and !'s until you have the tabs you need, then type **R** for the position of the right margin.

Your line should look like this:

```
   ..                                                       -
   L-----!---!-------------------------------------------------R   <
```

Note that the cursor column (the position of the cursor on the line) is displayed on the status line so you can easily calculate exactly where to put your tab stops.

Replacing the WordStar Ruler Line

When you have created a new ruler line, you can use it instead of the default ruler line that appears under the status line.

Step-by-step procedure

1. Make sure that INSERT is OFF. (You have probably learned the hard way that if you press **TAB** or **^I** with INSERT ON, and your cursor is in a line of text, you will move the text ahead of the cursor—usually you do not realize what has happened until you have done several tabs, by which time the text is all over the place!) If necessary, press **^V** to turn INSERT OFF.

2. Press **^I** or the **TAB** key.

You will find that the cursor is still following the tab positions on the default Wordstar ruler line; there is one more step before your own ruler line takes precedence.

3. Place the cursor anywhere on the special ruler line that you typed in and type ^OF. You will see the WordStar ruler line change to yours, and only *now* will ^I or **tab** move the cursor according to your ruler line's tab stops.

    Clearly, until you press ^OF to convert the WordStar ruler line to the format you typed in, *your* ruler line (as far as the software is concerned) could just be any line of text.

4. Now repeat the exercise for any other ruler lines you may need to use regularly; for example, create lines for documents such as minutes where you have a constant format from meeting to meeting, or for tables where you will always want the same spacing between columns. Give each file a name that describes to you the function of each different ruler line.

5. Just for interest, move the cursor to any line of text in your current file and press ^OF. You will see that the left and right margins are set according to the length and format of the line you have chosen. Try a very short line to prove the point. Move the cursor back to your ruler line and press ^OF to restore the line you want. This can be quite a useful way of creating temporary margins if, for example, you want to create a paragraph inset on both sides.

Using Standard Ruler Line Files

Having created the files containing the various ruler lines, you must learn how to use them.

Step-by-step procedure

1. Whenever you create a new letter file, before you type in any text, first type ^KR (the **READ** command from the BLOCK MENU).

2. You will be prompted for:

NAME OF FILE TO READ?

Answer with RULER-1.TXT, or whatever you decide to call the file, and when you press **Return** the ruler line will appear.

3. Place the cursor anywhere on the line, press ^**OF**, and you will convert the WordStar ruler line to the margins and tabs you need.

Now, when you save your letters, tables, or document files, the special ruler line will be saved with them. Each time you call up any file containing a special ruler, you will simply place the cursor on the line and press ^**OF**. This is much quicker and easier than typing in a new ruler line each time you need one.

Of course, you can put all your different ruler lines in one file. Then, when you read it in to your new file with a ^**KR** you can choose the line you need for a particular application, move the cursor to that line, press ^**OF** to convert the default ruler line, then erase the other ruler lines with ^**Y**.

After you have set a new ruler line in this way and saved it with your text file, unless you immediately exit from WordStar, each new file you open thereafter will have this same ruler line.

If you exit from WordStar and then call it up again, the default WordStar ruler line will reappear. This is another very good reason for saving an appropriate ruler line with every file you create—you will always have the right format for each letter or document.

Tables

If you are creating oversized tables there are several additional points to remember. If you have a wide-carriage printer, you can print out up to 132 columns across a page.

With a standard 80-column printer you could achieve the same result by printing out your large table in sections and pasting the sheets together later, or if you have a daisy wheel printer, you can get a 15-pitch wheel that will print 15 characters to the inch (compared to the normal 10 or 12). With some dot matrix printers you can use condensed printing to squeeze even more characters onto a line. However, this may not be compatible with WordStar files directly; you might have to use the CP/M command, **TYPE**, to use this facility.

Even if you think you will only use this table once, it is still worth setting up the ruler line and storing it with the file. If you want to go back at a later date and change any of the figures, you will simply put the cursor on the stored ruler line, press ^**OF** and you will have your very useful decimal tabs back to help editing.

Figure 6–2 shows the first five months of a simple income and expenses table. Ideally you should choose a table with headings

FIGURE 6–2 Example of a Portion of an
Oversized Table

MONTHLY INCOME AND EXPENDITURE

```
..
L------------------#--------#--------#--------#--------#----
```

	JAN	FEB	MAR	APR	MAY
INCOME:					
1. Unit A	92.95	126.75	367.00	665.00	1000.00
2. Unit B	365.50	440.65	575.00	850.00	1250.50
TOTAL	458.45	567.40	942.00	1515.00	2250.50
EXPENSES:					
1. Rent	125.00	125.00	125.00	125.00	125.00
2. Rates	75.00	75.00	75.00	75.00	75.00
3. Electricity	50.00	50.00	50.00	50.00	50.00
4. Car expenses	30.00	30.00	30.00	30.00	30.00
TOTAL	280.00	280.00	280.00	280.00	280.00

appropriate to some task in your organization and just use mine
as a guide to the technique.

If you may need to fill in more than one such table, it is worth
setting up a ruler line in a separate file (as discussed previously).
If not, simply open a new file called, say, MONTHLY.TBL and
store the appropriate ruler line with it.

Step-by-step procedure

1. Since you are going to be entering variable numbers of
   dollars and cents, your tab stops this time will be *decimal*

tabs—identified by the **#** symbol instead of the **!** for normal tab stops. You must extend the right margin **R** to COL 132—just press **^OR** then type in 132 when asked for right column number.

2. Directly under the WordStar ruler line type in the two dots followed by **^P**. Press **Return**.

3. Type **^OJ** to turn off right justification (you will find it easier to work with long lines and tabular material with justification off).

4. Now start the ruler line with an **L** and continue with minus signs up to column 24, allowing 20 spaces for the row headings and 4 more to take you midway through the 9 spaces for the first column. Now type a pound sign (**#**), usually found at Shift-3 on your keyboard, in column 24 (remember that the COL number is shown at the top of the screen in the status line, so you always know the cursor position).

5. Continue entering with minus signs and **#** at intervals of 9 spaces (COLS 33, 42, 51, 60, 69, 78, 87, 96, 105, 114, 123) until you have decimal tabs for each of your 12 months; then enter **R** at column 132.

6. Move the cursor to the new ruler line and type **^OF** to convert WordStar's ruler line. Since you are going to be "tabbing" it is probably a good idea also to turn INSERT OFF.

   Notice that as you move across the screen to add tabs past column 65, the screen automatically scrolls horizontally and, after you press **Return** and the cursor is at the beginning of the next line, you will see a new flag in the flag column of the screen—a + sign—indicating that the line extends beyond the usual 80 columns.

7. Now you are ready to start. To insert the month headings, tab to the first tab stop, back space one position, and type in **JAN** (the decimal point between your dollars and cents figures will now line up with the midpoint of each month heading).

8. Continue from tab to tab, inserting the months (don't forget to back space one position each time) until you reach **DEC**.

9. If you want to give your table a title, for example MONTHLY ACCOUNTS, type it in capital letters, then move the cursor back into the title with a **^A**, and to place

it directly in the center of your set margins, type **^OC**; the title is automatically centered.

10. Now you are ready to type in the row headings and the figures. If you have need for a real table like this, use your own headings and figures; if not, just copy the ones shown in the figure for practice.

11. Notice how the figures appear on the screen when you are using decimal tabs. They start at the decimal point and work from right to left (so that it does not matter if your dollars are units, tens, hundreds, or thousands). Then, after you type in the decimal point the normal mode (left to right) is restored—clever isn't it?

   Notice also that as you tab across to the next decimal tab position, the word DECIMAL appears on the status line.

When you have finished you might like to print out the table to make sure that it is completely to your satisfaction. You know enough now to feel confident in your ability to adjust the ruler line and if necessary move tab stops until you are satisfied with the output.

Remember that if you are going on to type in a normal text file you should restore right justification by typing **^OJ** (otherwise ragged right will remain until you exit from WordStar). Also remember to adjust the right margin back to the standard column 65.

You have learned some very valuable lessons in formatting by designing your own ruler lines. In theory there is almost no word processing task, however complicated it may seem, that cannot be achieved using WordStar.

Temporary Margins

There are times when you need to inset the left and/or right margins for a few paragraphs. This is quite straightforward in WordStar.

Step-by-step procedure

1. First you should set the right margin to column 59 (6 spaces less than usual) using **^OR**.

2. Then type **^OG**. You will notice that the ruler line at the top of your screen has lost its highlighting up to the position of your first tab stop.

3. You must have a tab stop for ^**OG** to use—so if you don't normally use tab stops, type ^**OI**, and then respond to the query by setting the tab to column 6.

4. From this point on, your lines will wrap to these margins until you press **Return**; then the right margin will remain as set, but the left margin will revert to column 1.

5. If you wish to inset even further, just press ^**OG** as many times as needed (remember, you must have tab stops for the second, or subsequent, ^**OG** to use). Watch the highlighting on the ruler line to see where your left margin will be, and then set your right margin accordingly with ^**OR**.

6. If you need a second inset paragraph, after pressing **Return**, just press ^**OG** again (leaving the right margin on 59), and so on, until you need to return to normal format.

7. To do this, reset the right margin to 65 (or whatever value you were using) and the normal ruler settings display.

Releasing Margins

Sometimes you need to squeeze one or two extra characters on just one line, or you may need to make a note in the margin of your document:

To avoid resetting margins and reforming the whole paragraph, you can use the ^**OX** command to release the margin. You will see the letters MAR REL appear in the status line; typing ^**OX** again turns MAR REL off. Remember *not* to reform the paragraph after you release the margin.

Line Spacing

To make your text double spaced (or triple, or more), use the ^**OS** command, and when you are prompted, enter the spacing you want.

It is a good idea to type and correct your whole document carefully before you alter the line spacing. It may even be worth saving your original, single-spaced document and then making a copy for the double spacing. Editing will be much easier on the single-spaced version.

You have now learned most of the onscreen formatting commands. In the next section you will learn more about formatting your printout.

STANDARD DOT COMMANDS

In Part One you learned that the function of the dot commands is to format your letter when it is printed out on paper. If you do not use dot commands at the top of your letter, then the default values are used by WordStar.

Following are the most common print formatting commands:

Dot Command	Meaning	Default Value
.MT	Margin at top	3 lines
.MB	Margin at bottom	8 lines
.PL	Paper length	66 lines
.PO	Page offset	8 columns
.OP	Omit page numbers	OFF, page numbers print

You may find that for most purposes the default values will produce quite satisfactory output. The form letter you typed in Chapter 3 used the default values. However, you will want to produce letters and documents using WordStar that look as good as anything you could manage on an electric typewriter. This is certainly possible, but it may take a little practice before you get everything just right. Here are a few guidelines to help you:

1. Always load the paper in the printer the same way, with the left edge as far to the left as it will go and with the top edge of the page just under the bar (for single sheets) or with the TOP OF FORM set so that the print head is right at the top of the page (for continuous-form paper).

2. Use the **.MT** command to determine the number of lines for the top margin (remember to allow adequate space if you are using letterhead; try **.MT 12**).

3. The page offset (**.PO**) command determines the width of the left margin; this will vary according to where your particular printer is set to begin printing. Trial and error is the only method here.

4. The right margin will be determined by your line length, so if you have a satisfactory left margin but the lines are too long, simply adjust the length in your text file using the ^OR command to bring in the right margin and shorten the line; then use ^B to reform the text to the new margin.

5. The default paper length of 66 lines should be correct for both continuous-form paper and single sheets. A **.PL** of 84 is com-

---

FIGURE 6-3 Standard Letter Format File

```
  ..        THIS IS MY RULER LINE AND DOT COMMANDS FOR A                    <
  ..        STANDARD LETTER USING SINGLE SHEET FEEDER                       <
  ..                                                                        -
  L-----!---!-------------------------------------------------R            <
  .PL 84                                                                    <
  .MT 12                                                                    <
  .PO 10                                                                    <
  .MB 26                                                                    <
  .OP                                                                       <
```

---

mon for single sheets in a single sheet feeder. Remember to use **.OP** if you prefer not to have numbered pages.

6. Use the file NEWLETT.TXT to try out these dot commands until you feel confident that you can produce a suitable format on the printed page.

7. It is probably a good idea to incorporate the dot commands with the ruler line files you have set up already. Call up your ruler line file for standard letters and add the dot commands to it. Change the comment at the same time. If your comment extends over more than one line, do not forget to put the two dots at the beginning of *each* line you wish *not to print*.

Note that your first dot must be in column 1, otherwise WordStar will assume that they are text to be printed and will not implement the instructions. Remember, if you are in column 1 when you type in a dot, a **?** appears in the flag column on the far right of your screen. This disappears when you type in the second dot (for a nonprinting comment) or an appropriate dot command.

You will again be using the **^P RETURN** when you type in the ruler line, giving a minus sign in the flag column. I have indicated below the appearance of the flags. Your file might look something like Figure 6–3.

When you are printing out a table, you may need to cover virtually the whole page area: to override the default values, make the top and bottom margins and the page offset all equal 0. Then make sure that the print head of your printer is lined up precisely with the top of the paper to achieve the maximum page length and, since there is no page offset, the left margin will also be minimal. You might like to try this out on the table you designed earlier in this chapter.

BLOCK OPERATIONS

You learned all the commands in the BLOCK MENU for saving files, and in some of the exercises you have used the ^KR command to read a file. Now you will have a look at some of the other operations in the BLOCK MENU.

Block Moves

You will probably find many uses for the BLOCK OPERATIONS. They enable you to move blocks of text around at will *within* your letter or document file, or *from* one file *to* another.

For example, if you are typing a letter and decide that one paragraph (or sentence, phrase, or single word), is out of place, you can mark it off as a *block* and move it around until you are satisfied. Then type ^B to reform the text.

The characters that mark off the block, ^KB at the beginning and ^KK at the end, are easy to remember if you notice that B and K are the beginning and end of the word BlocK.

Having marked the block you can move it with ^KV, delete it with ^KY, copy it with ^KC, or write it to another file with ^KW.

Step-by-step procedure

The best way to learn is to try out one of the BLOCK OPERATIONS on the text you have onscreen.

1. Position the cursor at the beginning of any line of text and type ^KB (this marks the beginning of the block of text).
2. Now move the cursor down a couple of lines and type ^KK (to mark the end of the block of text).
3. Move the cursor to the end of the document and type ^KC (this will copy the block of marked text at the new cursor position).
4. Note that once the markers (**B** and **K**) are typed, the whole marked block is highlighted on your screen. If you now type ^KY, the block will be deleted.
5. Shift the cursor back to the beginning of another line and mark a block as described in steps 1 and 2.
6. Now move the cursor down a couple of lines and type ^KV— the marked block will move to the new cursor position. If you want to leave the text in the new position, type ^KH

and the highlighting will be hidden. Then type **^B** to reform the paragraph.

7. If you want to move the block back, type **^KH** and the highlighting will reappear. Now move the cursor back to the original position and toggle **^KV** again and then **^KH** to hide the highlighting.

^KH is a toggle switch that turns highlighting on and off. Block commands will only be implemented, though, when the highlighting is on.

Column Moves

It is possible (with WordStar 3.3 or later versions) to mark a *column* block and to move it, copy it, delete it, etc. The command for this function is **^KN**, which turns COLUMN MOVE on. Try it out on the figures you typed into the table earlier in the chapter.

Step-by-step procedure

1. Move the cursor to the beginning of a block of figures and type **^KB**.
2. Shift to the end (and to the right of the block, as shown here) and type **^KK**. The whole column you have marked will be highlighted.

```
<B> 125.00
    75.00
    50.00
    30.00 <K>
```

3. Now move the cursor to a new position, and then type **^KC**. The block is *copied* at that position. Similarly you can *move* the block from its current position using **^KV**. If you wished, you could *delete* the marked column with a **^KY**.
4. When you have copied, moved, or deleted the column, type **^KH** to turn off highlighting as usual and remember to type **^KN** to turn COLUMN MOVE off.

If you ever mark a block of normal text, try to move it, and see a message on the screen:

BLOCK END MARKER BEFORE BEGINNING MARKER

you have forgotten to turn off ^**KN** after a previous column move. As soon as you type ^**KN** you will be able to move the block of marked text.

Writing a Block to Another File

A further useful block function is to write a block from the file you are working to another file created to contain the marked block. You may guess that the command for achieving this is ^**KW**.

Step-by-step procedure

1. Highlight a block of text from a file. You can use MONTHLY.TBL, transfering the ruler line from that table to another file (if you needed to set up a similar table with the same month headings, but different information). Also, assume that you do not want decimal tabs this time.
2. Type ^**KX** to save your current file and to exit back to DOS.
3. At the system prompt, type in **WS MONTHLY.TBL**. When the table displays, determine how much of the text will be useful for the new table—you want the same tab positions, but not decimal. Keep the month headings exactly as they are, but do not copy the rest of the table.
4. Make the changes to the ruler line now, in the MONTHLY.TBL file, and write the marked text to another file; then when you save the original file you do so with ^**KQ**, which saves it *without* the changes you have made. Your original file is restored to the format *before* you made the changes, and you have created a new file containing the required information in the format you need.
5. To convert the decimal format, change each **#** to **!** with the ^**QA** command. To the prompt FIND? respond with **#**, to REPLACE WITH? type **!**, and for OPTIONS type **5N** (or **12N** if you have 12 tabs).
   Then this:

```
. .
L--------------------#--------#--------#--------#---
              JAN     FEB     MAR     APR     MAY
```

will become this:

```
 . .
L--------------------!--------!--------!--------!--------!---
                     JAN      FEB      MAR      APR      MAY
```

6. Make sure INSERT is ON. Mark the beginning of the block you wish to move by moving the cursor to the first of the two dots at the beginning of your ruler line, and then pressing ^**KB**.

7. Now move the cursor down to the I of the word INCOME and press ^**KK** (this marked block includes the ruler line and **Return**).

8. Type ^**KW** and answer the request for a file name to write the marked text to with **SUMMARY.TBL** or a file name appropriate to your needs.

9. Type ^**KQ** and then **Y** to abandon the edited version of MONTHLY.TBL (leaving you with the original file just as it was and a new file SUMMARY.TBL).

10. Select **D** from the menu and have a look at the new file SUMMARY.TBL. You now have the ruler line and month headings all ready for you to use in a new table. Remember, you will have to add any dot commands at the top of the new file before you print it out (or remember to include these within your marked block of text before writing it to the new file).

There are many other uses for the ^**KW** command, which you will learn to use at appropriate times. One such example is using ^**KW** to write the name and address at the top of a letter you are typing to another file you will use for addressing the envelope. Remember that you obtained the same result in Chapter 5 by using the ^**KR** command to read the whole letter into a new file and subsequently deleting the contents of the letter below the address. It is more convenient to do it the way you have just learned; to mark the block containing just the name and address from your letter heading and then to write it with a ^**KW** to an envelope file (such as ADDRESS.ENV).

FILE OPERATIONS

There are several FILE OPERATIONS that you will need on occasion. These are commands you can carry out *while actually editing a file*, without having to exit to the MAIN MENU first. Some are useful in emergencies; some you may never need to use.

Most useful, almost certainly, will be the **^KR** command that you have learned to use to read another file from disk into your current file.

The **^KJ** command is usually used at times of distress, because you are trying to save a file at the end of editing and find you have run out of space—you need to delete files to make space on disk for saving the current file. Other commands, used less frequently, enable you to copy (**^KO**), to print (**^KP**), or to rename (**^KE**) a file while editing another file in WordStar.

These functions are described in more detail in the following sections.

Reading a File from Disk

You have used **^KR** to read a file stored on your disk into a new file (such as for inserting a standard heading or ruler line).

If you have the kind of business where there are standard paragraphs used in nearly every letter you send out, you can store these paragraphs in separate files and simply read them in to your current letter at the appropriate point.

You could type in your standard paragraphs, calling the files PARA-1.TXT, PARA-2.TXT, etc., according to your needs. Then when you wish to insert a paragraph into your current letter, type **^KR** and after the prompt NAME OF FILE TO READ simply type the PARA name and press **Return**.

The paragraph will appear at the cursor position; if necessary, use **^B** to reform the paragraph.

Deleting Files

One of the FILE OPERATIONS thatyou may need desperately one day is **^KJ**. Tthis will probably be on a bad day when nothing has gone right for you—you have just finished typing in a very complex and extremely long document that has tested your WordStar abilities to their utmost. With a sigh of relief you type **^KD** and as you turn away, the dreaded message appears on the screen: DISK FULL. Horror of horrors!

Has all that frustrating work been in vain? Well, probably not. You can dry your tears and use the **^KJ** command. This will allow you to get rid of one or more files that are not really required. (You *do* have a backup copy of all your important files, don't you?)

If you are not sure which files are stored on this disk, first type ^KF (a DISK OPERATION) and have a look at the file directory. If it is a long directory list, you may have to use ^Z to scroll the list to see extra lines of file names.

Choose some file names that you feel you can do without, and then press ^KJ and delete them one by one. Then when you judge you have sufficient space, try ^KD again. All things being equal, your file will be safely saved!

Unfortunately, we all seem to learn these lessons the hard way. But perhaps after a couple of these truly heart-stopping experiences, you will remember *always* to check how much space you have on a disk before you start a new file, especially if you know it is going to be a long document.

There is one fatal error that is extremely frustrating; if it ever happens to you, you will know why it is so important to save long documents at the end of each page or after every difficult word processing maneuver. It is a built-in hazard in CP/M, so your only safeguard is to be aware of the problem and to keep counting the number of files in your file directory. *You cannot have more than 64 files on any CP/M data disk.* This is particularly difficult on word processing data disks, where you tend to accumulate many small files. In MS-DOS the maximum number of files is 112.

Notice that there are six file names in each row in the file directory below the Wordstar OPENING MENU, so keep counting the rows. When you reach 10 rows (if you are a CP/M user), start looking for files to delete, or start a new data disk.

OTHER WORDSTAR COMMANDS

There are a couple of commands from the BLOCK MENU that you should know about, as both are very useful when you are working with long documents.

Place Markers

A block function that is handy for long documents is the PLACE MARKER. If you have an eight-page document, you can place a number on each page that you could quickly return to whenever you need to. On page 1 you would type ^K1, which appears as

<1>, on page 2, ^K2; and so forth up to ^K8 on page 8. To go back to page 3 from page 8, you would simply type ^Q3.

You can use ^K0 to ^K9 to mark up to 10 pages (or other appropriate positions) in a document. These markers are not saved with your file so you need not delete them. If you wish to hide a marker, just type the ^K command again (e.g. ^K1) and the <1> will be hidden: the ^Q1 will still function.

Save Often (^KS)

Another important point to remember when you are typing in long documents, as mentioned earlier, is to save your work at frequent intervals, such as the end of each page. To do this you simply type ^KS; when the file has been saved, a message appears telling you to type ^QP to go back to the position before the save.

Although this may seem to be a waste of valuable time, especially when you are in a hurry, it is very much quicker on that aforementioned bad day than typing the file in again from scratch. Most of us only make this mistake once!

WORDSTAR ON A COLOR MONITOR

It is quite common now to purchase a color monitor for your computer system. MicroPro has allowed for this possibility and included a BASIC program, WSCOLOR.BAS, which allows you to specify the color of text, the background color, and a separate set of colors (with or without highlighting) for the menus and screen messages.

To run the program, you will need a copy of WSCOLOR.BAS from the WS master working disk and a copy of the BASICA program from your MS-DOS master working disk on the same drive. Then you type:

```
BASICA WSCOLOR
```

and the screen will fill with the color options; try out some combinations until you find one you are comfortable with, following the simple instructions on the screen.

CONCLUSIONS

I hope you have enjoyed this in-depth tutorial in WordStar and that you now have the confidence to tackle your own everyday word processing problems. Although this chapter covers the most frequently used or most important functions, there are many more to learn. Much depends on your own needs and motivation to delve deeper into the reference manuals.

In the later tutorials you will see how WordStar is used in conjunction with CorrectStar and SpellStar (the proofreading system and spelling checker programs), with advanced DataStar, and with CalcStar, the electronic worksheet. You will learn a lot more about sorting files with FormSort and creating reports and summaries with ReportStar. Finally, you will learn some advanced MailMerge features and see how all the programs can be integrated in some very interesting and creative ways.

Do not forget to make a backup copy of your current data disk.

7

CorrectStar and SpellStar

Installing CorrectStar

Running CorrectStar

Word Counting Only

Installing CorrectStar in a Subdirectory

SpellStar Overview

Checking Disk Capacity

Running SpellStar

Supplementary Dictionaries

A Quick Spelling Check

There are currently two MicroPro programs for proofreading and checking for spelling mistakes or typing errors—the original SpellStar program and the newer system, CorrectStar. While SpellStar can run under CP/M or MS-DOS, CorrectStar, at the time of writing, is available only for IBM DOS or MS-DOS systems and will only work in conjunction with WordStar 3.3 or later versions.

CorrectStar has the following minimum hardware requirements: two floppy disk drives, with disk capacity of at least 320K each, and RAM (memory) of at least 192K. If you have a dual-floppy system, you will probably need to operate CorrectStar using a three-disk routine, described later; hard disk users will have no such problems. As MicroPro has included in the CorrectStar installation the facility to make use of a subdirectory, you will review the method of creating subdirectories (with MS-DOS version 2 or later) and how to copy files into them.

SpellStar, on the other hand, will run on a standard CP/M dual-floppy system, under CP/M 86, or with MS-DOS. You will need to use a three-disk routine if your disk capacity is less than about 190K or if you are checking large files.

The chapter describes the operation of both programs, starting with CorrectStar. If you are a SpellStar user, go straight to the heading SpellStar Overview.

INSTALLING CORRECTSTAR

You must install CorrectStar before you can start using it to check a WordStar file. If you have the WordStar OPENING MENU on screen, check the WordStar options. If the display reads:

```
S    Run SpellStar
```

then you know that CorrectStar is not yet installed on your system.

There are various ways to install CorrectStar on your MS-DOS system. You need to know which version of MS-DOS you have, and, if you have version 2 or later, you should learn how to create subdirectories.

This chapter starts with the simplest system. Users of IBM DOS or MS-DOS versions 2 or later should proceed to the section entitled Installing CorrectStar in a Subdirectory before returning to the Running CorrectStar section.

Installing CorrectStar for MS-DOS Version 1

If you have IBM DOS or MS-DOS 1, then installation will be the same for both dual-floppy disk and hard disk systems, once you have copied the distribution disks either to your hard disk or floppy disks.

If you have a hard disk system, copy the two CorrectStar disks onto one partition, making sure that you also have the three WordStar files on the same partition or drive (WS.COM, WSMSGS.OVR, and WSOVLY1.OVR). You can then go straight to the installation step-by-step procedure.

If you have a dual-floppy system, you need to make a copy of the two CorrectStar distribution disks and then add to the program disk the three WordStar files, WS.COM, WSMSGS.OVR, and WSOVLY1.OVR, from your tutorial disk. Then make a backup of that disk and boot the system from it.

Now you are ready to install CorrectStar. You will be confirming that the WordStar file you have is called WS.COM, that you have the three WordStar files on the same drive, that the drive is drive A, and, finally, that you are content to leave the AUTO-REFORM feature ON and the SOFTHYPHEN feature OFF.

If you have a hard disk drive that is not designated as drive A, you will have to answer **N** to the appropriate prompts as they appear during installation and type in the correct drive specifier for your system.

The AUTO-REFORM feature ensures that, if a word is replaced, edited, or removed during a CorrectStar session, the paragraph will be reformed automatically. You may need to disable this feature occasionally, but for the moment leave it ON.

The default for the SOFT HYPHEN feature is OFF. If you should decide in the future that you would like it ON, you can reinstall CorrectStar and change the default. For the moment accept the default OFF.

Step-by-step procedure

1. Next to the prompt type:

    CINSTALL

    and press **Return.**

2. You can now go through the installation procedure, answering the prompts as follows:

PROMPT	YOUR REPLY
Installed WordStar file: WS.COM Y/N	Y
WS.COM, CORRSTAR.OVR, WSOVLY1.OVR and WSMSGS.OVR should all be on same drive	press **Return** to confirm
The above files can be found on drive A Is this correct (Y/N)	Y
Drive and name of the Main Dictionary: A:MAIN.DCT Is this correct (Y/N)	Y
Drive and name of the Internal Dictionary: A:INTERNAL.DCT Is this correct (Y/N)	Y

```
Drive and name of the Personal Dictionary:
    A:PERSONAL.DCT
Is this correct (Y/N)                                          Y

Auto-reform feature is currently ON
Enter C to change or <RET> to leave as is               Return

The soft-hyphen feature is currently OFF
Enter C to change or <RET> to leave as is               Return
```

3. After the last **Return**, the screen message will tell you that CorrectStar is now being installed. If you have made any errors during installation, you will be prompted now to press any key to go back and correct the error. When you have done this, press **Esc** to end the installation.

4. Now if you type **WS** next to the prompt, you will see that the WordStar options include:

```
            S    Run CorrectStar
```

If you have a hard disk system, you are now ready to run your first spelling check on a WordStar file. You can go straight to the section below headed Running CorrectStar and follow the instructions for the three-disk routine, ignoring the instructions about changing floppy disks. If your hard disk drive is labeled A the instructions are correct for you; if it is labeled C (or any other) you will have to observe the drive specifications as they appear on the screen and make sure they are right for your system. If you made the appropriate corrections during installation, they should be correct now.

If you have a dual-floppy system, you must exit from WordStar and prepare the three disks required before you can run CorrectStar.

Preparing for the Three-Disk Routine

Insert your tutorial disk in drive A and the copy of the CorrectStar program disk, which you have just used for the installation, in drive B. Then you will make a copy of the CorrectStar Main Dictionary on a separate disk (the software requires 310K). You will also need the data disk you have been using for the exercises so far.

Step-by-step procedure

1. Disk 1 will be your tutorial disk. You must copy the following files from the installed CorrectStar disk in drive B to your tutorial disk in drive A:

WS.COM	CORRSTAR.OVR
WSMSGS.OVR	WC.EXE
WSOVLY1.OVR	INTERNAL.DCT

2. Note that you are deliberately overwriting the WordStar files on your tutorial disk with the newly installed versions from the CorrectStar disk. If you have space limitations, use a new formatted disk instead of your tutorial disk or delete some unwanted files. Label this disk CORRECTS-TAR DISK 1—PROGRAMS.

3. Disk 2 will be the data disk which, by now, should have a few letters and other files from the earlier exercises. Label it accordingly: CORRECTSTAR DISK 2—WORKING FILES.

4. Disk 3 is just a copy of the CorrectStar Main Dictionary disk, plus the Personal Dictionary from the copy of the CorrectStar program disk. Put a formatted disk in drive A and the Dictionary disk in drive B and copy MAIN.DCT from drive B to drive A.

5. Then remove the disk in drive B and replace it with the installed CorrectStar disk. Copy the file PERSONAL.DCT to the disk in drive A. Label this disk CORRECTSTAR DISK 3— DICTIONARIES.

Personal Dictionaries

Note that, for the moment, you have only one Personal Dictionary, and that it has no words in it yet—it was created during the installation process. Once you have completed your first spelling check, assuming you opt to add words to your Personal Dictionary, you will have a dictionary containing words pertinent to your particular needs.

The capacity of Personal Dictionaries is limited to about 1,500 words, so it is a good idea to plan ahead and see if there are specific types of words that should have their own dictionary, according to your business or profession. These could be legal, medical, insurance, journals, etc. Your additional Personal Dictionaries could be called for example, LEGAL.DCT, MEDICAL.DCT, and so on.

Although you cannot edit either the Main or the Internal Dictionaries, you can edit your Personal Dictionaries; this means that you need not add words *only* during a CorrectStar run, but can add lists of words any time from a Wordstar file to build up the dictionary of specialist terms you require.

RUNNING CORRECTSTAR

If you have a hard disk drive, you will be able to run CorrectStar directly.

The Two-Disk Routine

If you have 760K floppy disk drives, you will be able to run CorrectStar with two floppies—one with the programs and files for checking, the other holding the Main and Personal Dictionaries—unless you are checking some enormous files.

Just follow the instructions given here, ignoring the prompts to change disks. Once you have the WordStar OPENING MENU on your screen, just select **S** to run CorrectStar, then follow the instructions.

NOTE: If you get a message saying that your dictionaries cannot be found, you will have to run through the installation procedure again and check carefully the disk drives you entered as their locations.

The Three-Disk Routine

If your floppy drives are the 320K variety you will need to install the software with the three-disk system. This involves disk-swapping during the CorrectStar installation. Here's how it works:

Step-by-step procedure

1. Start with disk 1 in drive A and disk 2 in drive B.
2. Call up WordStar and type **L** to CHANGE LOGGED DISK DRIVES to drive B.
3. Select **S** from the OPENING MENU on drive B to Run CorrectStar. When prompted, type in the name of a file on drive B that you would like to check.

4. After you press **Return**, you will see the CorrectStar options menu and the request:

Please check your CorrectStar options

5. Next you will see listed the document file name you specified (B:FILE NAME), and the suggested name for your Personal Dictionary, A:PERSONAL.DCT. You can accept the default by pressing **Return** or enter any change (drive specifier, for example) at this stage.

6. Next you will be prompted to accept the default for the AUTO-REFORM feature; **press Return**. Then press **Return** again to accept SOFT HYPHEN insertion as OFF.

7. Press **Return** to begin the spelling check.

8. You will be asked to wait while the Internal Dictionary is loaded. Then you can see that your document is being checked.

9. When you are prompted to change disks, replace disk 1 in drive A with disk 3 (the Dictionaries).

10. When the first suspect word is found, it is displayed on the screen, and below it is the **Suggestion for change**; then you are asked: **What would you like to do?** You are given eight options: if you agree with the suggested correction, just press **Return** to accept it and you will see the word being corrected in your WordStar file. If the replacement word is longer or shorter than the original, you will see the AUTO REFORM feature working—doing an automatic *paragraph reform* on the text.

11. If you realize that the word shown is spelled incorrectly in the whole document, you should ask for global replacement by typing **G**.

12. If you accept that your word is incorrectly spelled, but do not agree with the suggested correction, you can enter your own correction from the keyboard, by typing **E** and then the correction, or you can press **N** to look at the next suggestion. You can continue typing **N** until you find the appropriate correct word, then type **C** to make the correction. If you wish to cycle back through the suggestions, press **P**.

13. If the suspect word is a specialist term or a person's name, address, or whatever, and you know you will be using the

word over and over again in your letters or documents, you should add the word to your Personal Dictionary—just press **A**.

14. If the suspect word occurs only once, you can either bypass it for this one occurrence, or type **I** to ignore it if it appears elsewhere in this document.

15. If at any time you need to interrupt the CorrectStar session, just press **^U**, then the **Esc** key when prompted, and you will exit CorrectStar and be returned to your WordStar file. If you are using the three-disk routine, you will be prompted to replace the WordStar disk, so remove disk 3 from drive A and replace it with disk 1. Press any key to redisplay WordStar.

Normally, you will go straight through your document, entering or accepting suggested corrections, adding words to your Personal Dictionary, and so on, until the CorrectStar session is complete at the end of the file. Then the system returns to WordStar, in Edit mode. You can make a final check through your file, if necessary, and then save it in the usual way.

CorrectStar is a sophisticated proofreader and spelling corrector program, yet it is very easy to use. At the end of the spelling check, you may have noticed a message that told you how many words were checked in the whole file and how many corrections were made. There may be times when you wish to know *only* how many words are in a file; you can then use the WORD COUNT program, WC.EXE.

WORD COUNTING ONLY

If you have the WordStar OPENING MENU on the screen, you can run the WORD COUNT utility using the **R** option to RUN A PROGRAM.

Step-by-step procedure

1. Select **R** from the OPENING MENU.

2. At the prompt NAME OF PROGRAM TO RUN? type **WC** and the name of a file to check. If you like, you can enter several file names, separated by a space; for example:

WC FORMLETT.TXT GENERAL.LBL BANK.DOC

if necessary, giving the drive identification as well.

3. You will see a heading for columns, for example:

Lines	Words	Characters	
21	356	1078	FORMLETT.TXT
127	675	2380	GENERAL.LBL
248	2085	19572	BANK.DOC
396	3116	23030	total

When the count is completed you will be asked to press any key to return to WordStar.

If you have a hard disk system, you will find this process is completed very fast (especially if you have a PC/AT or compatible). You can see how useful it could be for totaling all the words in each individual chapter of a book, for example, and then giving a grand total at the end.

You can also start the WORD COUNT utility from the system prompt by typing **WC** followed by the name (or names) of files you want counted, next to the prompt.

INSTALLING CORRECTSTAR IN A SUBDIRECTORY (MS-DOS 2 or Later)

The major difference between MS-DOS version 1 and more recent releases is the capability for creating subdirectories in later versions.

MicroPro has allowed for this subdirectory structure in the installation procedure for CorrectStar. The company suggests that you put the Main and Internal Dictionaries into a subdirectory called DICTNRY and then confirm this during the installation. In order for this procedure to work, the three WordStar files and CorrectStar have to be in the root directory.

If you would prefer to set your system up with all your word processing files in one subdirectory (as described later) and all your InfoStar files in another, you will have to install CorrectStar without creating the subdirectory for the dictionaries, and will have to include this information in CorrectStar during installation. The reason for this is that MicroPro has not allowed for the operation of WordStar and CorrectStar from *within* a subdirectory, and so the program is not designed to accommodate sub-subdirectories.

First the procedure for installing CorrectStar the MicroPro way is given, in which you keep your Wordstar and CorrectStar files in the root directory. Then the next section covers the installation of these programs within a subdirectory. It is up to you to decide which installation is best for your particular system.

Installing CorrectStar from the Root Directory

If you have a hard disk system, copy the two CorrectStar disks, making sure that you also have the three WordStar files on the same drive or partition (WS.COM, WSMSGS.OVR, and WSOVLY1.OVR). You can then go straight to the step-by-step installation instructions.

If you have a dual-floppy system, you need to make a copy of the CorrectStar program disk and then add to this disk the three WordStar files WS.COM, WSMSGS.OVR, and WSOVLY1.OVR from your tutorial disk. Then boot the system from your tutorial disk.

Now you are ready to install CorrectStar. During installation you will be asked whether your system has a hard or floppy disk, then to confirm that the WordStar file you have is called WS.COM, that you have the three WordStar files on the same drive, and that the drive is drive A. Also you must confirm that the Main and Internal Dictionaries are in a subdirectory called DICTNRY, and, finally, that you are content to leave the AUTO-REFORM feature ON and the SOFTHYPHEN feature OFF. Before you start installation you will create the dictionary subdirectory.

If you have a hard disk drive that is not called drive C, you will have to answer **N** to the appropriate prompts as they appear during installation and then type in the correct drive specifier for your system.

The AUTO-REFORM feature ensures that, if a word is replaced, edited, or removed during a CorrectStar session, the paragraph will be reformed automatically. You may need to disable this feature occasionally, but for the moment leave it ON.

The default for the SOFT HYPHEN feature is OFF. If you should decide in the future that you would like to have it ON, you can reinstall CorrectStar and change the default. For the moment accept the default of OFF.

Step-by-step procedure

1. Boot your system and next to the prompt type:

    MD DICTNRY

2. Then type **CD DICTNRY** to go into the subdirectory and copy in the dictionary files, MAIN.DCT and INTERNAL.DCT, from your root directory. To do this type:

    COPY *.DCT

    Remember, the backslash indicates the root directory.

3. If you have floppy disks, you would make your DICTNRY directory on the same drive as your CorrectStar programs (drive A), then copy the dictionaries into it from drive B.

4. Now you are ready to call up the installation program. Next to the prompt type:

    CINSTALL

    and press **Return.**

5. You can now go through the installation procedure, answering the prompts as follows and/or changing drive labels where necessary:

PROMPT	YOUR REPLY
Enter disk type used: H for hard, F for floppy	H or F
You have selected (H or F) Is this correct Y/N)	Y or N
Installed WordStar file: WS.COM Y/N	Y
WS.COM, CORRSTAR.OVR, WSOVLY1.OVR and WSMSGS.OVR should all be on same drive	press **Return** to confirm
The above files can be found on drive C Is this correct (Y/N)	Y
Drive, path, and name of the Main Dictionary: C:\DICTNRY\MAIN.DCT Is this correct (Y/N)	Y
Drive, path, and name of the Internal Dictionary: C:\DICTNRY\INTERNAL.DCT Is this correct (Y/N)	Y

```
Drive, path, and name of the Personal Dictionary:
    C:\DICTNRY\PERSONAL.DCT
Is this correct (Y/N)                                           Y

Auto-reform feature is currently ON
Enter C to change or <RET> to leave as is                  Return

The soft hyphen feature is currently OFF
Enter C to change or <RET> to leave as is                  Return
```

6. After the last **Return**, the screen message will tell you that CorrectStar is now being installed. If you have made any errors during installation, you will be prompted now to press any key to go back and correct the error: when you have done this, press **Esc** to end the installation.

7. Now if you type **WS** next to the prompt and look at the OPENING MENU, you will see that the WordStar options include:

```
              S   Run CorrectStar
```

That completes the installation of CorrectStar in a root directory. To actually run the program, turn back to Step 3 of The Three-Disk Routine and start your spelling check.

Installing CorrectStar from within a Subdirectory

The use of subdirectories is especially convenient on a hard disk system; however, you can use them just as easily on your floppy disks to help organize your files and available disk space efficiently. In Chapter 2 you created a subdirectory to use as a tutorial working area. As you may remember, when you first boot up your system, and the system prompt is on the screen, you are automatically in the root directory. If you type **DIR** next to the system prompt, you will see a listing of the directory of files in the root directory. Any subdirectories you have already created will be included right at the end of the directory listing with <DIR> next to the chosen subdirectory name.

You created the TUTORIAL subdirectory in Chapter 2, with its sub-subdirectories, WORDTUTE and DATATUTE. Now you will create another one called WORDPRO (for word processing) to contain the WordStar, MailMerge, and CorrectStar files. If you create three more sub-subdirectories, called LETTERS, DOCS and

LABELS, you could use these later on to store your own files of letters, documents, and so on.

You may remember that the structure of root directories, sub-directories, and sub-subdirectories can be likened to an upside-down tree, where the trunk is the main directory and the branches are the various levels of subdirectories.

Once you have created the WORDPRO subdirectory, with its associated sub-subdirectories, you will have this structure:

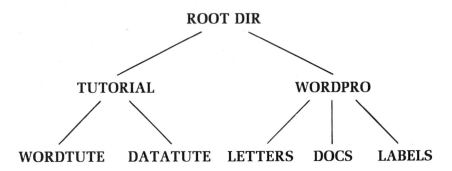

You will start by copying the three WordStar files, and the MailMerge and CorrectStar files, into the new subdirectory WORDPRO; then you will install CorrectStar for this system. In this exercise I assume that you have a hard disk labeled drive C (if you have something different, remember to write in the changes).

Step-by-step procedure

1. Start by making the directories you need using the MKDIR command; boot up your system and next to the prompt type:

    MD WORDPRO

2. After you press **Return**, type **DIR** next to the prompt and you will see WORDPRO <DIR> at the end of the list on the screen.

3. Next you have to change directories by typing:

    CD WORDPRO

4. Now you are now inside the WORDPRO subdirectory.

5. If you need to check your position in the directory system at any time, you can type **CD** next to the prompt, and you will be given the current directory location. Remember, a backslash \ means the root directory.

   Go ahead now and make the three sub-subdirectories. Next to the prompt type, in turn:

   `MD LETTERS`

   then, after pressing **Return**:

   `MD DOCS`

   and finally:

   `MD LABELS`

6. While you are in the WordPro subdirectory, you can copy in the files you need from your TUTORIAL subdirectory:

   `COPY    \TUTORIAL\WS*.*`

   and:

   `COPY    \TUTORIAL\MAILMRGE.OVR`

   Note the positions of the backslashes. If your files are on a tutorial floppy disk, use the usual copying command to copy them into the WORDPRO subdirectory.

7. Copy the CorrectStar programs and dictionaries from the two master working disks. Now if you check the directory of WORDPRO you should see the following files:

WS.COM	WC.EXE
WSOVLY1.OVR	INTERNAL.DCT
WSMSGS.OVR	MAIN.DCT
MAILMRGE.OVR	CINSTALL.EXE
CORRSTAR.OVR	

8. Now you are ready to install CorrectStar. Next to the prompt type:

CINSTALL

and press **Return.**

9. You can now go through the installation procedure, answering the prompts as follows, and/or changing drive labels where necessary:

PROMPT	YOUR REPLY
Enter disk type used: H for hard, F for floppy	H or F
You have selected (H or F) Is this correct (Y/N)	Y
Installed WordStar file: WS.COM (Y/N)	Y
WS.COM, CORRSTAR.OVR, WSOVLY1.OVR and WSMSGS.OVR should all be on same drive	press **Return** to confirm
The above files can be found on drive C Is this correct (Y/N)	Y
Drive, path, and name of the Main Dictionary: C:\DICTNRY\MAIN.DCT Is this correct (Y/N)	N
Enter drive, name, and path of Main Dictionary:	**C:MAIN.DCT**
Drive, path, and name of the Internal Dictionary: C:\DICTNRY\INTERNAL.DCT Is this correct (Y/N)	N
Enter drive, name, and path of Internal Dictionary:	**C:INTERNAL.DCT**
Drive, path, and name of the Personal Dictionary: C:\DICTNRY\PERSONAL.DCT Is this correct (Y/N)	N
Enter drive, name, and path of Personal Dictionary:	**C:PERSONAL.DCT**
Auto-reform feature is currently ON Enter C to change or <RET> to leave as is	Return
The soft hyphen feature is currently OFF Enter C to change or <RET> to leave as is	Return

10. After the last **Return**, the screen message will tell you that CorrectStar is now being installed. If you have made any errors during installation, you will be prompted now to press any key to go back and correct the error: when you have done this, press **Esc** to end the installation.

11. Now if you type **WS** next to the prompt and look at the OPENING MENU, you will see that the WordStar options include:

```
S    Run CorrectStar
```

You are now ready to run your first CorrectStar spelling check. Turn back to step 3 of The Three-Disk Routine; if you have a floppy disk system, you may need to turn back to the previous section on preparing disks for the three-disk routine for running CorrectStar.

You should back up the installed WordStar and CorrectStar files right away. Also, if you have any other versions of WordStar or CorrectStar, either on floppy disks or other areas of your hard disk, it is a good idea to overwrite them with these new versions.

Remember that you will now be running WordStar from inside your WordPro subdirectory. At the end of each session, after exiting from WordStar, you could copy all your .TXT files into the LETTERS subdirectory, any .DOC files into the DOCS subdirectory, and .LBL files into the LABELS subdirectory. You can then delete these files from your WordPro directory.

You may find that you want different, or additional, subdirectories for your particular business—go ahead and create what you need. By keeping similar files grouped together in this way, you will find "housekeeping" that much easier; you can check the subdirectories from time to time and remove any extra files. And you can back up these areas more easily onto their own floppy disks when they are grouped logically.

SPELLSTAR OVERVIEW

SpellStar is used in conjunction with WordStar text files as a proofreader and spelling checker. It will help you to locate typing errors (it *knows* you did not mean *tpying*!) but it does not know any grammar, so if you type *witch* when you meant to type *which*, the mistake will not be drawn to your attention. On the assumption that you would only rarely need to use the word witch in normal business life, you could actually remove that spelling from the dictionary if you wished.

SpellStar comes with a 21,000-word dictionary. Most of the packages sold have an American dictionary built in, but there are also English, French, and German dictionaries available on disk now (you should contact your dealer if you are interested in this option). There are also some dictionaries of specialist terms, but you will probably find it much more satisfactory to compile your own for your company's specific needs. This is very easy to do with SpellStar.

Another useful function of the SpellStar software is that as it proofreads your text file it also counts the number of words. You are even told how many *different* words you have used—a guide to how varied a vocabulary you have. It is often useful, and sometimes imperative, to know the number of words in a newspaper article, scientific abstract, book for publication, prize essay and so on. In many such situations there may well be a minimum, or maximum, number of words required.

CHECKING DISK CAPACITY

The SpellStar dictionary occupies nearly 100K of disk space. Unless you have very large capacity floppy disks or a hard disk, you will need to create a new master working disk that has the three WordStar programs on it; also the SpellStar dictionary, SPEL-STAR.DCT, and the SpellStar overlay file called SPELSTAR.OVR. The file called SAMPLE.TXT should be on a data disk in drive B. Note that although the program is called SpellStar the program files are written with only one L—SPELSTAR. This is because a file name cannot be more than eight characters in length.

You will run SpellStar by inserting the program disk in drive A and the data disk in drive B. Then when you call up WordStar you will change logged disk drives so that you should not have the problem of running out of space.

If you need to check very large document files, you may need to use *three* disks—one with your WordStar program files and overlays (WS.COM, WSOVLY1.OVR, WSMSGS.OVR, and SPEL-STAR.OVR), a second with the SpellStar dictionary (SPEL-STAR.DCT) and the remaining SpellStar programs, and a third for your text files.

There is a file on the SpellStar distribution disk called SAM-PLE.TXT that is provided as an example of a spelling check.

RUNNING SPELLSTAR

Once you have prepared new master working disks, you are ready to use the software on a WordStar text file.

Step-by-Step Procedure

1. Boot up your system from the tutorial disk. At the A> prompt type:

WS

2. Select **L** from the OPENING MENU, and press **B** and **Return** when asked for the new logged drive.
3. Press **S** to call up the SpellStar option.
4. Type in SAMPLE.TXT when you are prompted:

NAME OF FILE TO CHECK/ADD TO DICTIONARY?

5. Now you will see the SpellStar Operations Menu, giving you some options:

```
C    -   Check spelling
M    -   Maintain dictionary
X    -   Exit to WordStar no-file menu
```

Operation?

To carry out a spelling check now, you will select **C**. If you had typed in a file full of words to add to the dictionary, you would select **M** to go straight to dictionary maintenance (which includes adding or deleting words from the SpellStar Main Dictionary).

6. When the process is complete, you would press **^X** to go back to WordStar and then **^X** again to exit the operating system.

The Spelling Check Process

Press **C** to select the spelling check operation and your screen will display the SpellStar SPELLING CHECK OPERATION menu shown in Figure 7–1.

You will find that the defaults for the CURRENT VALUES are the current disk drive and file name you specified.

Note that because you changed logged disk drive the drives given are all B. It does not matter that the dictionary is actually on A (the program finds it anyway).

FIGURE 7–1   SPELLING CHECK CONTROLS Menu
                  is SpellStar

```
     SPELLING CHECK CONTROLS              CURRENT VALUE

D  - Use another main dictionary =       B:SPELSTAR.DCT
S  - Add supplemental dictionary =
F  - Change file to be checked   =       B:SAMPLE.TXT
W  - Change work drive           =          B:
```

Under the SPELLING CHECK CONTROLS menu you will see:

```
       <Return>  -  Start spelling check
              X  -  Exit to Operations Menu
```

```
Control to change?
```

To start the spelling check, press **Return**.

Now you will see this checklist as SpellStar proceeds with the proofreading:

```
Number of words in document.........: 422
Number of different words...........: 261
Number of words in main dictionary..: 21027
Number of words in supplement.......:
Number of dictionary words checked..: 8798
Number of misspelled words..........: 28
Total number of misspellings........:
```

You will see the numbers changing quickly as the proofreading progresses. The dictionary is organized in such a way that it checks the words in order of their length, starting with two-letter words. So although it may seem a little slow to get going, it speeds up when it gets past the more commonly used short words and usually stops well before it reaches the figure for Number of words in main dictionary unless you happen to have used a lot of the really uncommon 20 letter words!

Now you are given some more options:

```
Enter ''L'' to list the misspelled words.
Enter <Return> to flag errors in your text.
Enter ''R'' to abandon the check and restart.
```

Since you wish to see a list of misspelled words, type **L**. The list (all in capital letters) will appear on the screen.

Notice that some of the words look quite correct, especially if you used one of your own text files for the spelling check. They are called "misspelled" by SpellStar simply because they are not in the Main Dictionary supplied with the software. Others are clearly misspelled or typing errors.

Error Correction

Having listed the words, continue with the next option:

Enter <Return> to flag errors, ''R'' to restart.

Press **Return**; you will notice the disk is accessed as SpellStar busily checks through the text file.

The software is totaling the errors and putting in the "flags." (Next to every occurrence of an error, SpellStar puts an **@** sign.) Now you will see the Total number of misspellings filled in and you will get the message:

SpellStar has flagged the misspellings in the text.

and, below that:

If you changed disks at the beginning of this program, please insert the original disk before continuing.

This will apply to you if you are operating a three-disk system. Then finally:

Enter <Return> to correct errors in text, ''R'' to restart.

You can choose to flag the errors in the text for correction at a later stage. To do so, press **R** to restart and then **Return** to go back into WordStar. You will find that the file you save will be listed in the directory with the extension .@@@. When you return to edit the file, remember to call up the file with the .@@@ extension and then proceed normally with error correction and editing, as detailed here.

When you have finished you will have three files with the extensions .TXT, .BAK, and .ADD.

If you want to correct the errors now, press **Return**. After a moment or two your letter will appear on the screen, with all the errors flagged with @ signs. You will see some new options on-screen that relate to making the necessary corrections.

Notice that the status line at the top of the screen shows the drive and file name on the left, and on the far right, the possible Action you may wish to select. Next to that there is a flashing cursor, waiting for your selection.

At the top of your letter are the action options:

```
F  - Fix word          D  - Add word to dictionary
B  - Bypass word       S  - Add word to supplemental dictionary
I  - Ignore word
```

Now you will notice that the @ sign at the first error has disappeared and the cursor is flashing over the first letter of the word. As soon as you decide what to do with the flagged word and select an action, the @ sign in front of the next error will disappear and the cursor will start flashing over *its* first letter.

If the first word is a proper name, select **I** to say that you ignore it. As soon as you press the **I**, you will see the letter appear briefly in the status line next to action?

Continue on with the next errors, ignoring all proper names, until you come to a genuine error or typing mistake. Press **F** to fix the error; you will go automatically into WordStar; now you can use any of the normal cursor control and editing commands to correct the mistake.

When you are satisfied, press ^L to go to the next flagged error. You will find the actions list restored and the cursor flashing over the first letter of the next word.

When you come across a flagged word that you feel is worth adding to the dictionary, press **D** to add it to the Main Dictionary or **S** if you want to create a Supplement. When you select **D** or **S** you will get the prompt:

```
                Add to Dictionary?  (Y/N)
                Add to Supplement?  (Y/N)
```

You must type **Y** to confirm that you wish to add the word to the dictionary.

The next flagged error will now flash. If you encounter a word that you want to check before making corrections, you can bypass it for the time being by typing B, and then correct it or add it to the dictionary later. Continue thus until you have corrected the whole document.

You can use all the usual WordStar editing facilities at this stage, just as you would when correcting a normal WordStar file. You are not bound to change only the flagged "errors' in the text. Use ^ B to reform paragraphs as you go along.

When you have finished, you will get the message:

```
Spelling Check Completed *** Press ESCAPE Key
```

and the WordStar MAIN MENU will reappear at the top of your screen. Now exit in the usual way, using **^KD** if you wish to continue in WordStar or **^KX** if you want to exit to the operating system.

If for any reason you want to abandon the spelling corrections you have done, you can press **^KQ** and the file would be saved in its original, prechecked form, with all the flag characters restored and the extension **.@@@**. The flag characters would be printed out with the file if you decided to print it at this stage.

Adding Terms to the Dictionary

You will notice that the file directory shows a file named SAMPLE.ADD (or your file name with the extension .ADD). This is the file containing the words you elected to add to the dictionary during error correction by selecting action **D** or **S**.

Even if you had decided not to add *any* words to the dictionary the .ADD file would still have been created. If you are short of space on your disk, you should erase such excess files. You can do this using the **Y** option to delete a file in WordStar or using the ERA function built into CP/M (DEL for MS-DOS users).

If your .ADD file contains words you want to keep, these are added during a *dictionary maintenance* session. Select **S** from the WordStar OPENING MENU to call up SpellStar again. Enter the .ADD file's name in answer to the first query. This time you should select **M** from the OPERATIONS MENU to MAINTAIN DICTIONARY. Now you will see on your screen the DICTIONARY MAINTENANCE menu for controls and options menu (see Figures 7–2 and 7–3).

FIGURE 7–2 DICTIONARY MAINTENANCE MENU
for Controls

```
               SpellStar - Dictionary Maintenance

    DICTIONARY MAINTENANCE CONTROLS              CURRENT VALUE
F - Change word file to use                 = B:SAMPLE.ADD
D - Change dictionary to update             = B:SPELSTAR.DCT
U - Change name of new or updated dictionary = B
W - Change work drive for sort              =     B:
```

For this first file you can accept the control defaults listed under CURRENT VALUE. You will learn the other controls in later exercises.

You can also accept the defaults under options for this session, so just press **Return** to start. You will see something like the following summary:

```
SpellStar is now creating/updating your dictionary

Number of words in file......................: 11
Number of different words in file............: 11
Number of words in dictionary being updated..: 21032
Number of words added to dictionary..........: 11
Number of words deleted from dictionary......:
Number of words in new or updated dictionary.: 21043


If you changed disks at the beginning of this program,
    please insert the original before continuing.
```

FIGURE 7–3 DICTIONARY MAINTENANCE OPTIONS

```
DICTIONARY MAINTENANCE OPTIONS
N - Create a new dictionary                     =  NO
A - Add words                                   =  NO
T - Delete words                                =  NO
C - Combine add/delete                          =  YES
S - Use ''S'' words from ''.ADD'' file          =  NO
L - List dictionary words                       =  NO

<Return> - Start dictionary maintenance
    X    - Exit to operating system

Control or option to change?
```

Then you will be reminded to press **Return** to go back to WordStar or **R** to restart dictionary maintenance. You would *restart* if you have several files to add to, or delete from, the dictionary. You would select **F** to change the work file name (simply overtype the previous name) and then carry on with the next dictionary maintenance session.

SUPPLEMENTARY DICTIONARIES

If you use a lot of specialist terms that are not in the SpellStar Main Dictionary, you can create a new supplementary dictionary for yourself. You may also add the words to the Main Dictionary, but this has two disadvantages.

First, the Main dictionary is already very large and occupies a lot of disk space. You would be increasing the size still further, which also increases the time it takes to complete a dictionary maintenance. Second, there is always the risk that you will damage or destroy your Main Dictionary in error. You can easily recopy SPELSTAR.DCT from your master working disk, but you will then have lost any changes and additions you have previously made.

If you do decide to keep only the Main Dictionary, you must remember to make a back up copy *every time you update* it, just in case you are unlucky enough to erase it.

Creating a Specialist Supplementary Dictionary

In WordStar, create a file with an appropriate name, such as LEGAL.TXT, MEDICAL.TXT, or FINANCE.TXT, according to your specialty.

Type in all the specialist terms you can think of, including all parts of verbs, singular and plural nouns, adjectives, etc. Save the file with a ^**KD** and then select SpellStar from the WordStar menu.

Press ^**R** to enter the file name for checking. Then select **C** to run a spelling check. At the end of the check, list the "misspelled" words. You may find that some of your special words are in the Main Dictionary, so you need to mark only the new words when you go on to the next stage, which is correcting the flagged words in the text file. For each word select action **S** to mark it for adding to a supplementary dictionary.

When you have finished the corrections, save the file with ^**KD**. Then select SpellStar again. Enter the file name; now choose

M to run dictionary maintenance. Select **D** to change the dictionary to update and press the Space Bar over SPELSTAR.DCT to leave that option blank.

Now select **U** to enter the name of the new dictionary and enter a name with the extension .SUP. From the options, select **N** and change the default to YES to create a new dictionary and **S** to add the S words from the .ADD file.

Now press **Return** to accept the rest of the defaults and to start adding your word file to the newly created dictionary supplement. The status line shows the name of your new supplementary dictionary on the right-hand side. The dictionary maintenance summary is the same as for the last maintenance run you did.

When this is finished, you will see the number of words in the new dictionary and the message reminding you to press **Return** to go back to WordStar or **R** to restart maintenance.

Combining ADD AND DELETE

If you ever needed to create documents with British spelling, you could achieve it without going to the expense of purchasing the English dictionary. You could make a copy of the standard dictionary, giving it a name that implies that it has a dual purpose (AM-ENG.DCT), then use the combined ADD AND DELETE option in SpellStar: where words in your file already exist in the dictionary you are given the option to delete them—any new words are added automatically.

Step-by-step procedure

1. Create a WordStar file containing as many pairs of British and American spellings of words as you can think of. Save it, then select **S** to run SpellStar. Select **M** to run dictionary maintenance and accept all the defaults.

2. As the words are checked against the SpellStar main dictionary, you will be given the option to delete existing words (American spellings), and the new British spellings will be added automatically.

3. Note that if you include a word for deletion that is not in the Main Dictionary, it will be *added* instead! To avoid this, you should run a spelling check on your word file first.

Remember, whenever you create a very long file you must make sure you have enough space left on the disk before you start any maintenance runs.

A QUICK SPELLING CHECK

Once you are more familiar with SpellStar operation, you will find that you can run a spelling check, correct the errors, and add words to the dictionary fairly quickly. However, if you are in a hurry and do not have time to do this all in one session, you can achieve the same results in stages.

Step-by-Step Procedure

1. Assume you have typed a three-page document of great importance that must be printed and shipped immediately. You want to be absolutely certain that it does not contain any spelling mistakes or typing errors, but you do not want to go through the usual process of flagging errors for correction, since frequently these are not real errors but simply unrecognized words. There is a quick solution to this problem.

   As soon as you have saved the file, select **S** to run SpellStar and then **C** to check spelling.

2. When the spelling check is complete, select **L** to list the "errors" some of which will be real errors (not just new words or unrecognized proper names), which you will want to correct.

3. Note the details of words to be corrected and then exit to WordStar without flagging the "errors" in the text. Use **^QF** to find the words that you noted for correction and make the changes; check for more than one occurrence of the *same error* by pressing **^L** (which repeats the previous **^QF** command).

4. If there was only one occurrence, the cursor will now be at the end of the document; press **Esc** and then type **^QF** again.

5. After entering the next word to find, remember to use the **B** option to search backwards through the file. Continue until you have corrected all the spelling mistakes and typing errors, then save and print your file in the usual way.

6. At your convenience you can return to SpellStar to run the spelling check, flag the errors, and then run dictionary maintenance so that new words can be added to the appropriate dictionary.

You may prefer to work this way, using the "quick check" technique to proofread and check your documents and letters, making the corrections of genuine errors in WordStar. You can then "batch" run spelling checks and dictionary maintenance on several files at the end of each week, for example.

This tutorial has covered the everyday uses of SpellStar. Some additional specialized options are discussed in the SpellStar manual. Happy proofreading!

8

CalcStar Tutorial

Introducing CalcStar
The CalcStar Menu
Entering a CalcStar Table
Designing Your Own Tables
Sales Forecasting
Converting Calcstar Files to DataStar Format
Conclusion

CalcStar enables you to produce analyses and reports on all kinds of numeric data. MicroPro calls its program an *electronic report generator*, though it is similar to other *electronic spreadsheets*. You can enter columns of figures—monthly sales figures, for example—then manipulate them to produce sales projections for the next half year, sales tax figures, or a profit and loss account.

The major advantage of this kind of computer program over the pencil, paper, and electronic calculator is that, with very little experience, you can manipulate the figures on the computer screen using the extensive editing and formatting facilities available, and only print out your report when you are completely satisfied with the results. For example, when you have entered several columns of figures, you can change just one value and then have your computer recalculate all the other entries that are dependent upon the single value you have changed. Or you might like to see the effect on your overall sales figures of decreasing your profit margin on one item.

CalcStar is by far the easiest program to operate in the MicroPro family; it also has a readable, easy-to-understand manual. This tutorial will introduce you to the program and its new terminology and will help you through some areas that might otherwise be a little difficult to follow. This chapter also explains how CalcStar can be linked with other MicroPro programs.

You will start by entering some data you are already familiar with, the price list information you entered in Chapter 7. You can compare the ease of entry and manipulation of the data with the previous method with DataStar. It will illustrate immediately one of the possible drawbacks of this program—the limited size of the model you can generate. In DataStar you could go on adding stock items to your PRICELST file almost *ad infinitum*, but in CalcStar you are limited to about 200 items if you use the same form layout. Having said that, the program should prove more than adequate in normal use, and if you need a more sophisticated financial planning package, MicroPro provide this in the form of PlanStar (for IBM and compatible machines).

Clearly, CalcStar was not intended for the entry of large numbers of stock items. Later in the chapter we will look at ways of performing economic projections, which is the kind of problem CalcStar is designed to handle.

As with the other software, you should have the original distribution diskette and a backup copy tucked away safely, and you should use your working master of the CalcStar master disk in drive A and the data files data disk in drive B. If you have a hard disk system, you can copy the CalcStar files into the tutorial partition of your hard disk.

INTRODUCING CALCSTAR

To load the software, boot up your system and at the prompt type:

CS

and press **Return**.

The screen will display the CalcStar MAIN MENU and, below that, the blank table with rows numbered from **1** to **255** and columns labeled from **A** to **DW**. You can see the first 10 rows and columns A to F in the *window*, if you turn off the help screen the window enlarges to show 15 rows. You can shift the window at will to view any part of the CalcStar table.

The cursor is not the usual shape, but appears as two inward-pointing highlighted arrowheads marking the left and right margin of each "box."

In CalcStar the table is called an *array* or *matrix* which simply means a table formed of equally spaced columns and rows; the position where a column and row intersect is called a *coordinate* (as in map reading) and the box at that position is called an *element* of the array. Altogether, there are 32,385 elements in the whole CalcStar array; of these only about 750 can be used for any one model.

Try out some cursor movements now and learn a few of the very basic CalcStar commands. If you press the **Return** key, the cursor will move across the screen from column to column. Note the *cursor location indicator* at the bottom of the table. As you move the cursor, it indicates the current coordinate position (such as D1).

Note also the *direction indicator*, which remains unchanged at L–R, this indicates that the cursor will move from left to right when you press the **Return** key. The commands in CalcStar are capital letters preceded by a semicolon. You can change the direction by pressing **;O**. Now the direction indicator will read T–B, and the cursor will move from top to bottom when you press **Return**.

At the bottom of the screen, below the line containing the cursor location and direction indicators, are three more important indicators: type:, contents:, and edit:.

When you type in your first *entry*, the *edit* box displays what you have entered, and the *type* shows whether it is a *text* or *numeric* entry. As soon as you press **Return** to load your entry into its appropriate location, the edit box will clear and the *contents* will now tell you what you have entered at that location.

Once you have filled in a section of table, you will find this very useful; every time you move the cursor into a particular location, the contents box will tell you what is entered there. This is not so important when the entry is text, but it is extremely useful when the entry is a calculation.

THE CALCSTAR MENU

Now you will learn about the menu in detail. On the left are the cursor control characters, which perform basically the same movements as in other MicroPro programs. The ^**S** and ^**D** commands move the cursor to left and right a column at a time; and the **^E** and **^X** move up and down a line at a time. The **^Z** moves the cursor from any position in one row down to column A in the next row (when the *order* is left to right), or from any position in one column to the top of the next, when the order is top to bottom.

The **Tab** key is extremely useful, since it will move the cursor back to coordinate A1 (the top left-hand corner of the CalcStar screen) from any position in the array. Try it out now.

Step-by-Step Procedure

1. Move the cursor to D6 using the cursor control keys (remember that you can change the direction of cursor movement using **;O**). Now press the **Tab** key; if you look at the bottom left corner of the screen you will see goto> A1. You have the option of pressing **Return** and accepting A1 or of overtyping A1 with any other coordinate.

2. Try out both options and see how quickly you can move around the array. If you enter **DW255** as one option, the cursor will move to the extreme right-hand corner of the array, into the element number 32,385.

3. The next section of the menu shows all the CalcStar commands. As mentioned earlier, these are implemented when you press the semicolon followed by a command letter. You have used one of these already—the **;O** to change order (that is, to change the cursor direction from the default of L–R to T–B). Inadvertently, in using the **Tab** key you have used another command, **;G** for goto.

By the end of the tutorial you will have used the basic commands, so I will not go through them one by one now. One of the nicest features of CalcStar is that virtually everything you need to know to operate the program is displayed in the menu. Once you are familiar with the functions of these control characters, you will hardly ever need to look anything up in the manual—a relaxing change after the complexities of DataStar.

The last part of the menu, headed *MISC*, shows four more handy functions:

The ? allows you to use CalcStar as a calculator (not to be confused with ;?, the command that tells you at any time how much space you have left for your model). You simply type in the formula for your calculation; you can use all the usual calculator functions—including addition, subtraction, multiplication, division, and percentages—followed by ?.

You must use the * (asterisk) for multiply by, a slash sign for divide by, and the usual signs, +, -, and % for the rest. For example:

$$(9*9)/(3*3)?$$

You should use parentheses where necessary to ensure that the calculation is performed in the order of precedence that you intended.

Experiment with some calculations until you are familiar with this function and see how useful it can be.

Another useful function key is **Esc** which cancels a command if you make a mistake. The other functions under MISC will be explained later in the tutorial.

ENTERING A CALCSTAR TABLE

Now you will design a table to hold the same price list information as you entered previously with DataStar. This is a simple way to cover the basic commands you need to know when you design any CalcStar table.

You will need four columns of the appropriate widths, headed CODE, DESCRIPTION, SIZE, and PRICE, as before.

Labeling the Columns

For each column you must determine the width required; decide whether the heading should be centered, left justified or right justified; and, for numeric fields, what degree of precision is required (that is, if you use a decimal point, how many zeros do you want after it?).

The default width is 10 columns. Text is normally *left justified*, and numeric data, *right justified*; and the default for precision is two decimal places—just what you want for the PRICE field (for dollars and cents) but not required for the SIZE field (centimeters).

Start with the CODE field. Since there is a function that allows you automatically to update a number from one row to the next; change the format of the code to all numeric, that is, start at 100001 and increment to 100050.

You need the 1 at the beginning of the code number, because otherwise CalcStar converts 000001 to the form 1 (with a precision of zero; **1.00** with the default precision of 2). You cannot use the original codes (such as U1/10010), since this would be interpreted as a text entry and you could not then make the number increment automatically.

The exponential form will be used if there are not enough spaces for the number of digits you have entered. In order for the code 100001 to be entered exactly as written here, not converted to an exponential form (such as 1.00e05), you need a column width of eight (two more than the number of digits you wish to enter) and a precision of zero.

Step-by-step procedure

Here's how you achieve that:

1. Move the cursor to Column B1. Adjust the column width to 8 by typing **;F** (for Format) and then select **W** (for Width) and enter **8** (you may choose any width between the limits 3 to 63). Notice that the type: now reads (empty, but allocated).

2. Press **;F** again. This time select **P** for Precision and type **0** (options are 0 to 12).

3. To center the heading CODE, type:

/CCODE.

4. Your entry will appear next to **edit.** Then when you press **Return**, the **/C** ensures that the word CODE will be written in the *center* of column B1.

5. Did you notice that as soon as you pressed the / the type: displayed text:? Then, when you pressed **Return**, it displayed text:centered and the **contents:** read 'CODE'.

The edit: position is now clear, ready for the next entry. But the cursor is still in the same location—do not forget to press **Return** after each entry is satisfactorily entered, or you will simply overtype the entry you have just made. This can seem a nuisance, but it is useful when you need to make a change or correct an error in the data you have entered *before* it appears in the form.

6. Try entering some codes. See the result, then change the precision back to the default value of 2 and watch the results.

Move the cursor to coordinate B3. Type **000001** next to edit:—notice that type: reads numeric as soon as you press the first **0**. Press **;F**, select **P**, and enter **2** for the value.

7. Now type **100001** next to edit and see what you get this time.

8. Change the precision back to zero—type **;F**, select **P**, and enter **0**. This is the format you will use for entering data values in the CODE column.

9. On now to the other columns. For the description column you will want a width of 36 and no other format changes. Go ahead and move the cursor to **C1**, type **;F**, select **W** and enter **36**.

10. Now type:

/CDESCRIPTION

and when you press **Return**, the centered column heading will appear.

11. Go straight on to D1, adjust the width to **7**, accept the default Precision of **2**, and center the heading PRICE.

12. If you ever forget to type the **/C** at the beginning of a heading, you can type it in afterwards. Enter **PRICE** and press **Return**; you will see the heading appear at the top of the column. Now, with the cursor at the blank edit: line, type **/C** and you will see the heading realigned.

13. Finally, go on to E1, adjust the width to **5**, and right justify the heading by typing **/RSIZE**. Then change the Precision to zero, since you will be entering centimeters with no decimal places.

14. Now press **Tab** (or **;G**) and then **Return**, to go back to coordinate A1. It would be a good idea to save your table at this point, just in case anything goes wrong later.

15. Press **;S**, enter **CSPRICES** next to the request for a file name, press **Return** when asked for a password, and then **A** for A(ll). The table will now be saved and then you can continue to the next stage.

Labeling the Rows

It is not essential to label the rows, but it will give you some more practice and helps to make up for the fact that previously, in

DataStar, the code included the price code information (U1, F2, S3, etc.).

Step-by-step procedure

1. With the cursor in A1 adjust the width to **12** and enter the heading **PRICE CODES**.
2. Change the order to T–B with **;O**, then move the cursor to A3 and enter **ULTIMA:**. Then leave three spaces and type **U1** (if you leave three spaces after the colon, U1 will be in the right-justified position).
3. Now move the cursor to A4 and enter the price code **U2** making it right-justified. Continue entering the Ultima codes—U3 and U4, remembering to *right justify* them.
4. On the next line type in **SUPREME: S1** (this time leave two spaces after the colon so that S1 will be in the right-justified position) and then the other price codes on subsequent lines, S2–S4. Finally, do the same for **FINESSE:** and its price codes.
5. That is the end of the labeling. Save your form again by pressing **;S**. This time when you enter **CSPRICES** for the file name, you will get the message

`File exists.  Destroy old contents (Y,N)?`

You must type **Y**, then press **Return** when asked for the password and finally, enter **A** for A(ll).

Entering Data

Now that you have saved all the column and row headings, you can start entering data. First, you will learn how to enter the formula to make the code number increase by one from one row to the next.

Step-by-step procedure

1. Move the cursor to B3 and check the entry of the first code number, 100001.
2. Change the Order to T–B using **;O** (if necessary) and move the cursor to B4. Enter the formula:

1+B3

and when you press **Return**, the B4 entry will read 100002.

3. To make the code number increment all the way down the column, you will use the **COPY** command.

4. Move the cursor to B5 and type **;C**. You will be asked:

From coord (>coord):

Type **B4**.

5. Then in response to the next query:

To coord (>coord):

Type **B5>B52**

6. Finally you see the query:

R)elative or N)o adjustment

7. Type **R** to indicate that it should be relative (that is one will be added to the previous number each time). If you had entered No adjustment, one would have been added to the value in B4 all the way down the column.

   What this all means is: copy the formula from the box B4 into all the boxes from B5 to B52, updating the coordinate each row (that is, B5 = 1+B4; B6 = 1+B5 etc.).

8. For a few moments nothing seems to happen, but then you will see the numbers fill in all the way down the column. Press the **Tab** key (or **;G**) and overtype A1 with **B52** to see that it has incremented correctly.

9. Now you can go on to the description column and copy the first description in **C3** from **C4** to **C14** (remember, there are only 12 identical descriptions for each item).

10. Move the cursor back to C4. Press **;C**, answer **C3** to the query From coord and then **C4>C14**. Again, it takes a few seconds before the columns fill up with the data.

11. Go to the SIZE field and copy the **100** in E3 from E4 to E14. The procedure is exactly the same as for the description, except you will be asked:

R)elative or N)o adjustment

since this is a numeric field. The answer must be **N**, since you want identical contents for each of the 12 rows.

12. Your table is now almost complete. It remains only to fill in the prices one by one.

In real life, you may find that there would be a fixed percentage difference in price between each of the four price codes. Then you would enter the first price for each range, move the cursor to the next row, type in a formula (such as 110%D3) and then use the COPY command to fill in D5 and D6 (with *relative* adjustment).

Since you are not going to use this data seriously, you could try out that technique now, if you like; you do not have to keep to the format you used in DataStar.

One obvious advantage of this would be the ease of updating the prices whenever there was a change. You would need to change only the first price in each block of four, then you would press ;R and the other dependent fields would be automatically recalculated (assuming the *percentage difference* remained the same).

Quitting and Loading

Once you have filled in all the prices, save your form again, then type **;Q** to quit the program. You will be asked to confirm that you want to quit by typing **Y**, then you will find yourself back at the operating system prompt.

Now to reload your file.

Step-by-step procedure

1. At the prompt, type **CS**. When the table appears, type **;L** and then **CSPRICES** for the file name.

2. You will be asked to confirm that you wish the program to be loaded from position A1, simply press **Return** and after a few seconds, you will see a series of dots (to indicate that the program is being loaded) and your table will appear.

This is the way that you would start any CalcStar session if the file you need is saved on disk.

Printing out the CSPRICES Table

Make sure that your printer is powered on and online.

Step-by-step procedure

1. To print the Table, press **;P**. You will have to confirm that you wish to accept the default of printing the output to the printer (the alternative would be to send it to a file on disk), that the table should be printed starting from A1 and finishing at the end of the table.

2. Then, enter whether the form length is continuous or single sheet and specify the width of the printer you are using (the default is 132 columns). If you have an 80-column printer, enter **80** here and all of the form as designed should fit on a single width of paper.

3. When you press **Return** after the last query, you will be given the option of typing in a title for your Table. You may have as many lines of title as you wish, but if you only need one line, when you press **Return** to refuse the second line the system will assume that you do not want the third line either and the table will then print out right away.

4. For this table, enter the title, **CALCSTAR PRICE LIST** then press **Return** and use the equals sign to underline the heading.

5. Now press **Return** to go to the next title line. When you are asked for the title again, press **Return** once more to start printing the table.

6. If you would like a blank line between your titles and the table, press the **Space Bar** once and then **Return**, before the final **Return** to start the printer.

The output from a CalcStar table is well laid out and can often be included in documents and reports without further formatting. At the end of this chapter you will learn how to convert data entered in a CalcStar table to DataStar format. This could be very useful if you wanted to use a CalcStar data file as a slave file for a DataStar form.

DESIGNING YOUR OWN TABLES

You now know enough commands to try designing some CalcStar tables of your own. Try to think of a simple problem that could make life easier for you if you had it in CalcStar format.

Almost any material you normally prepare in tabular form is suitable: sales figures, budget details and forecasts, salary and tax records, or sales tax calculations and returns.

TABLE 8-1 Sales Analysis

```
        SALES - ACTUAL & TARGET
        =======================
```

	JAN	FEB	MAR	APR	MAY	JUN
	1	2	3	4	5	6
ULTIMA:						
SALES	1100	1150	1250	1310	1450	1590
COSTS	840	910	990	1050	1190	1310
% PROFIT	23	20	20	19	17	17
TARGET:						
SALES	1050	1137	1237	1312	1487	1637
% PROFIT	20	20	20	20	20	20

In the next section you will design a monthly sales analysis and learn some of the more advanced features in CalcStar, so make sure you are really familiar with what you have learned so far.

SALES FORECASTING

Now you will design a table that has the 12 months of the year as column headings and data on sales, costs, profit percentages, and target figures as column bodies.

You will enter data for the first six months and then try out the system of forecasting that is part of the CalcStar program. It uses a statistical procedure called *linear regression*, but you do not need to know the math—just follow the instructions and all will be revealed to you.

You will produce projections of the sales, costs and profit margins for the remaining six months of the year. Then you can apply a simple calculation to work out by how much you would need to increase sales to maintain a particular level of profits.

Call up CalcStar and prepare to enter the months at the top of 12 columns. You will use three letter abbreviations for most of them and the columns will need to have a width of six. This way you can display all the months from January to December on one width of 80-column paper. See Tables 8–1 and 8–2 for the final result.

Column A must have a width of eight and will contain the row headings. Columns B to G, inclusive, will have a width of

TABLE 8-2 Sales Forecasting

```
                              SALES FORECAST
                              ==============


         ACTUAL FIGURES                     PROJECTION
         ==============                     ==========


           JAN     JUN ***   JUL   AUG   SEPT   OCT   NOV    DEC
            1       6  ***    7     8      9     10    11     12
 ULTIMA:            ***
    SALES  1100   1590 ***   1649  1746  1844  1941  2039   2136
    COSTS   840   1310 ***   1373  1466  1559  1651  1744   1837
            23      17 ***    15    14    13    11    10      9
                   ***
 TARGET:           ***
    SALES  1050   1637 ***
  % PROFIT   20     20 ***
```

six and the abbreviated month names right-justified in each. Column H will have the minimum width of three and be filled with asterisks to divide the table into two parts; the left-hand side, with the first six months, contains the *actual* figures and the right hand side will hold the *projections*.

Start now with the details for adjusting the widths of the first two columns and for putting in the headings; then you can finish the rest of the table by yourself.

Step-by-Step Procedure

1. With the cursor in A1, press **;F**, then type **W** and **8** for the width. Then press **;F** again and change the precision to zero.

2. Move the cursor to B1. Adjust the width to **6** and the precision to zero. Enter the month, **JAN**, right-justified (**/ RJAN**).

3. Repeat for the other months through to G1, JUN; then with the cursor in H1, make the width **3** and enter asterisks as a heading.

4. Continue from I1 to N1, adjusting the widths and precision of each column as before and putting in the abbreviated month headings. At this point save your table; type **;S** and give the file a name—say, SALES.

5. Now number the months; move the cursor to B2 and enter **1**, to C2 and enter **2**, to D2 and enter **3**, right through to N2, **12**. You will need these numbers for some of the linear regressions later. Note that the numbers are automatically right-justified; do not try to center them with a /C or you may lose your whole table.

6. Move the cursor back to A3 and type in the first heading, **ULTIMA:**. Then move down to A4 and enter **/RSALES**, then to A5 and enter **/RCOSTS**, and then to A6 and enter **/R% PROFIT**.

7. You must put in the headings for target sales and profits. Move the cursor to A8 and type **TARGET:**, then to A9 and enter **/RSALES**, and move to **A10** and enter **/R% PROFIT**.

8. Now you are ready to enter some numbers, but first you must save the table as constructed so far. Press **;S** and remember that when you type in the file name this time, you will get the message telling you that the file already exists and you must confirm that you wish to overwrite (destroy) the old contents.

9. Look at the Sales Analysis Table (Table 8–1) and copy out the numbers entered under the first six months for each of the row headings.

   In order to calculate the target figures for the first six months, you must enter two very simple calculations. Target sales is calculated from the figure for actual costs and is based on the fact that the target profit margin is to be 20 percent.

10. Move the cursor to B9 and enter the formula:

    5/4*B5

    the figure 1050 will appear at B9.

11. Now move the cursor to **C9**, use the COPY command **;C**, and respond to the prompts as follows:

    From coordinate: B9
    To coordinate: C9>G9
    R)elative or N)o adjustment: R

12. You will see the figures for target sales for the first six months, as shown in Table 8–2. Now you can apply the

formula that will enter the figure for target profit. Move the cursor to B10 and enter the following:

(B9-B5)/B9*100

you will see the figure 20 appear at B10.

13. Now use the COPY command again, copying the formula in B10 from coordinates C10 to G10 (relative). You will see the figure 20 appear in each column.

You may wonder why you did not simply type in the result, 20, instead of bothering with a calculation. The advantage of using a formula is that if at some later date you wish to change the calculation for target sales to achieve a higher or lower profit margin, you can use the **RECALCULATE** command to adjust all the other figures at the same time.

Now you are ready to try out the technique for obtaining projections for the second half of the year.

Linear Regression

Using the linear regression function built in to the CalcStar program, you will be able to calculate the predicted sales for the remaining six months of the year from the figures you have entered for January to June. You can then make the same projections for the costs and the profit margin. Finally, you will calculate the level of sales required to maintain the profit margin at 20 percent.

Linear regression is simply a mathematical statistical technique that replaces the graph paper and pencil. Imagine that you had plotted on a graph the actual sales figures achieved for each month, and then drawn through these points (by eye) the best possible straight line. You would only achieve something close to the computer prediction for that line, even if your data were fairly close to a straight line to begin with. Then if you used an extension of your rather inaccurate line to cover the next six months, you could end up with some very suspect predictions.

Linear regression is designed to fit a straight line extremely accurately through your data—even when the data are widely scattered. So although in theory it would not be difficult to do the statistics yourself, it could be both tedious and inaccurate compared with just typing the numbers into your model and letting the computer do the work.

We will begin by computing the regression function for sales against time. The figure will be stored in the computer and then recalled as required to produce the desired projections. The actual *value* of the regression function is not of any interest to you at the moment and need not be displayed in the table.

Step-by-step procedure

1. Move the cursor to I4 and type in the following formula:

   +regr(B2>G2,B4):'':''

   The leading + ensures that the entry is treated as numeric.
       The part inside the parentheses means calculate the regression function for sales (B4 to G4) over the first six months of the year (B2>G2).
       The part after the first : suppresses the screen display of the regression function—it is stored in the computer memory but does not appear on the screen. (You can make it display if you would like to know what the actual value is simply by ending the entry after the second bracket.)

2. Now for the fun: with the cursor still at **I4**, type in the following:

   +proj(7)

   and a number will appear that represents the *projected amount for sales in July* based on the actual figures for January to June.

3. Move the cursor to J4 and enter the formula to obtain the projection for the eighth month—+**proj(8)**.

4. Repeat up to +proj(12) for the remaining months.

5. Now you can do the same for the costs column and for the percent profit, remembering to move the cursor to I5 and I6 respectively, and entering the appropriate coordinates in the formula for calculating the regression function. B2>G2 remains the same for all three functions, since the months of the year represent the *independent variable*. The actual figures for costs and percent profit are the *dependent variables*, so you will need to enter **B5** for costs and **B6** for the percent profit in the formula.

It is clear from this particular example which variable is dependent and which is independent—obviously, the sales figures vary with the months. (It would be difficult to imagine that the months varied according to the sales figures!)

In case you should want to use these regression functions again in another CalcStar session, you should move the cursor right past the edge of your current form—say to column R—and enter the formulae once more.

At coordinate R4 enter:

```
+regr(B2>G2,B4)
```

Now you will see the regression function print out. Repeat for costs and percent profit at R5 and R6.

Have a look at More Functions later in the chapter to see how to use this function when you call up an existing CalcStar form.

Analyzing the Data

If you examine Tables 8–1 and 8–2, or the first half of your table on the screen and compare the sales achieved with the target sales, you will see that they look quite close. You can see that the percent profit has slipped a little, but the situation seems acceptable.

However, when you examine the projected figures for the second half of the year, it is obvious that some drastic action is called for immediately. Either costs must be reduced or sales must be increased. If there is no way to increase the volume of sales without further increases in costs, then there will have to be a price rise.

You can easily calculate the sales figures that must be achieved in order to keep the profit margin steady at 20 percent by continuing along the row with the **COPY** command from I9 to N9. You can then work out how much you would need to increase the price of each item you sell to achieve this increase.

More Functions

When you come to design your own tables and work out real regression functions, you will find it necessary to display and store the actual figure for the function with your table (as mentioned previously).

Whenever you return to the form to update figures and work out new projections, you will move the cursor to the appropriate regression function and type **;R** to load the value of that function into the computer's memory. You should then complete any projections or other analyses with that function before you go on to the next, since only *the last function used* is stored in memory.

To carry on to the next projection, you simply move the cursor to the next appropriate regression function calculation and press **;R** again.

Step-by-step procedure

Try this out now:

1. Move the cursor to R4 and press **;R** to load the regression function into the computer memory. If you did not enter the function earlier, do it now—enter the formula:

   `+regr(B2>G2,B4)`

   and the actual regression function will display at R4.

2. While you have this value stored, either because you just entered it, or because you pressed **;R** to load it, you could calculate the *slope* of the line through your data. Move the cursor to S4 and type:

   `+slope()`

   and the slope value will display at S4.

3. The slope tells you by how much the dependent variable (sales) increases or decreases in relation to the independent variable (months). In this case it tells you that with each month which passes, sales increase by 97 units (the units would be dollars in the case of sales).

4. Now move the cursor to R5 and repeat the regression calculation for costs this time, and then go on to calculate its slope as well. Finally, move to R6 and do the same for percent profit. This last slope value shows you that the profit margin *decreases* by something over 1 percent per month.

Printing Out the Final Table

Now that you have analyzed your data and made the projections, you probably wish to print out the table to keep.

Step-by-step procedure

1. First, save your form. Then press **;P** and go through the prompts, accepting defaults where appropriate, as you did previously.

2. You should give the paper width as **99** (if you are using an 80-column printer and 12 pitch) and you will find that all 12 months will fit exactly on the page. After the first page is printed, containing the main table, the second page will print out, showing the extra columns you entered to display the regression functions and slopes.

3. If you prefer, or if you have a 10 pitch printer, you can print out the *first page only* by entering **P** for partial at the appropriate query in the sequence. Then be prepared to enter the top left and bottom right coordinates of the part of the table you wish to print.

4. Have a look at Table 8–2 to see the printout of page 1, then go ahead and enter titles as follows (make sure your printer is on and online): for the first title line, enter **SALES FORE-CAST** (it will automatically be centered for you); press **Return** to go to the second title line and underline the title with a series of equals signs.

5. Press **Return** to go to title line 3 and just enter a space with the **Space Bar**, then press **Return** again. This will bring you to the fourth title line (with a blank line between it and line 3).

6. Enter **ACTUAL FIGURES** and then space across to a position that looks reasonable (unfortunately, there is no status line to tell you where you are), and type in **PROJECTIONS**.

7. Now press **Return** to go to the fifth title line and underline each of these headings. Finally, enter a blank line if you wish by pressing the **Space Bar** once before the **Return**, then press **Return** once more and your table will print.

You can see how easy it is to manipulate the figures once you have entered your basic table. You could go on to recalculate the projected costs, for example, assuming that the rate of inflation would not increase so rapidly over the second half year as it had over the first (or vice versa).

The best way of learning the other capabilities of the CalcStar program is to start entering some data of your own. I have taken you through the areas where you may have found a little difficulty at first—now you must practice on your own data to explore the other functions available.

CONVERTING CALCSTAR FILES TO DATASTAR FORMAT

You may wish to use the CalcStar data in a ReportStar report, for example, where it would need to be in DataStar format. This is easy to achieve.

Step-by-Step Procedure

1. Clear the screen of the FORECAST table, after you have saved it (press **;S** again if you are not certain). To clear the screen type **;D** for delete and then **A** for all. Confirm by typing **Y**; the screen will clear.
2. Now press **;L** and load the CSPRICES table, confirming that it should be loaded from coordinate **A1**.
3. You will now "print" the file to disk, at the same time the CalcStar program automatically converts the data to comma-delimited fields (that is, DataStar format).
4. Press **;P**. This message will appear:

To which file? PRINTER

5. Overtype PRINTER with **>CSPRICES**.
6. Then overtype the A1 with **B3** (the first data field) and make the bottom right coordinate **E14**. The disk drive active light will come on and the screen will tell you that it is Writing Data file.
7. Under this message you will see dots appearing, as happens when a file is loading, to show you that the process is continuing. Next you will see End of report and you will be asked to Hit space bar to continue.
8. The display of the table will appear. You can press **;Q** to exit and confirm by typing **Y**.

Now you could use the FormSort **/N** option (see Chapter 10) to create an index File from this data file. For the moment, satisfy yourself that the data file has been created correctly by using the TYPE command. At the prompt type:

```
TYPE CSPRICES.DTA
```

and you will see the list come up on the screen, showing the comma-delimited fields.

After you have made a copy of the PRICELST.DEF form (called CSPRICES.DEF), and created an index file (using FormSort/N), you can call up DATASTAR CSPRICES and scan through the data that you originally entered in CalcStar.

CONCLUSION

The format of the CalcStar printout is very acceptable and will probably suffice for most report purposes. You can tidy up the forms if you wish by reading the **.PRN** files into WordStar, where you can edit them as usual. In Chapter 12 you will learn how you can include data from CalcStar forms in a report created with WordStar and MailMerge.

That completes the CalcStar tutorial. There are many other possibilities for using CalcStar that you will have the fun of finding out for yourself. I hope you have enjoyed the tutorial and feel inspired to go on to greater things with the help of the MicroPro CalcStar manual.

9

InfoStar I: Advanced Form Design

As you saw in Part One, InfoStar is divided into three main programs: FormGen, for form design, DataStar for data entry and retrieval, and ReportStar for sorting data and producing reports.

This chapter will cover advanced form design with FormGen. In the next chapter, you will learn data entry and retrieval with advanced forms in DataStar and the sorting and report generation programs, FormSort and ReportStar.

PRINCIPLES OF ADVANCED FORM DESIGN

In Part One you designed a simple, basic form to enter customer names and addresses. I hinted then that there were some very advanced features in FormGen that could revolutionize the way you store and retrieve such data.

In this tutorial you will design three interrelated forms. Work right through these examples before you try to create a form, or group of forms, more appropriate to your own specific needs. You may find that there is just too much to learn in one session, so take your time and make sure that you understand each section before moving on to the next. The techniques may seem a little complicated at first, but you will soon get the knack once you have worked through a few examples.

Having mastered the basic principles, you should have little trouble designing your own forms or, if you are lucky, adapting some of the examples in this chapter, if they happen to be similar to your own requirements. On your DataStar master disk you will find another set of examples for an invoicing system that you will be able to work through after you have completed this tutorial. You may find it useful, if you need an invoicing system in your business, to make a copy of the related files and use them for your own purposes.

Advanced form design in InfoStar allows you to define data-fields very precisely and to assign various special attributes to them, which are then implemented during data entry. First the terminology will be explained: What is meant by "datafield definition" and "assigning attributes"? Why do we need these attributes? What function do they perform?

Datafield Definition

Datafield definition is the process of endowing all or some of the fields in a form with specific characteristics, called *attributes*, which control the way that data is subsequently entered into a form. It is eminently possible to use forms that have not had special attributes assigned to any fields—like the form you designed in Part One. You can carry on using that simple form quite happily, and there are many other situations where similarly simple forms would be quite adequate.

However, in a business situation, the person who designs the form and decides how it is to be used is frequently not the person who fills in the data. By careful manipulation of the attributes assigned to each datafield, the designer (who may be an office manager or department head) can keep considerable control over the way that data is entered by someone else (or maybe by the entire staff).

So the first reason for datafield definition is control over the data entry process and reduction in errors at the data entry stage, particularly where different people will enter the data.

Equally important, though, is the second reason. It is possible by the use of certain attributes to perform quite complicated internal calculations, for example, and even to link together several forms. These are very sophisticated techniques that greatly enhance the usefulness of DataStar.

Assigning the Attributes

Having designed a form and entered the background text of field names and field lengths, you will go on to datafield definition and specify the precise characteristics of each field in turn. This is the technique of assigning attributes to the datafields. You will learn most of the attributes available in InfoStar as you design the three interrelated forms later in this chapter.

You can specify, for example, that lowercase letters will be converted automatically to uppercase, or that only numbers may be entered in a particular field, so that an error message appears if letters are entered by mistake. You can define calculations, such as the totaling of certain items and the automatic calculation of sales tax at the current rate (the tax rate could be stored in a separate file and updated whenever necessary). These attributes are all easy to understand and simple to apply.

When you design a set of *linked forms*, as you will be doing in this chapter, there are some additional principles involved. Think of the main form as the *master* and the subsidiary form as the *slave*; the slave form contains data that will be slotted automatically into specially defined datafields in the master form on demand. You will use special attributes to link the master and slave forms together.

Index Fields

To summon the appropriate slave form, one datafield in the master form must be defined in such a way that it will be recognized by the slave, thereby linking the two forms together.

In DataStar terminology this field that links the master form to the slave is known as the *index field*. When the index field in the master form is filled in (during the data entry phase of DataStar) the named slave form is called up and the data it contains is made available to the master form.

Derived Fields

In order for the data from the slave form to be automatically slotted into the correct fields in the master form, each field in the master form that is to hold data *derived* from the slave form must be prepared by having the appropriate attributes assigned to it.

Summary

The master form is linked to its slave form via an index field. The contents of the index field must be entered into the master form by the operator during data entry.

As soon as the index field in the master form has been filled in, the data contained in the slave form is entered *automatically* into the predefined derived fields in the master form.

THE DESIGN PROCESS

Now that you have an overview of the techniques involved, you can start thinking about the design of your three linked forms. I will take you through the processes of form design and datafield definition in three stages.

Stage 1

First, we will go through the design of the master form, QUOTES, assigning attributes to those fields that are *not* linked to either of the two subsidiary forms. This will give you a feeling for how the assignment process works in the simplest case, including the special attributes associated with key fields.

In stage 1 you will cover:
The FormGen screen
Simple attributes
Key field attributes

By the end of stage 1 you will be able to design business forms for your own use, assigning various attributes to control data entry, including automatic internal calculations.

Stage 2

You will then design the two slave forms—both very short and straightforward—and you will learn how these are prepared for use in conjunction with the master form. You will cover a little new ground in stage 2, and the repetition of some of the lessons learned in Stage 1 should help to reinforce your appreciation of the datafield definition process.

By the end of the first two stages, you will have met most of the commonly used attributes and will be able to design quite complex forms. You may prefer to stop at this stage and practice the design of forms for your own use before you go on to the final stage of linking forms together.

Stage 3

Finally, you will go back to the QUOTES form and finish the datafield definition process, completing the links with the subsidiary forms. In stage 3 you will cover:

Index field attributes
Derived field attributes

Then you will list the field attribute definitions.

That's enough theory—time to get on with the examples. If you are using a floppy disk system, you will boot up from your tutorial disk and have a separate data disk in drive B. If you have a hard disk, continue to use whatever method you have devised, according to whether you have user areas, partitions, or a tutorial subdirectory. You should remember to pencil in any necessary changes in drive specifications in the following tutorial and exercises.

STAGE 1: THE MASTER FORM

Boot up your system from the tutorial disk (or hard disk). Next to the prompt type:

FORMGEN QUOTES

The default FormGen help screen is help screen 4; read through it and then type ^J to turn to help screen 3, which has the main cursor control and other control characters at the top.

The FORMGEN Screen

Before you start actual form design, you should learn something about the limits of the FormGen screen and how to find your way around it. Most of the cursor control keys are the same as in WordStar.

Step-by-step procedure

1. Help screen 3 lists the cursor movement characters; start by moving the cursor down the screen a line at a time with **^X**.

2. Watch the status line and note the change in line number as you move down the screen (in FormGen the first line is 000). When you reach line 016 and press **^X** again, the cursor will return automatically to the top of the screen. You have reached the default length limit of 17 lines (with help screen 3 in place).

3. Remember that the line number shown in the status line will be 016, but as the line numbering starts at 000, this is actually line 17.

4. Type **^J** twice to rotate the screen to help screen 1. Even though you now have much more screen in view, the default length remains 17 lines. Test this by moving the cursor with **^X** as above. You will learn later how to increase the screen length, but for now type **^J** until you have help screen 3 back again.

5. Now use **^D** to move the cursor across the screen from left to right. Again, watch the status line at the top of the screen and note the change in column number as you move the cursor across.

   When you reach column 79 the cursor will return to column 0 at the beginning of the next line. This is the default screen width.

   You can easily increase either the width or the length of the screen to accommodate your form design, within the maximum of 255 columns wide or 255 lines long (not both at the same time!).

6. The maximum number of fields you may have, whatever the length or width of the screen, is 245. This should be enough for most complex form designs, but you should bear these limits in mind whenever you start the form generation process.

The line buffer

Since there is no way of telling when you are reaching the end of your form (needless to say you are never watching the status line at the crucial moment), you can insert a marker to show where it is.

Step-by-step procedure

1. On the first line of the screen type

END

2. With the cursor still on the line, type ^P and then ^Y to delete the word END.

3. You will see END printed at the bottom of the screen, and if you move the cursor down to the E of END you will find, if you check the status line, that you are in LIN 016 (that is, line 17).

4. Press ^X again; the cursor will move back up to line 000.

5. Now press ^N. This inserts a line, just as in WordStar. You will see END appear again at the bottom of the screen. If you press ^N three more times, END will be written on all four inserted lines.

6. If you move the cursor down to the E of END at the bottom of your screen with ^X, you will find it is now in line 020.

7. Move the cursor back to line 000 (just press ^X once more) and press ^Y to delete the four lines you inserted containing the word END.

   When you pressed ^P you filled the line buffer with whatever was on the cursor line (that is, stored the contents of that line in the memory of the computer). The content of the line buffer was simultaneously printed out on the last line of the form. The line buffer can hold only one line at a time, so you will change the contents every time you press ^P.

   When you pressed ^N after filling the line buffer with END, you simply typed out the contents of the line buffer *at the cursor position*, inserting a line as you did so.

8. Once END is deleted, if you now press ^P to fill the line buffer with a blank line and *then* press ^N, you will "type

out' blank lines at the cursor position, inserting a blank line with every ^N. You will also have an extra blank line at the bottom of the form, created when you filled the line buffer. You can delete it later.

This is a good way to increase the length of your form before you start your design, if you have calculated that you are going to need more than the default length of 17 lines.

The QUOTES form (see Figure 9-1) will need 45 lines. Remember, the contents of the line buffer is a blank line.Using ^X, move the cursor down to the line above END.

9. Now press ^N repeatedly; as lines are inserted you will see the word END disappear off the bottom of the screen.

10. Move the cursor down again with ^X (the screen scrolls automatically at line 14 and then every 6 lines thereafter); and continue inserting lines with ^N until END is on line 045.

11. Now move the cursor down to line 046 and delete the extra blank line you inserted earlier; next time you press ^X the cursor will move back to the top of the form. (If the cursor goes beyond line 046, you have inserted some extra blank lines; remove these with ^Y until the cursor is on the E of END in line 045, and when you press ^X the cursor will move to 000.)

12. Try increasing the screen width by moving the cursor with ^D until you reach column 078. Insert columns with ^B. You will then be able to move further to the right with ^D until you reach the new width limit you have set.

Remember that when you press ^B you insert a column all the way down the screen, so don't do it after you have started entering field names—you could get a surprising result.

13. For most purposes the default width is adequate; to re-move the extra columns, move the cursor back to column 078 and press ^T to delete them. Again, don't do this once you have entered part of your form.

Now you are satisfied with the form boundaries, you can go on to enter the form.

FIGURE 9–1 Quotes Form Listing and Field Attribute Definitions

---

```
              FIELD NUMBERS

     QUOTE NUMBER:    _____1    CLIENT NUMBER:    ___2

     CLIENT DETAILS:
     TITLE (Mr/Mrs/Ms): ____3  INITIALS: ____4  LAST NAME: _____5

     STREET:    _____6 CITY: _____7
     STATE:    _8  ZIP: ___9
     TEL AREA CODE: _____10    TELEPHONE NUMBER: _____11




             DESIGN: _____12  PRICE CODE: *
             ======================================

 QTY   CODE           DESCRIPTION           SIZE   UNIT    TOTAL
                                            (cm)   PRICE   PRICE

  *   _____15 _____16  __17  _____18  _____19
  -
  *   _____21 _____22  __23  _____24  _____25
  -
  *   _____27 _____28  __29  _____30  _____31
  -
  *   _____33 _____34  __35  _____36  _____37
  -
  *   _____39 _____40  __41  _____42  _____43
  -



                          TOTAL FOR FURNITURE    _____44
                          ====================================




 This quotation is valid for 30 days from:

 DATE:    _____45




 SIGNED:   _____46
 POSITION: _____47
```

The scenario

Imagine you own a company that sells customized bedroom furniture direct to the public. You have a showroom where customers can see examples of your three ranges of bedroom furniture: Finesse, Supreme, and Ultima. Your computer is near the entrance, and as the customers walk in you invite them to give you their names and addresses so that you can put them on your mailing list. These entries will be made on the CLIENTS form.

Hopefully, after browsing around for a while, they will ask for more details on a particular range of furniture. You offer to produce a quote for them on the spot—all the details of price, style, etc., are stored in the computer (on the PRICELST form). You already have the customers' addresses; if they would like quotes for three or four different ranges, that is no problem at all (you have a QUOTES form set up for just this purpose).

Keeping records

Next to the computer you will need a note book in which you enter today's date, and under that a consecutive list of client numbers, starting at 0001. As customers give you their surnames, you jot them down adjacent to the next client number, then enter their full details into the CLIENTS form on the computer, entering the same client number to identify them. If they return subsequently for a quote, you could put a **Q** next to their number and name in your note book.

This is a very simple way of keeping a record of what you have on disk. Even though you have a computer, there are still some things that can be done quicker and more conveniently by hand.

The importance of the CLIENT NUMBER is that it is the link between your CLIENTS form and the QUOTES form. Similarly, the CODE will be the link between your PRICELST (price list) form and the QUOTES form.

That is the scenario—now for the forms creation process.

The QUOTES form

You will start by designing the QUOTES form, since it is the structure of this master form that will determine the structure of the two subsidiary forms (CLIENTS and PRICELST). You will design it in such a way that it can be printed out directly after filling in the details the client requires and handed to the client on the spot without having to exit from DataStar and go into WordStar or ReportStar. The technique of entering data and printing out forms will be covered in Chapter 10. However, it is important to plan the layout of the form at the form generation stage so that it will have a reasonable appearance when printed out, so now is the time to insert lines to divide the screen into blocks and perhaps underline where appropriate.

It is advisable to design your form on paper first—the more complex the design, the more important this is. Look at the print-out of the completed QUOTES form (Figure 9–1) so that you can see the kind of format you are aiming for. Note that the field numbers are inserted automatically during the printout phase; you enter the field names and the field lengths only.

Step-by-step procedure

1. Use uppercase letters for the field names and insert a couple of spaces between the field name and the blanks (create them with ^Q) that determine the length of the field. Space the form out as attractively as possible. Note that the client details at the top of Figure 9–1 are inset on left and right and that there are a couple of blank lines separating this first section from the listing of the furniture items.

2. There are tab settings with default tabs every 8 columns in FormGen; if you wish you can easily change these settings. For example, to achieve the inset of client details, move the cursor to the first tab at column 8 with a ^I (or the **Tab** key) and press ^U to remove the tab at that position.

3. Now, move the cursor back to column 5 and press ^U again to set the tab in the new position. This will give you the correct inset for entry of the client details at the top of the QUOTES form.

4. Tab to the first tab stop, type **QUOTE NUMBER**, insert two spaces, and then press ^Q six times to enter the field length of six characters.

5. Insert four or five spaces and then type **CLIENT NUMBER** followed by four ^Q 's. Leave a blank line and then enter

the field names and fields for the client details, fields 3 to 11. The field lengths (number of times you press ^Q) are:

Field 3: 5	Field 8: 2
Field 4: 5	Field 9: 5
Field 5: 15	Field 10: 5
Field 6: 27	Field 11: 8
Field 7: 26	

6. Note that the DESIGN and PRICE CODE fields (fields 12 and 13, lengths 15 and 1, respectively) have been underlined (with the equals sign) to act as a heading for the second section of the form. There are some more blank lines to separate the last section of the form.

7. Go ahead and fill in the top part of the form until you reach the line that contains QTY, CODE, DESCRIPTION, SIZE, etc. Stop there and note the following points:

    Five lines of items have been entered as an example. You may well need more when you come to fill out a real form for yourself. Remember, you may have a maximum of either 255 *lines* or 255 *columns* in a form; but the most important figure to remember is that you cannot have more than 245 *fields*.

8. You can see from Figure 9–1 that the QUOTES form can accommodate another 198 fields before it run out of space, or a further 33 lines of furniture items (6 fields to the line).

9. Now, to finish off the form, type in the headings, then press **Return** and enter the field lengths by pressing ^Q repeatedly for one line only.

    Field lengths:

Field 14: 1	Field 17: 4
Field 15: 8	Field 18: 7
Field 16: 35	Field 19: 7

10. With the cursor still on the line, press ^P (to fill the line buffer), then press ^N four times. You will see four more identical lines appearing below the one you typed in. Note that the lines are slow to appear, so allow time to complete

the process. If you inadvertently add extra lines, you can delete them with ^Y.

11. Insert two more blank lines and then type in the TOTAL FOR FURNITURE field (length of 8) and underline it as before.

12. Insert some more blank lines and type in the rest of the form, copying the format in Figure 9–1.

Field lengths:
Field 48: 8
Field 46: 18
Field 47: 18

If your format is identical to this one, you will find that you are typing POSITION directly above END; if not, it doesn't matter too much. You can either go back and delete some blank lines or insert some blank lines with ^N if you are running out of space (remember to fill the line buffer—^P—with a blank line before inserting lines).

Don't forget that you want the form to print out on one sheet of standard paper, so don't increase the length too much.

13. After you type **POSITION** and the field length you must move the cursor to the line below the word END, then press ^Y to delete any excess lines.

14. Continue until the cursor rests on the E of END. Delete that line too and then press ^X to return to the top of the form.

15. Now, finally, you must designate the key field(s) and stage 1 of the form creation is over. Move the cursor to the first dash of the LAST NAME field and press ^K. The field will fill with asterisks. Move back with ^A into the INITIALS field and press ^K again. This makes the LAST NAME and the INITIALS the key fields (in that order).

16. Make sure your printer is powered on and online, then press ^W to print it. Now you can compare your result with the form shown in Figure 9–1.

17. You are only interested in the first page of the printout; which is the listing of the form structure with the field numbers. So after the first page is finished, press ^C to

indicate that the form edit is done and then **B** to return to the operating system.

Sometimes the printer will not stop immediately; just keep pressing ^C until it interrupts successfully.

18. Press the online button to take the printer offline. (Do not switch the printer offline until you have pressed ^C or you may find that the computer will ignore your attempts to communicate with it.)

If you ever do this by mistake, and find that whatever key you press the screen remains unchanged with a stationary cursor, the computer is "hung': usually if you just turn the printer back on again, communication is restored and you can exit with ^C in the usual way.

If worse comes to worse, press **Reset** to cold boot the system.

It might be a good idea to take a short break now—drink a cup of coffee and just read through the next section on attributes before you actually try to implement the instructions. By the time you have worked through the basic QUOTES form attributes, you should have a good understanding of the procedures involved and will begin to appreciate the degree of control you can exercise over the data entry process.

Simple Attributes

If you exited from FormGen at the end of the last session, prepare to restart now.

Step-by-step procedure

1. At the prompt type:

   FORMGEN QUOTES

   and press **Return**. Your form will appear on the screen with help screen 3 above it.

2. Type ^J to change the help screen to level 2; this lists the control characters you will need for datafield definition.

3. Move the cursor into the first field—QUOTE NUMBER— and check the status line at the top of the screen. It should show you the number of the datafield the cursor is in—

001 and the length of the field—006. The cursor must be positioned on the dashed line, not on the field name, to be in the field.

4. With the cursor in the first field, you start the definition process by pressing ˆR. (If you press it when the cursor is not in a field, you get a warning message that tells you so.)

5. Most of the form now disappears, leaving just the line containing the field you wish to define (or sometimes one or two more lines).

Notice that you now have help screen **R** at the top of the screen, with a new menu of control characters. Although the controls look familiar, remember that now they will apply *only to the field you are currently defining.*

6. The field definition process is a series of prompts to which you must respond, either by accepting the default answer supplied or by typing in your own. To accept a default, you simply press **Return**. To return to the previous item in the list (to make changes, for example) you press ˆE. The other controls, will be explained at appropriate points in the tutorial.

NOTE: If you have an earlier version of InfoStar you will find that some of the prompts appear in a different order than that shown here, and some are missing completely. Tables 9–1 and 9–2 show you a complete list of the prompts as they appear in versions 1.0 and 1.6, respectively.

7. After the first prompt type the first field name. Note that the field number is already inserted by default; to enter the field name, you must press **Return** to bypass the 001. If you have an earlier version of FormGen, there will be no field number option, so just type in the field name, **QUOTE NO.**

Field number/name: 001/QUOTE NO

You may not use the same field name twice; the name may be up to 32 characters in length and of mixed numerals, letters, and spaces as long as it starts with a letter.

8. The main reason for choosing to enter field names is to prepare to use MicroPro's program, ReportStar, later on. Press **Return** to continue.

TABLE 9-1 Listing of Attributes—FORMGEN Version 1.0

	Field name:
	Field order:
	Key order:
KEY FIELDS	Tie breaker field? (Y/N)
	Refuse duplicate keys? (Y/N)
	Copy attributes of field:
	Field derived? (Y/N)
	Allow operator entry? (Y/N)
	Calculated/File? (C/F)
	Index field number:
DERIVED FIELDS	Item number in file:
	Verify/calculate order:
	Numeric/String? (N/S)
	Enter String/Algebraic expression for field:
	Intermediate field? (Y/N)
	Required? (Y/N)
	Right justify? (Y/N)
	Pad field? (Y/N)
	Enter pad character:
	Floating character? (Y/N)
	Enter floating character:
	Verify field? (Y/N)
	Sight/Retype/File? (S/R/F)
INDEX FIELDS	Keep file in memory? (Y/N)
	Enter file name:
	Enter file disk drive (-/A/B...):
	Enter file key field number:
	Batch verify? (Y/N)
	Check digit? (Y/N)
	Range check? (Y/N)
	Enter/change minimum field value:
	Enter/change maximum field value:
	Edit mask? (Y/N)
	Entry Control Character Codes:
	Content Control Character Codes:
	Record edit characters? (Y/N)

---

9. The next prompt is:

Processing order: 001

Note that in the earlier versions of FormGen this prompt

TABLE 9–2 Listing of Attributes—FORMGEN Version 1.6

Field number/name:

KEY FIELDS
Key order:
Tie breaker field? (Y/N)
Refuse duplicate keys? (Y/N)

Processing order:
Copy attributes of field:

Field derived? (Y/N)
  Calculated/File? (C/F)
    Index field number/name:
     Item number in file:
DERIVED FIELDS
  Numeric/String? (N/S)
  Enter String/Algebraic expression for field:
  Intermediate field? (Y/N)
  Allow operator entry? (Y/N)

Required?/Optional/Unused
Right justify? (Y/N)
Pad field? (Y/N)
  Enter pad character:
Floating character? (Y/N)
  Enter floating character:

Verify field? (Y/N)
  Sight/Retype/File?
INDEX FIELDS
    Keep file in memory? (Y/N)
    Enter file name:
    Enter file disk drive (-/A/B...):
Batch verify? (Y/N)

Check digit? (Y/N)
Range check? (Y/N)
  Enter/change minimum value:
  Enter/change maximum value:

Edit mask? (Y/N)
  Entry control character codes:
  Content control character codes:

Record edit characters? (Y/N)

---

is Field order.

As you know from the printout of the QUOTES form, the fields are numbered in order from 1 to 47. The default order for data entry is that order, but you have the option to change it if you want to. For example, if you changed

001 to 047, you would find that at data entry you would type the quote number in last. Since the quote number is going to be entered automatically, and updated by one on each new record, we will make its processing order **002**. Just overtype the 001, so it now reads:

Processing order: **002**

10. The next statement is:

Copy attributes of field: /

You will use this option later, but for now just press **Return** twice to bypass it. If you have an earlier version of FormGen, there will be a default (001) that you can accept by pressing **Return.**

11. The next query is:

Field derived? (Y/N)   **Y**

As you can see on your screen, the default answer is No; you have the option to overtype the N with a **Y** to signify that the field is derived. For the QUOTE NUMBER the answer will be because you are going to make this number autoincrement, that is, you will not enter it in the form during data entry. Instead, the number will automatically increase by one every time you fill in a new quote. So overtype the N with a **Y.**

12. As mentioned earlier, a field is *derived* if it is the result of an internal calculation within the form rather than manually entered by you *or* if the value for that field is drawn from an external file linked to the main form (as will be covered in detail later).

13. The next prompt is:

Calculated/File (C/F)   **C**

If you accepted the default, F, here it would imply that the QUOTE NUMBER would be filled in by accessing an external file. However, this field is to be calculated, so type **C.** (Note that in earlier versions of FormGen the prompt

Allow operator entry appears in this position. Accept the default N.)

14. The next prompt is:

    Numeric/String (N/S) **N**

    Clearly, our calculation is numeric, so accept N and press **Return**.

15. Then you are prompted:

    Enter algebraic expression for field calculation:

    Note that "QUOTE NO =" is already entered for you. Now you must type in the calculation you wish to perform. In this case you want the QUOTE NUMBER (field #1) to increase by one every time you type in a new quote. Type the following to perform the calculation:

    QUOTE NO = QUOTE NO + 1

    This means that when the first quote is typed, the value for QUOTE NO starts as zero. Zero plus 1 equals 1, so the number for the first quote becomes 1. When you start the second quote, the value for the first field is now 1, and 1 plus 1 equals 2—so the quote number becomes 2—naturally enough!

    Since the first field is itself part of the calculation that determines the value of the field, it is known as a *self-referenced field*.

16. The next question is:

    Allow operator entry? (Y/N)   N

    You must accept the default, N (by pressing **Return**), because the entry is to be automatic.

17. Next you are asked:

    Right justify (Y/N)   Y

    If you answer Y then the numbers will be aligned to the right side of the field; if you reply N, they will be justified on the left. Generally speaking, it is a good idea to right justify numeric fields, so type **Y**.

18. Then you are prompted:

> Pad field? (Y/N)   Y

If you type Y here the field will be padded (filled out to its full extent) even if you have just one figure in a field of nine spaces. Type **Y**.

19. The next prompt is:

> Enter pad character: 0

The default pad character is a space (-), though you can use anything you like. Often zeros or asterisks are used.
   You should enter a **0** (zero) here.

20. Now the display asks:

> Floating character?   (Y/N)   N

You would say Y here if the field were dollars, for example, and you wished to have a dollar sign automatically inserted for you. In this instance, accept the default **N**.

21. Next you are prompted:

> Verify field? (Y/N)   N

If you say Y here, you will be asked whether, during data entry, you wish to *verify* the field.
   Verification can be achieved in three different ways: *visually* (the cursor moves to that field before you exit the data entry process and you check it by eye), by *retyping* the data when the cursor returns to the field, or by having the data in the field checked against an *external file*.
   In this instance, since the value will be entered automatically, you can accept N by pressing **Return**.

22. The next prompt asks:

> Check digit? (Y/N)   N

In DataStar the *check digit* is used to improve the accuracy of numeric data—hardly necessary in the case of the QUOTE NO.

Accept **N**.

23. Then the display prompts:

> Range check? (Y/N)　　　N

The range check allows you to specify the maximum and minimum values that can be entered in a field. For example, a cents field would have to have a value between ·.00 and .99.

Accept **N**.

24. Then you are asked:

> Edit mask? (Y/N)　　　N

The *edit mask* gives you extensive control over the data entry process. You can define very precisely what may or may not be entered into a field, character by character, by careful use of this option.

You will make use of it later, but for the first field you do not need it, so accept **N**.

25. Finally, the display prompts:

> Record edit characters? (Y/N) N

If you answer Yes the pad characters you asked for will be saved along with your file. If you reply No these characters are removed before the file is saved. One consideration is space—clearly, saving all the edit characters in a long form with many attributes can considerably increase the file space occupied. Also there may be times when the extra pad characters can be a nuisance for certain applications—particularly extra zeros.

Accept the default **N**.

Well, that is the end of the first field definition. I can assure you that by the time you have defined all the fields in the QUOTES form, you will be assigning attributes like an old hand.

Note that at any point in the field definition process, you can press ^J and get a help message on the screen, similar to the notes I have given you here for defining the first field.

As a final check to help familiarize you with the sequence of queries, you should type **^R** with the cursor still in the first field and look through the attributes one more time.

When you go through the list again you will see the answers you made are now the *default values*—check them against the following list below, pressing **Return** to go from one item to the next.

Query	Answer
Field number/name:	001/QUOTE NO
Processing order:	002
Copy attributes of field:	/
Field derived? (Y/N)	Y
Calculated/File? (C/F)	C
Numeric/String? (N/S)	N
Enter String/Algebraic expression for field:	
QUOTE NO=QUOTE NO+1	
Allow operator entry? (Y/N)	N
Right justify? (Y/N)	Y
Pad field? (Y/N)	Y
Enter pad character:	0
Floating character? (Y/N)	N
Verify field? (Y/N)	N
Check digit? (Y/N)	N
Range check? (Y/N)	N
Edit mask? (Y/N)	N
Record edit characters? (Y/N)	N

Now you can move the cursor to the next field with **^F**. Note that field 002 is the link or index field to the CLIENT form, so you will leave its definition until stage 3.

Key Field Attributes

Now that the simple attributes have been entered, you can advance to the key field attributes.

Step-by-step procedure

1. Using **^F**, move past field 003, which will also be defined in stage 3, to field 004. You may remember that the INITIALS field is the second of the key fields. You will assign the attributes for key field status now, then you will return to this field in stage 3 to add the attributes that make it a derived field.

2. Press **^R** to start the definition process:

Field number/name:	004/INITIALS
Key order:	002
Tie breaker field? (Y/N)	N
Refuse duplicate keys? (Y/N)	N
Processing order:	004
Copy attributes of field:	/
Field derived? (Y/N)	N
Required?/Optional/Unused	O
Right justify? (Y/N)	N
Pad field? (Y/N)	N
Floating character? (Y/N)	N
Verify field? (Y/N)	N
Check digit? (Y/N)	N
Range check? (Y/N)	N
Edit mask? (Y/N)	N

Note that when you are assigning attributes to key fields, there are some extra queries. The key order determines the precedence given to a key field where more than one key field has been specified (if you had only one key field, you would not see this query).

The same applies to *tie breaker field*—when there is more than one key, you are given the option of specifying that the lower order key field can be made unique.

In practice, since the lower order key field is the INITIALS field in the QUOTES form, every time you entered an initial or group of initials that happened to be identical to previously entered initials, then a character would be inserted automatically into that field to make it unique. However, in the case of initials there are so many potential duplicates that if you implemented this option the operation of the file could become very slow.

In this instance you must respond **N** to the tie breaker.

3. The option to refuse duplicate keys will appear for any key field. In many cases you would enter Y to this query, but in the case of initials, for the same reasons given above, you must say **N**.

4. For all the remaining attributes you can accept the default values. Now go on to field 005, the LAST NAME, which is also a key field.

5. Note the responses in the following list. This is key order 001, which means that the LAST NAME field will take precedence over the INITIALS field in all sort procedures that make use of the index file. (You will learn more of

this in the next chapter.) In practice, you will accept all the default values.

Field number/name:	005/LAST NAME
Key order:	001
Refuse duplicate keys? (Y/N)	N
Processing order:	005
Copy attributes of field:	/
Field derived? (Y/N)	N
Required/Optional/Unused	O
Right justify? (Y/N)	N
Pad field? (Y/N)	N
Floating character? (Y/N)	N
Verify field? (Y/N)	N
Check digit? (Y/N)	N
Range check? (Y/N)	N
Edit mask? (Y/N)	N

Note also that fields 4 and 5 are both derived fields, so you will return to them again in stage 3 to finish off assigning attributes. You should also leave fields 006 through 011 (all derived fields) until stage 3, so move the cursor with ^F to field 012 and press ^R to begin the field definition process.

Remember that if you make an error when responding to any of the items, or press **Return** and move on to the next item by mistake, you can return to the previous item by pressing ^E.

6. Again, following are the queries and answers—simply go through the list item by item either pressing **Return** to accept defaults or typing in the appropriate response where required.

Field number/name:	012/DESIGN
Processing order:	012
Copy attributes of field:	/
Field derived? (Y/N)	N
Required/Optional/Unused	R
Right justify? (Y/N)	N
Pad field? (Y/N)	N
Floating character? (Y/N)	N
Verify field? (Y/N)	N
Check digit? (Y/N)	N
Range check? (Y/N)	N
Edit mask? (Y/N)	Y
(explained below)	

Note that you have accepted most of the default values;

you have said, however, that the field is required (the form cannot be completed unless that field is filled).

7. Having entered Y to the edit mask, you will now specify the attributes that ensure that the characters typed in will be converted automatically to uppercase, even if you enter them in lowercase. First, learn the entry control character codes that guide your entries. They begin:

! means you must enter a character   _ means you may enter or leave blank

(All the codes are listed on the screen each time you select edit mask).

The use of the entry control mask characters can force you to enter characters in a specific position in a field during data entry, or you can have automatic alignment of a decimal point, or an automatic copy of the contents of a field from one record to the next.

You will use all these possibilities during the course of designing your three forms, but for field 012 none of these entry controls is required, so just press **Return** to leave the entry control mask and you will come to the second edit mask—this time the content control mask.

8. Use the content control character codes that guide your entries. They begin

A = A-Z only   a = a-z only

The content control mask allows you to define the type of data that can be entered in every individual space in each field. For example, if you insert a capital A in every space in field 012, then only capital letters (A–Z) could be entered there—lowercase letters would be rejected. A capital B in every space in field 012 would allow a space between one or more words, but still only A–Z in uppercase letters. A capital A in the first space would allow only a capital letter in the first space, but any character (or nothing) in the remaining spaces.

The D option allows the entry of uppercase letters and spaces but also automatically converts any lowercase letters entered to uppercase—that is the meaning of the characters:

$$a-z \rightarrow A-Z$$

You could use this option for field 012, so that however the names Ultima, Finesse, or Supreme were entered they would be converted automatically to all uppercase; by allowing for a space, you also leave some flexibility for later ranges, which may have two-word names. If you wished to allow for numbers as well, you would choose option H.

Enter the **D** (as shown below) or **H** in field 012 and press **Return**.

```
DESIGN  _____        Entry Control
DESIGN  DDDDDDDD        Content Control
```

9. The final query is

```
Record edit characters  (Y/N)     N
```

If you enter Y the edit characters will be stored with your file. Since you will have many edit characters in the QUOTES form, accept the default, **N**.

10. Now press **^F** to go on to field 013 and then press **^R**.

In this case, you should specify that this field is required and that it must be a numeral only:

```
Field number/name:                        013/PRICE CODE
Processing order:                         013
Copy attributes of field:                 /
Field derived? (Y/N)                      N
Required/Optional/Unused                  R
Right justify?  (Y/N)                     N
Pad field?  (Y/N)                         N
Floating character?  (Y/N)                N
Verify field?  (Y/N)                      N
Check digit?  (Y/N)                       N
Range check?  (Y/N)                       N
Edit mask?  (Y/N)                         Y
```

Now, in the entry control mask enter ! to say that a character must be entered here.

11. Then in the content control mask, choose option **9**, which specifies that you may enter only 0–9 in this position:

```
PRICE CODE  !            Entry Control
PRICE CODE  9            Content Control
```

12. Accept the default for Record edit characters.

13. Type **^F** to go to field 014, QUANTITY. You should enter the same attributes as for field 013.

    This brings you to another new option. When you press **^R** to start the definition process, the third item is:

```
Copy attributes of field:    /
```

In this instance, you can type **013** and the attributes from field 013 will be copied automatically to field 014. As soon as you type the numbers before the slash, the field name, PRICE CODE, will be entered after the slash (in the more recent versions).

In the earlier versions, just enter the field name.

```
Field number/name:                    014/QTY 1
Processing order:                     014
Copy attributes of field:             013/PRICE CODE
Field derived? (Y/N)                  N
Required?  (Y/N)                      Y
Right justify?  (Y/N)                 N
Pad field?  (Y/N)                     N
Floating character?  (Y/N)            N
Verify field?  (Y/N)                  N
Check digit?  (Y/N)                   N
Range check?  (Y/N)                   N
Edit mask?  (Y/N)                     Y
```

14. After you enter 013 in response to Copy attributes of field: you can simply press **Return** and see that the other attributes have been copied, including the entry control and content control characters. You can use this copy function whenever two or more fields have identical attributes.

15. When you have accepted the default for the last query, you should press **^R** again. Now you will see that the Copy attributes of field: says 014. There is no mistake—once the attributes have been copied from field 013, the number is automatically updated to 014.

Go straight to field 019 since field 015 (the other index field) and Fields 016 to 018 (the other derived fields) will be filled in automatically from the third form, PRICELST, and will be dealt with in stage 3.

Field 019, the TOTAL PRICE for that line, is obtained by the simple equation:

FIELD 19 = FIELD 14 * FIELD 18

That is, the Total Price is equal to the Unit Price multiplied by the quantity ordered (note the use of the *asterisk* for a multiplication sign).

Once you have entered the field Names for these fields, the calculation will appear as:

TOTAL PRICE 1=QTY 1*UNIT PRICE 1

16. Move the cursor with ^F to field 019 and then press ^R to assign the appropriate attributes and the calculation.

Field number/name:	019/TOTAL PRICE 1
Processing order:	019
Copy attributes of field:	/
Field derived? (Y/N)	Y
Calculated/File? (C/F)	C
Numeric/String? (N/S)	N
Enter String/Algebraic expression for field:	
TOTAL PRICE 1=#18*QTY 1	
Intermediate field? (Y/N)	N
Allow operator entry? (Y/N)	N
Right justify? (Y/N)	Y
Pad field? (Y/N)	Y
Enter pad character:	-
Floating character? (Y/N)	Y
Enter floating character:	$
Verify field? (Y/N)	N
Check digit? (Y/N)	N
Range check? (Y/N)	N
Edit mask? (Y/N)	Y

Note that this time you have asked for the following field attributes: right-justified, padded, and a floating character—the dollar sign ($).

17. Now, in the edit mask, you can arrange automatic decimal point alignment. Choose the decimal point option (.) in both the entry control and the content control masks and in the latter, the 9 option to allow only numbers 0–9 to be entered.

The decimal point should be in the third space from the right, leaving two spaces for the cents, as shown below:

```
TOTAL PRICE  ____.__      Entry Control
TOTAL PRICE  _999.99      Content Control
```

Now, when the TOTAL PRICE field is filled in, the dollars and cents will be right-justified, the decimal point between dollars and cents will be aligned, and there will be a dollar sign to the left of the dollar amount entered.

18. Accept the default for record edit characters.

19. You will leave the other four lines of QTY, etc., until stage 3, so move the cursor to field 045, the DATE, and press **^R**.

20. The date can be entered in many different ways, but if you may sort by date later using FormSort, the way it is entered must be standardized. One method is:

10/01/85

= This is the 1st of October 1985. To produce this format, you can accept all the defaults except

```
Required/Optional/Unused   R
Edit mask? (Y/N)           Y
```

21. In entry control choose option " (constant in this position) for the third and sixth spaces in the field, where you will enter the slashes (/) which separate the month from the day and the day from the year. If you like, in content control you can enter **9** in each position where the numbers must be inserted. This summarizes what will appear on your screen:

```
DATE  __''__''__        Entry Control
DATE  99/99/99          Content Control
```

An alternative technique for ensuring easy sorting would be to make three individual date fields for the day, month, and year. You should try both methods when you design your own forms.

22. Fill in attributes for fields 046 and 047 (both are required and should have the edit mask). You may like to use the *automatic copy* option for the manager's name and position. This would mean that once these fields have been entered on the first customer quotation in any one session, they will be copied on every form automatically thereafter. The Y option achieves this but also allows you to make changes when necessary (you might get a new manager!).

```
SIGNED    YYYYYYYYYYYYYY  Entry Control
SIGNED    _____  Content Control
```

You may be tempted to use a content control character here—for example, a lowercase **d** allows upper- and lowercase letters and spaces only. However, if you then try to enter a name like O'Brien, you will not be allowed to type the apostrophe. It is safer to allow *any character* to be entered in name fields.

Remember, when you come to assign attributes for the POSITION field you can make use of the item Copy attributes of field:. You will enter **046** to copy the attributes of the SIGNED field.

23. Type ^C to end the definition process. Exit and save the QUOTES form by typing ^C, and then select option **B**, which will save the form and boot the operating system, bringing you back to the prompt.

By now you should be finding the procedure much easier, if not yet automatic.

STAGE 2: THE SLAVE FORMS

In this section you will design the slave forms and define various attributes, but you will leave the special attributes that apply to the index field until stage 3. The only point you need to remember about index fields at this stage is that they must be key fields.

The CLIENTS Form

Now you will create the second form, called CLIENTS.

FIGURE 9–2 Clients Form Listing and Field Attribute Definitions

```
            FIELD NUMBERS

CLIENT NUMBER   ___1
TITLE  (Mr/Mrs/Ms)   ___2  INITIALS   ___3  LAST NAME  _____4
STREET      _____5    CITY  _____6
STATE   _7_                              ZIP   ___8
TEL AREA CODE   ___9   TEL NUMBER   _____10
```

Step-by-step procedure

1. Type **FORMGEN CLIENTS** and prepare to design the new form. Look at Figure 9–2, which shows the layout of the 10 fields making up the CLIENTS form. The key field will be CLIENT NUMBER; it is this field that will link the CLIENTS form to the QUOTES form.

2. Type **^J** to rotate the help screens to help screen 3. Proceed with the form design—you can manage now without detailed instructions. If there is anything you are not sure of, look back at the instructions for the QUOTES form.

    NOTE: It is *vital* that all fields common to both the CLIENTS form and the QUOTES form have identical field lengths, so count them out now.

3. When you have finished entering the field names and field lengths, remember that you must create at least one key field before you save the form. Move the cursor to field 001 and press **^K**.

4. Although you can go straight on to field definition, it is a good idea to save your form first, just in case you have a small tragedy along the way. You do not want to have to start over again! Type **^C** and then choose option **C** to save your form and continue; after saving, your form will reappear on the screen and you can resume.

5. With the cursor in field 001 again, type **^J** to rotate to help screen 2 and press **^R** to enter the field definition process. Go through the list, entering the following attributes:

```
Field number/name:                          001/CLIENT NUMBER
Refuse duplicate keys? (Y/N)                       Y
Processing order:                                 001
Copy attributes of field:                          /
Field derived? (Y/N)                               N
```

```
Required/Optional/Unused                          R
Right justify?  (Y/N)                             Y
Pad field?  (Y/N)                                 Y
    Enter pad character:                          -
Floating character?  (Y/N)                        N
Verify field?  (Y/N)                              N
Check digit?  (Y/N)                               N
Range check?  (Y/N)                               N
Edit mask?  (Y/N)                                 Y
```

When you elect to Refuse duplicate keys, as in the CLIENT NUMBER field, it will then be impossible to type in an identical number. An error message will be displayed and you will be forced to change the number to something unique. Although this option is not suitable for all key fields (such as the INITIALS and LAST NAME fields discussed earlier), clearly it is essential for the CLIENT NUMBER.

The attributes assigned to CLIENT NUMBER will ensure that it must be entered, it is right-justified, the field is padded with blanks, and that it has both entry control and content control characters defined.

In the edit mask section, you will specify that at least one character must be entered and that where characters are entered, they must be numeric:

```
CLIENT NUMBER  ___!      Entry Control
CLIENT NUMBER  9999      Content Control
```

That completes the definition of the first field in the CLIENTS form.

6. Now go on to fields 002 through 006 and enter the field names. As soon as you have typed in the name, press **Return**, then type ^C to end the definition of the field, then ^**F** to move to the next field, and ^**R** to start the definition process. You can save time by typing these three commands one after the other—^**CFR**—after you press **Return**.

7. When you reach the STATE field, number 007, enter the field name, make the field required, and enter **Y** to the edit mask. Press **Return** to bypass entry control, and enter **CC** in content control (which will ensure that however you type in the State details, they will be converted to uppercase letters).

8. Go on to field 008 ZIP, now. Again, enter field name, make the field required, and enter **9** five times in content control of the edit mask to ensure that only numbers can be entered in this field. As an extra precaution, since ZIP is such an important field, you can put exclamation points in each field position to require that they all be filled: The edit mask will be:

```
ZIP    !!!!!          Entry Control
ZIP    99999          Content Control
```

Accept the default for record edit characters.

9. Now on to TELEPHONE AREA CODE. You must assign the attributes that make the field required, that insert the parentheses automatically, and that make the middle three field positions numeric only. To achieve this, you will put quotes in the first and last positions in entry control to specify that there will be constants in these positions. Then in content control, enter the parentheses and enter 9 in each of the other three positions:

```
TEL AREA CODE ''___''   Entry Control
TEL AREA CODE (999)     Content Control
```

10. The last field is TEL NUMBER. Assign the attributes to make the field required and to insert an automatic space between the first three digits and the second four.

To do so, you must insert quotes in position four in entry control. In content control, press the **Space Bar** once, then enter 9 for each blank to make the seven digits numeric only:

```
TEL NUMBER  ___''____   Entry Control
TEL NUMBER  999 9999    Content Control
```

Since this is the last field in the CLIENTS form, you may remember that it must be filled in order for MailMerge to work correctly. You have said that the field is required; if you have a client who has no telephone number, you will need to fill the field with zeros. The same applies to the TEL AREA CODE field.

FIGURE 9–3 PRICELST Form Listing and Field
Attribute Definitions

```
                 FIELD NUMBERS

CODE _____1  DESCRIPTION _____2
SIZE ___3       PRICE        _____4
```

---

11. You have completed the CLIENTS form, so type ^C and
    select **B** from the options to get back to the A> prompt.

You can go straight on now to design the PRICELST form, or
take a break and look back over the last few pages and marvel at
how much you have learned so far!

The PRICELST Form

Now you will design the last of the three interrelated forms.

Step-by-step procedure

1. After the A> prompt type **FORMGEN PRICELST**, then ^J to
   reach help screen 3. Look at the form design in Figure 9–
   3—the simplest so far and well within your capabilities by
   now.
   Remember—you must have identical field lengths for
   fields common to QUOTES and PRICELST—Count them
   now!

2. Fill in the design, making CODE the one key field. Save
   the form with ^C and type C to Continue.

3. Move the cursor to field 001 and type **^R**. You must enter
   field names for all the fields. In addition, for field 001, you
   should refuse duplicate keys (CODE is the key field) and
   to make CODE a required entry. Go ahead and assign those
   two attributes and then accept the edit mask.

4. You want to specify that the first character of CODE will
   be a letter, that it may be entered as lower- or uppercase,
   and that lowercase will be converted automatically to uppercase—option **C** in content control.

```
         CODE  _____           Entry Control
         CODE  C_____           Content Control
```

5. The only attribute for field 002, in addition to entering the field name, is that it is required. Go ahead and assign that attribute.

6. Field 003 is required, must be right-justified, should be padded with blanks, and should have entry control and content control masks as follows:

> SIZE ___!   Entry Control
> SIZE 9999   Content Control

7. Field 004 is required, should be right-justified, padded with blanks, must have a floating dollar sign, and should have decimal points aligned.

Field number/name:	004/PRICE
Processing order:	004
Copy attributes of field:	/
Field derived? (Y/N)	N
Required? (Y/N)	Y
Right justify? (Y/N)	Y
Pad field? (Y/N)	Y
Enter pad character:	-
Floating character? (Y/N)	Y
Enter floating character:	$
Verify field? (Y/N)	N
Check digit? (Y/N)	N
Range check? (Y/N)	N
Edit mask? (Y/N)	Y

8. Then in Edit Mask:

> PRICE ____.__   Entry Control
> PRICE _999.99   Content Control

9. That completes the PRICELST form, so press ^CB to return to the prompt.

In the final stage, you will learn how to link the slave forms to the master.

You may feel that it would be more profitable now to design some forms for your own particular applications. This is a good idea, since it will help to reinforce the new techniques you have learned so far, and you may even be able to follow the instructions for linking forms together using your own models instead of the examples here. Look ahead to Designing Your Own Forms in this chapter.

STAGE 3: LINKING THE FORMS TOGETHER

The last stage in the design process is to return to the QUOTES form and make the links between it and the two new forms. Remember, the fields that link the Master form to its slave forms are called *index fields* (in the QUOTES form these are CLIENT NUMBER and CODE), and the fields in the master form that are then filled automatically are called *derived fields*.

Index Field Attributes

The first phase of stage 3 is assigning attributes to the index fields.

Step-by-step procedure

1. After the prompt type **FORMGEN QUOTES**.
2. Move the cursor to field 002, CLIENT NUMBER, and press **^R**.

   This is the first index field, the link between QUOTES and CLIENTS. Remember, you assigned processing order 002 to the QUOTE NO field, so make this one 001.

Field number/name:	002/CLIENT NUMBER
Processing order:	001
Copy attributes of field	/
Field derived? (Y/N)	N
Required/Optional/Unused	R
Right justify? (Y/N)	Y
Pad field? (Y/N)	Y
Enter pad character:	-
Floating character? (Y/N)	N

3. So far, you have encountered nothing that you have not covered already. Now for the new feature:

Verify field? (Y/N)	Y
Sight/Retype/File	F
Keep file in memory? (Y/N)	N
Enter file name:	CLIENTS
Enter file disk drive (-/A/B...):	-
Check digit? (Y/N)	N
Range check? (Y/N)	N
Edit mask (Y/N)	Y

4. The entry control and content control will be:

```
CLIENT NUMBER  ___!      Entry Control
CLIENT NUMBER  9999      Content Control
```

5. Accept the default for record edit characters.

In the first part, you specified that the CLIENT NUM-BER should be required, right-justified, and padded with blanks.

The second part says that the field must be *verified* by looking at the external file called CLIENTS on the current disk drive.

NOTE: The index field in your Master form *must* be a *Key Field* in the slave form.

6. Now, when CLIENT NUMBER is filled in the QUOTES form, the number will be *verified* in the CLIENTS form, and all the CLIENT DETAILS information will be entered automatically into the appropriate positions in the QUOTES form. However, there is one last step before this automatic entry can occur.

You have connected the master form, QUOTES, to the slave form, CLIENTS, via the index field, CLIENT NUM-BER. To complete the definition process, now assign the appropriate attributes to the CLIENT DETAILS fields in the QUOTES form so that they will accept the data from the CLIENTS file. These are the attributes for derived fields.

7. Move the cursor to field 003 and press ^**R**. The answers to prompts should be:

```
Field number/name:                       003/TITLE
Processing order:                         003
Copy attributes of field:                 /
Field derived? (Y/N)                      Y
   Calculated/File?  (C/F)                F
   Index field number:          002/CLIENT NUMBER
   Item number in file:                   002
   Intermediate field? (Y/N)              N
   Allow operator entry? (Y/N)            N
Right justify?  (Y/N)                     N
Pad field?  (Y/N)                         N
Floating character?  (Y/N)                N
Verify field?  (Y/N)                      N
Check digit?  (Y/N)                       N
Range check?  (Y/N)                       N
Edit mask?  (Y/N)                         N
```

Now you have assigned the special characteristics to the

first derived field, TITLE in the QUOTES form, which ensure that the correct information is loaded into it from the CLIENTS file.

Explanation

The most important point is that the field is derived from an external file. Because of this, you will not allow operator entry.

Because you can confirm that the derivation of this field is not via an internal calculation but is from another file, you type F. Then you state how this field is linked to the external file. In fact it is via field 002 (the index field) in the QUOTES file, called the CLIENT NUMBER, so you type in 002. In recent versions of FormGen, the field name is then automatically filled in for you.

Then you are asked for the item number of the TITLE field (in the external file): it is item number 002 in the CLIENT file—so you overtype the default value of 001 with 002.

This terminology is a little confusing: there is nothing in the prompts to remind you that *index field number* refers to the master file, and that *item number in file* refers to the slave file (though it helps, in recent versions, that the field name is entered automatically as soon as you type in the field number). It is obvious, though, that you must specify which field in the slave file is going to supply the data for the derived field in the master file, and also how the master and slave forms are linked. You will just have to commit to memory the meaning of these two prompts. The practice in the next few pages will help this process.

Finally, in that section you are asked if there is need for an intermediate field; you accept the default value, N.

The remainder of the queries are defaults. You do not need to control the content of the field in the QUOTES form, since the data is being entered from another file.

Derived Field Attributes

We dealt with the Key field attributes earlier, so it remains only to assign those associated with derived fields.

Step-by-step procedure

1. Move the cursor to field 004 and type ^**R**.
2. All attributes will be the same as for the TITLE field, except that the processing order will be 004. We can't use copy attributes of field: because this is a key field.

3. The Index field number will still be **002** (the CLIENT NUMBER field) since this is the link between the QUOTES form and all of the CLIENT DETAILS that are required.

4. However, the Item number in file will be **003** (the INITIALS field is third in the CLIENTS file).

```
Field number/name:                              004/INITIALS
Processing order:                               004
Key order:                                      002
   Tie breaker field (Y/N)                        N
Refuse duplicate keys (Y/N)                       N
Copy attributes of field:                         /
Field derived? (Y/N)                              Y
   Calculated/File? (C/F)                         F
   Index field number:                  002/CLIENT NUMBER
   Item number in file:                         003
   Allow operator entry? (Y/N)                    N
```

Again, the rest will be defaults.

5. Now move the cursor to field 005, the LAST NAME, and press ^R.

This should be Processing order 005 and key order 001. The Index field number must remain 002 (the CLIENT NUMBER field on the QUOTES form), but the Item number in file: is now 004 (the LAST NAME is item 4 in the External File). All the other attributes are as the list shows.

Have you been able to follow what we are doing? Even if you still have some lingering doubts, all should become clear by the time you have finished this set of attributes and then those that link the QUOTES form to the PRICELST file.

6. Carry on as before through Fields 6, 7, 8, 9, 10, and 11, remembering that the Index field number will be 002 throughout, but you must update the Item number in file as you go along.

That completes the attributes that link the QUOTES form to the CLIENTS form. Press on to assigning attributes to the DESCRIPTION, SIZE etc., to link QUOTES to PRICELST in the same way.

7. Move the cursor to field 015—CODE—which is the second index field that links the QUOTES form to its other slave, PRICELST. Press ^R.

8. Remember, the previous INDEX FIELD for the link to the CLIENT form was 002, CLIENT NUMBER. You handle this one in precisely the same way:

```
Field number/name:                                    015/CODE 1
Processing order:                                           015
Copy attributes of field:                                     /
Field derived? (Y/N)                                          N
Required/Optional/Unused                                      R
Right justify? (Y/N)                                          N
Pad field? (Y/N)                                             N
Floating character? (Y/N)                                     N
```

9. OK so far? Now for the new link:

```
Verify field? (Y/N)                                          Y
   Sight/Retype/File?                                        F
   Keep file in memory? (Y/N)                                N
   Enter file name:                                    PRICELST
   Enter file disk drive (-/A/B...):                         -
Check digit? (Y/N)                                           N
Range check? (Y/N)                                           N
Edit mask? (Y/N)                                             Y
```

10. In the edit mask for CODE you must simply specify that the first character entered must be a letter and that if a lowercase letter is entered, it will be automatically converted to uppercase (as in PRICELST):

```
       CODE  _____       Entry Control
       CODE  C_____       Content Control
```

11. Accept the default for record edit characters.

12. Having assigned the attributes to the index field that links the CODE in the QUOTES form to the PRICELST form, you must now finish the job by assigning the appropriate special characteristics to the derived fields that will be filled automatically when a code number is entered: DESCRIPTION, SIZE and UNIT PRICE.

   Move the cursor to field 016, the first DESCRIPTION, and press ^R. Once again, you will be filling in the items relating to derived fields.

```
Field number/name:                              016/DESCRIPTION 1
Processing order:                                           016
```

```
Copy attributes of field:                          /
Field derived? (Y/N)                               Y
  Calculated/File?  (C/F)                           F
  Index field number:                              015/CODE
  Item number in file:                             002
  Intermediate field? (Y/N)                         N
  Allow operator entry? (Y/N)                        N
```

13. Accept the defaults for all the remaining queries.

    As soon as you type **Y** to the query, Field derived? you will get the other items related to derived fields.

14. Note that the Index field number is 015 (the CODE in the QUOTES form) and that the Item number in file is 002 (that is, DESCRIPTION is the second item in the PRICELST file).

15. Continue thus for fields 017 and 018, remembering to enter the field names, SIZE 1 and UNIT PRICE 1, respectively, and to update the Item number in file to 003 and 004 respectively (the items SIZE and UNIT PRICE are third and fourth in the PRICELST file), and to keep the index field (the CODE) as 015.

16. In addition, field 017 should be right-justified and padded with blanks and field 018 should be right-justified, padded with blanks, and have a floating dollar sign.

    You have already assigned the attributes to field 019, so that almost completes the form definition process—you may breathe a sigh of relief!

    To finish off, you will save your form as it is now and then delete the four lines following the first line of QTY 1, CODE 1, etc. (to which you have just assigned attributes). When you recopy them, they will automatically take on the attributes already assigned to fields 14 to 19, inclusive.

17. Type **^CC** to save the form and continue. Move the cursor down to the second line of the item list and press **^Y** to delete the whole line; repeat for the other three identical lines.

18. Now move the cursor back to the first line of the item list and press **^P** to fill the Line Buffer and then move the cursor down to the next line and press **^N** to insert a whole line. Remember it takes a second or so for the inserted lines to appear.

19. Continue pressing ^N until your four lines are restored.

20. Now move the cursor to the second DESCRIPTION field, press ^R, and enter the field name, DESCRIPTION 2, and then check through the remaining attributes. You will find that the correct field numbers have been inserted in the appropriate positions and that all the attributes match up correctly with those of Field 016. Amazingly clever!

21. Check through each field in turn, adding to each field name the appropriate number (add 2 to each on the second line, 3 to each on the third line, and so on). Once you are satisfied that the attributes have copied correctly, you don't need to look through all the prompts; just press **Return** after entering the number after the field name, then ^C to end the definition, and ^F to go to the next field, then ^R to start the new definition. Remember, you can type these commands one after the other while holding down the control key—^**CFR**.

22. The last field to define is 044, the calculation of TOTAL FOR FURNITURE. Move the cursor to this field and press ^R. Note that the field is derived and calculated. Just go through and enter the field names or numbers for the calculation:

TOTAL FOR FURNITURE = FIELD 19 + FIELD 25 + FIELD 31 + FIELD 37 + FIELD 43

Field number/name:	044/TOTAL FOR FURNITURE
Processing order:	044
Copy attributes of field:	/
Field derived? (Y/N)	Y
Calculated/File? (C/F)	C
Numeric/String? (N/S)	N
Enter String/Algebraic expression for field:	
TOTAL FOR FURNITURE=TOTAL PRICE 1+TOTAL PRICE 2+TOTAL	
PRICE 3+TOTAL PRICE 4+TOTAL PRICE 5	
Intermediate field? (Y/N)	N
Allow operator entry? (Y/N)	N
Right justify? (Y/N)	Y
Pad field? (Y/N)	Y
Enter pad character:	-
Floating character? (Y/N)	Y
Enter floating character:	$
Verify field? (Y/N)	N
Check digit? (Y/N)	N
Range check? (Y/N)	N
Edit mask? (Y/N)	Y

23. The edit mask should be as follows:

```
TOTAL FOR FURNITURE  _____.__        Entry Control
TOTAL FOR FURNITURE  _9999.99         Content Control
```

24. Accept the default for record edit characters.

That absolutely completes the datafield definition process for all three forms.

LISTING THE FIELD ATTRIBUTE DEFINITIONS

It remains only to list out to your printer the full form listing and field attribute definitions (earlier you printed out the first page only of this listing).

Step-by-Step Procedure

1. With the QUOTES form still on the screen, type ^W to list it.
2. When the listing is completed, save this form with ^C and select **B** to boot the operating system.
3. Next, call up the CLIENTS form and list that with a ^W.
4. Finally, having saved CLIENTS, call up **PRICELST** and list that too.

You will find a copy of all these listings in Appendix A at the back of this manual, so you can compare them with your own.

You now have a detailed summary of all the attributes you have assigned. Keep the listings next to you; you will need them later in the DataStar and MailMerge chapters.

You have learned a great deal in this rather long and arduous chapter. You must quickly design some forms of your own and try out your newly acquired skill. You will soon forget these hard-learned lessons if you do not give yourself a lot of practice.

Remember that here is a demonstration program on your DataStar master working disk; the master form is called ORDER and it is linked to two subsidiary forms, CUSTOMER and OKS-TATES. The best way of learning about these forms is to call each of them up in turn in FormGen and check through the attributes assigned to each field (by typing ˆ**R** in each field in turn). You will find a few extra ones in addition to those covered in this tutorial.

Make a note of any that you might like to use in form designs of your own.

DESIGNING YOUR OWN FORMS

This section summarizes the principles you will need to understand before you will be able to design good advanced forms yourself. Turn back to Tables 9–1 and 9–2 which list the field definition prompts in the order that they appear. You can use them as a reference list for assigning attributes.

You will never get all of these in one field definition! In these two tables I have marked the items that apply to special fields: key fields, derived fields, and index fields. If you accepted the default value for every prompt during the field definition process, you would see only the items that are **not** inset. Whenever you choose not to accept the default, you will get the extra items shown inset on the list.

Index Fields

The link between any master form you may create and the slave form that you want associated with it is the index field. If you intend to have more than one slave form, then you will have more than one index field in the master form.

The examples from the QUOTES form are the CLIENT NUMBER, which linked the QUOTES master form to the slave CLIENTS form, and the CODE, which linked QUOTES to the slave PRICELST form. These were the two index fields on the QUOTES form.

The vital attribute that *must* be assigned to an index field is file verification:

```
Verify field (Y/N)      Y
Sight/Retype/File       F
Enter file name:
Enter file disk drive:  _
```

You then must give the name of the external file that is to be verified (CLIENTS or PRICELST) and, in early versions, you must enter the appropriate key field number (such as field 001 for both in this example), and accept the default for the disk drive.

Derived Fields

Once you have established the index fields in your master form, you must then go through the fields that will be filled in automatically by access to the slave forms. These derived fields (since they are not *entered* by you) have essential attributes assigned under the Derived field:

> Derived field (Y/N)   **Y**
>
> Calculated/File   **F**
>
> Index field number:
>
> Item number in file:
>
> Intermediate field?
>
> Allow operator entry   **N**

You then enter the Index field number in the master file. This number must be the field number of the index field connecting master to slave (such as 002, CLIENT NUMBER, in the QUOTES form). The Item number in File query is asking you to enter the Field number of the item you are deriving *in its own file*; for example, in the case of the TITLE field (003 in the QUOTES form), it is derived from field number 002 in the CLIENTS form, so you would enter 002 as an answer.

You can see that it is now a very straightforward cross-indexing problem for the computer. As soon as you fill in the index field in the master form, this is used as a cross reference to the external file containing the required information. This information is slotted into the appropriate positions in the master form (Fields 003 to 011 in the QUOTES form) since these positions have been identified by the special attributes assigned to them (they have been defined as derived fields, linked to the master form through the index field).

COPYING FORMS

To make a copy of any of the definition files in this tutorial or the demonstration files on the DataStar disk, you should call up WordStar. Use the **O** option from the OPENING MENU to copy a file, give the name of the file to copy from (here **QUOTES.DEF**), and then give the name of the file to copy to. You can make minor changes in FormGen, but for major changes you should use the Data Base Restructure program (InfoStar version 1.6 or later).

CONCLUSION

DataStar is a powerful program. If you had to hire a software consultant to write, for your specific needs, the programs required to achieve the results outlined in this tutorial and the next on data entry, it would probably cost you more than you paid for your microcomputer. Yet, with no programing experience at all, you can solve any similar problems in your own business situation using InfoStar.

Lots of practice on real life problems is the key to mastering these techniques. Good luck!

10

InfoStar II: Data Entry and Reports

Now that you have created your three new forms and finished assigning attributes, you can reap the fruits of your labors in the Data Entry phase. You will find you can enter and retrieve large amounts of data very easily and quickly using the forms you set up in Chapter 9.

Once you have data entered and have learned how to retrieve it, you should know how to display it. You looked at the Quick Report program in the InfoStar tutorial in Part One; now you will see how to produce customized reports and summaries from your data. Finally, you will use database restructuring to modify one of your existing forms.

Before starting this session, if you have a floppy disk system, boot up from your tutorial disk, with a separate data disk in drive B. Now copy all your .DEF files. If you have a hard disk system you can do the same, copying the files from your tutorial user area or other system setup. By now you should be used to working with your program disk in drive A and your data disk in drive B. It is a good idea to keep separate data disks for word processing data (letters, documents etc.) and for data processing (forms, data files, reports, etc.).

CALLING UP DATASTAR

You will start by entering data into the slave forms that consist of some stock items and prices and a few client names and addresses. Then we will try some quotes.

Step-by-Step Procedure

1. Boot up your system from the tutorial disk and insert a separate data disk in drive B. At the prompt type:

   DATASTAR B:PRICELST

2. After the usual few lines of information appear on the screen you will be asked:

   Enter Disk Drive to Use For Data File (PRICELST.DTA) (A/B..)
   Enter Disk Drive to Use For Index File (PRICELST.NDX) (A/B..)

   You probably remember from the DataStar tutorial in Part One that every time you enter data into a form, the record itself is stored in the data file (.**DTA**) and information about its key fields is stored in the index file (.NDX). This process is built in to the DataStar program and occurs quite automatically.

   You must enter the appropriate disk drive (A to P) for each of these files. As you wish to save your data and index files on the data disk in drive B, you must enter **B** in answer to the two queries. Even if you have a hard disk, this is good practice.

3. Now your PRICELST form will appear on the screen. Notice that, since you have not yet entered any data into the form, you are automatically in *add mode* (see top left hand corner of the screen).

DATA ENTRY

If you look at my examples, you will see that I have carried on where you left off with the scenario outlined earlier in the advanced form design tutorial. Of course, if you have some real data to enter that would be useful to you later, then use your own details instead of these.

Remember, you have three ranges of bedroom furniture—Ultima, Supreme and Finesse (in descending order of cost). These are now further subdivided into four price levels within each range.

You can enter just enough items in each range to make a reasonable stock list for testing the QUOTES form later. The examples in this chapter contain 5 different furniture items in each of the 12 design range/price level categories, for a total of 60 entries. Not so arduous a task as you might imagine. There are so many useful short-cuts available to you when entering data into a DataStar form that you can complete the entry of 60 items much quicker than you could type them on a typewriter (or you *will* be able to when you are fully conversant with the program).

Step-by-Step Procedure

You can get started now. You should have the PRICELST form on the screen in front of you and the cursor should be in the first field. In InfoStar version 1.0 and earlier versions of DataStar, if you completely fill a field the cursor moves automatically to the next field; if you do not fill it, press **Return** to move to the next field. In 1.6 and later versions, you must always press **Return** to move from one field to the next.

When you come to the first right-justified field, SIZE, the cursor moves to the right hand side of the data field. As you enter data, the cursor shifts to the left. Similarly, with the PRICE field, the cursor sits on top of the decimal point with the floating dollar sign on its left. As you enter figures the cursor stays where it is, the dollars fill in from the right, and then *after you enter the decimal point*, the cursor and the data you enter return to their normal mode, moving from left to right.

If you notice a mistake before you have saved the record, you can use the usual DataStar cursor control keys to get back to any field and make the necessary changes. Remember that ^**A** moves the cursor *back* a field at a time, ^**F** *forward* a field at a time, and ^**S** and ^**D** do the same a character at a time.

If you notice that you have left out a few characters and you need to insert them, you can use **^V** to make as many spaces as you need, and then you can type the characters in the space created (you must have noticed that in DataStar you are always working with INSERT OFF). To delete characters, you can use **^G**.

Remember *not* to use **^E** to move up a line. In DataStar **^E** signifies that you wish to Exit the current mode (in this case Add mode) and you will then lose what you have entered in that particular record.

If you do it by mistake, don't worry: Just press **A** to get back to Add mode and continue entering data for that record.

1. Enter the first code number, **U1/10010**; then the description of the first item, **Dressing table, mirror and lights;** the size in centimeters, **100**; and the price, **$125.00**.

2. Your form will look like this:

```
CODE  U1/10010   DESCRIPTION  Dressing table, mirror and lights
SIZE  100        PRICE        $125.00
```

3. After entering data in the last field, press **^B** or **Return** and read the message that appears at the top of the screen. Press **Return** again to file the data. If you have made a mistake in entering the data, press any key to go back to the top of the form and start again, or press the **Del** key to delete that whole record.

   You will have noticed the effect of the attributes as you entered the size in centimeters into a right-justified field and the floating dollar sign in the right-justified PRICE field. Now you are seeing the attributes you assigned in action.

   The code number here includes the range and price level information (U1 is Ultima, price level 1). The rest of the code number could be anything, but you should set it so that it is easy to remember, such as 10010 for item 1, 10020 item 2, 10030 item 3, and so on.

   When you set up a system for yourself, if you need a code to cover hundreds or thousands of items (a large stock list or an inventory, for example) you might find it better to start from 00001, 00002, 00003, etc., through to a theoretical maximum of 99,999.

4. At the end of each record entry, you can press either **^B** or **Return**. The **^B** is useful in that you can press it at any time, to signify that you have finished that entry. So if you have to go back and make a correction in a record, you do not have to press **Return** repeatedly to reach the end of the form before saving it. You can press **^B** even if your changes are in the first field (as long as all the other fields have been filled correctly).

5. Practice using the cursor controls to move around your form until they are second nature to you. The ability to enter large amounts of data quickly is partly dependent upon knowing the control characters by heart. Only lots of practice will achieve this, so keep at it!

6. Enter the next code, **U2/10010** (which is price level 2 in the Ultima range).

7. Now, to enter the description, which is exactly the same as the last one, you simply press **^C**, and that field is copied from the previous record.

8. You can press **^C** for SIZE as well, which is also the same as last time.

9. Enter the new price, **$155.00**, and then **^B** and **Return** to save the record, as before.

   You can see how quick data entry can be when several items in a record are the same as the previous ones and you can copy them with **^C**. Continue thus for codes U3 and U4, just entering the codes and the new prices (**$190.00** and **$215.00** respectively) and **^C** for the rest.

10. The other two ranges can be entered the same way. The codes for Supreme will be **S1** to **S4/10010**; the DESCRIP-TION and SIZE fields will be the same as for Ultima, so you can use **^C** for this data.

11. The prices will be, in ascending order, **$105.00**, **$130.00**, **$165.00**, and **$195.00**.

   Similarly for Finesse, codes **F1** to **F4/10010** and prices, **$95.00**, **$120.00**, **$140.00**, and **$175.00**.

   You have now entered all 12 variations on the dressing table item and, hopefully, you feel confident of what you are doing. You are beginning to appreciate the power of the datafield attributes you assigned in Chapter 9 and to see how quick data entry can be.

12. Proceed to the second furniture item:

```
Description: Master wardrobe, fitted
   CODE  U1/10020   DESCRIPTION  Master wardrobe, fitted
   SIZE   150        PRICE        $225.00
```

13. Starting at U1/10020 go right through to F4/10020 (another 12 records) filling in a size of 150 cm and using the prices that follow.

U1/10020	$225.00
U2/10020	$255.00
U3/10020	$285.00
U4/10020	$305.00
S1/10020	$195.00
S2/10020	$225.00
S3/10020	$255.00
S4/10020	$285.00
F1/10020	$175.00
F2/10020	$195.00
F3/10020	$225.00
F4/10020	$255.00

Do not worry if you press ^C by mistake in a field that is not a duplicate of the previous record. You can get back to the field in the usual way with ^A and make corrections.

14. That completes the master wardrobe series. Go straight on to the:

```
Description:   Matching top cupboard
```

remembering that the size is the same as for the master wardrobe (150 cm). The new codes are U1/10030 to F4/10030 and the matching prices are:

U1/10030	$95.00
U2/10030	$115.00
U3/10030	$130.00
U4/10030	$155.00

S1/10030	$85.00
S2/10030	$105.00
S3/10030	$125.00
S4/10030	$140.00
F1/10030	$75.00
F2/10030	$95.00
F3/10030	$110.00
F4/10030	$130.00

15. Go on to items with the code ending /10040:

      Description: **Bridging unit with doors & shelves**

The size will be 250 cm and the prices:

U1/10040	$200.00
U2/10040	$235.00
U3/10040	$260.00
U4/10040	$295.00
S1/10040	$175.00
S2/10040	$205.00
S3/10040	$240.00
S4/10040	$270.00
F1/10040	$155.00
F2/10040	$190.00
F3/10040	$225.00
F4/10040	$235.00

16. The fifth and final item is:

      Description: **Headboard with stereo & lights**

The codes will run from U1/10050 to F4/10050, the size will be the same as the bridging unit, and the prices:

U1/10050	$425.00
U2/10050	$465.00
U3/10050	$495.00
U4/10050	$525.00

S1/10050	$385.00
S2/10050	$415.00
S3/10050	$455.00
S4/10050	$485.00
F1/10050	$345.00
F2/10050	$375.00
F3/10050	$405.00
F4/10050	$455.00

You have finished entering all 60 records in the PRICELST file. With practice, you will be able to enter that amount of data in about 15 minutes (in fact, maybe you did).

You probably made some minor mistakes in your data entry, so probably you observed some of the built-in safeguards coming into play. For example, if you tried to type in a duplicate code number, you saw the message:

```
Key already exists—enter new key
```

You can see how easy it would be to make errors in data entry if you did not get these warnings. Since that is the end of data entry in the PRICELST form, you can press ^E to **exit,** then go on to data retrieval.

DATA RETRIEVAL

Before entering data in the other forms, you should try out the various methods by which you can *retrieve* data entered in a DataStar form. These techniques were described briefly in the tutorial in Part One, but I will remind you of them now.

When you type ^E to exit the current mode you are presented with a menu of different modes. Try each of these in turn to familiarize yourself with their use; type ^E now.

Select **D** from the menu to scan the file in data order. Press ^N to go on to the next record or ^P to look at the previous record. The records will appear in the order you originally entered them. If you had to edit any records as you went along, then the edited records will be out of order.

When a record is edited in DataStar the revised record is saved and becomes the last record in the data file. The previous version is not deleted, but is automatically marked in such a way that it does not appear during any scans or other uses of the data. If you look at the data file in WordStar, you will see all such edited records marked with a tilde (˜) in place of the first character in the record, or with the first character missing.

NOTE: You must *never* delete these marked records from the data file in WordStar. In fact, you must never edit an original data file *in any way* in WordStar. If you want to edit data it must be done in DataStar or on a *copy* of the original file.

Clearly, there must be a way of getting rid of the marked records from time to time; otherwise your file would become unwieldy and slow to operate. These deleted records still occupy space in your file and also disturb the order of the file. You can clean up your files (called *file maintenance*) using the FormSort program. This sorts your file into key field order, removes any records marked for deletion, and automatically creates a new matching index file. You will do this later on in the chapter.

Let's go on now to try the other data retrieval methods.

Press ^E again, but this time select **I** from the menu to scan the file in index order. Note that records will appear in numerical order by code, starting with the last record you reviewed. When you have finished, press **^ED** to go back to Scan mode, D.

Remember, the index file stores only the information relating to the key field(s). Every time you enter a new record or edit an existing one, the index file is automatically and simultaneously updated.

Your DataStar form will only operate when you have both a data file and an index file. If you should ever erase your index file by mistake, you can create a new one from your data file using FormSort, which is described later in this chapter.

Now press ^E and select **S** for edit scan mask (or **M** in InfoStar version 1.0 or earlier—check your help screen to be sure). All fields will fill with asterisks; type **U1** in the first two spaces in the CODE field. Then press **^B**. The form will fill with a record starting with U1 (such as U1/10010).

If you look at the status line you will notice that you are now in Scan mode (D). You can now scan through all records starting with U1 in the code field by pressing **^N**. The next record will be U1/10020, the next will be U1/10030, and so on to U1/10050. If you press **^N** again, you will get the message:

End of file Press ESC

Press the **Esc** key and you will return to U1/10010.

Now type ^**ES** (or ^**EM**) again, and enter **F4** in the first two spaces (you can overtype U1) and press ^**B**. Now when you press ^**N** you will move through all the items starting with F4.

Before you exit from Edit Scan Mask mode, you must clear the mask: in later versions you can simply press ^**Y** and any entry you have made will be cleared; then you must press ^**B** to end the entry before going on to another mode. In earlier versions of DataStar, you have to move the cursor to each entry and delete it with ^**G**, then press ^**B** to end the entry. If you ever forget to clear the mask, you may have problems when using other scan modes thereafter.

You can see that the Edit scan mask can be an extremely useful facility. For example, you may forget the surname of someone on file, but remember that it begins with Under (such as Underwood or Underhill). You could simply type in Under in the last name field in Edit Scan Mask mode, press ^**B** and then scan through all the people whose surnames begin with Under until you find the one you want.

Now try out the Select by Key Mode: press ^**E K** and type in a code number (remember, CODE is the key field in the PRICELST form). The form will fill out with the record that precisely matches the code you typed in.

Once your record selected by key is on the screen, you might need to look at records on either side of it. Just type ^**EI** to use the Scan in Index Order mode, and you will be able to use ^**N** to look forward in the file and ^**P** to move backward.

If you make a mistake when entering the key, you will get the message:

Key not found. Hit ESC to re-enter key.

Just press the **Esc** key and enter the correct code number. To enter a new Key, you must type ^**EK** again.

That completes the coverage of Scan modes. You can go on to enter data in the other forms now. Perhaps you should take a break first and review progress.

ENTERING DATA IN THE SLAVE FORMS

Now that you have entered data in PRICELST, you are ready to input similar data in the other slave form.

Step-by-Step Procedure

1. To exit from the PRICELST form type ^**EE**. You will find the cursor back at the prompt (if you have InfoStar version 1.0 or earlier, you must type ^**EEC**).

2. Go on now to the CLIENTS form and enter a few names and addresses. At the prompt type:

DATASTAR B:CLIENTS

Again, you will be asked for the disk drives for the data and index files. Enter the appropriate drive, as before.

3. The CLIENTS form will appear on the screen, with the cursor in field 001 and in Add mode. You need to enter five or six names and addresses, just enough to provide some practice later with the QUOTES form.

   Remember that the CLIENT NUMBER is the key field in the CLIENTS form and is the link to the QUOTES form. Numbering can start at 0001, allowing for a maximum of 9999 clients. When you are setting up a system of your own later you may need higher numbers than this, so remember to leave space for an extra digit.

4. It is common in name and address forms to have several blank fields; sometimes you just do not have all the information. To skip a field, just press **Return** to go on to the next. Whenever you skip a field in DataStar, a comma is automatically inserted in the file.

   Following is a sample list of the five names and addresses to enter. Note that the *extra commas* indicate blank fields. When entering data into your form, you need only press **Return** and the commas are inserted for you, whether you enter data or leave a blank field. Enter some genuine names from your own files into the CLIENTS form. Or, to match this chapter's examples, enter the names I have used:

```
0001,Ms,J M,Smith,1 Main Street,New Haven,CT,06453,(203),524 4455
0002,Mrs,B N,Jones,5 West Street,Manchester,CT,06040,(203),649 3766
0003,Ms,G L,Dyer,10 South Street,Springfield,VA,22151,(703),234 6677
0004,Mr,D D,Bowman,21 The Avenue,Denver,CO,80224,(303),997 8899
0005,Mrs,V T,James,2 The Green,Providence,RI,02906,(401),271 9911
```

Hopefully you did not have any trouble filling in the CLIENTS form. You can see how much easier it is to enter data into a predesigned form than to type it out on paper. When you are more experienced you will be able to enter this kind of data at a rate of at least 50 or more records per hour (if you are a skilled typist, you could manage two to three times this rate).

ENTERING DATA IN THE MASTER FORM

The next stage is to call up the QUOTES form. Exit from the CLIENTS form by typing ^EE (or ^EEC) which will return you to the prompt. Now that you have some data entered in your two slave forms, you can try preparing some quotes.

Step-by-Step Procedure

1. At the prompt type:

DATASTAR B:QUOTES

2. Fill in the disk drives to use for the Data and Index files and prepare to enter the first CLIENT NUMBER.

   Remember that the QUOTE NUMBER field is to be completed automatically and updated by one each time you type in a quote, so as you call up the form you will see the cursor in field 002, CLIENT NUMBER.

3. Enter a CLIENT NUMBER in field 002, say **0005**. As soon as you press **Return**, the cursor moves to field 012, and the details you entered for this client (in the CLIENTS form) appear automatically, filling fields 003 to 011.

4. Enter one of the three designs in field 012, say **ULTIMA**, and one of the four price levels in field 013, say **2**.

5. Assume for this first quote that the client is interested in buying all five items in this range and price level, so type **1** under QTY and **U2/10010** under CODE in fields 014 and 015.

6. As soon as you enter the CODE into field 015, the DE-SCRIPTION, SIZE, UNIT PRICE and TOTAL PRICE fields are filled in automatically from the PRICELST file (in the earlier versions the TOTAL PRICE details do not fill until after you press ^B).

7. Now fill in the second line (such as QTY **2**, CODE **U2/ 10020**) and watch the magic repeat itself! Carry on through to U2/10050.

8. Finally, enter today's date and your name and position at the bottom of the form. Type **^J** to turn off the help screen (so that you can see more of your form) and press **^B** to inform the system that the form is complete.

   If by any chance you have entered something incorrectly or left out a required field, you will be reminded of it as soon as you press **^B**. You will not be able to save this record until everything is correct.

   Did you make any mistakes this time that were picked up by DataStar? For example, if you entered F for Finesse in the QTY field you would get the message:

```
0-9 only allowed - re-enter field
```

   You should always test your form with a varied but limited amount of data before filling in thousands of records. At this early stage it is little trouble to make changes, but if you go ahead too fast and then want to change your mind about some detail of the form design, you may have to abandon all the data already entered and start again. In versions 1.6 and later of InfoStar there is a specific program for restructuring your databases that is described toward the end of this chapter. If you have an earlier version of InfoStar, you can use a combination of MailMerge and FormSort to achieve the same result; this technique is described in the MailMerge chapter of Part Two.

9. Carry on entering CLIENT NUMBER and DESIGN codes until you have a dozen or so quotes prepared and you are quite familiar with using the form. You are bound to make errors at first. For example, if you find that you have typed in a Client number and no data appears on the QUOTES form:

   a. Are you sure you have chosen a CLIENT NUMBER that exists in your CLIENTS form?

   b. Have you typed the number correctly? Have you forgotten one of the leading zeros, for instance?

   Similarly, you may find that when you enter the CODE for an item of furniture, nothing appears. Check carefully that you have entered the details correctly.

10. Note that after the first entry, the contents of the fields SIGNED and POSITION fill in automatically.

    Note also that with the attributes assigned as they are, you are forced to fill in all five lines of furniture items on each quote; you could change the attributes if you wished to force entry of only one or two items. You would have to change the Required option to **N** and remove any entry control characters that specified that data must be entered.

11. You should practice the Data Retrieval and Scan modes on this new form until you are familiar with them. There is no point in entering data efficiently only to find you are not able to retrieve it at will!

PRINTING OUT A QUOTE

To print a quote to hand to a customer, like the example in Figure 10-1, select the particular record you wish to print, make sure your printer is online, and press ^U. As soon as the quote has printed, press ^E. Otherwise, if you are using the Scan mode, the subsequent records will print out too. This can be useful if you have prepared several quotes for the same client; you can select their record by key, and then when you press ^U all their records will print consecutively.

Although this direct printout from DataStar is adequate for handing to a client on the spot, you will want to use ReportStar to create much more attractive reports and summaries, as you will see later in this chapter.

DATA ENTRY IN BATCH MODE

You may find it very useful to use *Batch mode* for data entry under certain circumstances. Batch mode allows you to enter data, as the name suggests, in batches that can be checked at a later time for errors before being incorporated into the main data file.

The QUOTES file serves as an example, though in the scenario you have been following it would not be entirely suitable since calculated fields (in this case just the QUOTE NUMBER—though in earlier versions of the program it include the calculations of prices, also) would not be entered until the *verification* stage. However, it serves to demonstrate the use of batch mode, so let us proceed.

FIGURE 10–1 Sample Printout of Quote

```
    QUOTE NUMBER: 000003      CLIENT NUMBER: 0002

    CLIENT DETAILS:
    TITLE (Mr/Mrs/Ms): Mrs      INITIALS: B N    LAST NAME: Jones

    STREET: 5 West Street              CITY: Manchester
    STATE: CT    ZIP: 06040    TEL AREA CODE: 203    TEL NUMBER: 649-3766



                  DESIGN: SUPREME      PRICE CODE: 4
                  ======================================


    QTY   CODE        DESCRIPTION              SIZE   UNIT    TOTAL
                                               (cm)   PRICE   PRICE


     1   S4/10010  Dressing table, mirror and lights   100   195.00   $195.00
     1   S4/10020  Master wardrobe, fitted             150   285.00   $285.00
     1   S4/10030  Matching top cupboard               150   140.00   $140.00
     1   S4/10040  Bridging unit with doors & shelves  250   270.00   $270.00
     1   S4/10050  Headboard with stereo & lights      250   485.00   $485.00




                               TOTAL FOR FURNITURE        $1375.00
                  ======================================


    This quotation is valid for 30 days from:

    DATE: 10/01/85




    SIGNED:   James Justice
    POSITION: MANAGER
```

If you are the only person who uses the QUOTES form, you may choose to enter the quotes for any one day in a batch file labeled with the date, which you can check later at your convenience. If several different people are entering quotes, it would be a good idea to use their initials as well as the date in the batch file name, for example, **JD1001** would be JD's entries for the 1st of October.

Step-by-Step Procedure

1. To enter Batch mode, select **B** from the menu. You will see the following message:

   ```
   Enter disk drive (A/P...): _
   Enter name of batch file: _____
   ```

2. You should enter the disk drive you wish to use for the batch file (probably the current drive) and then type in a name for your batch file, for example, JD1001 (you may choose a name up to eight characters in length).

3. The status line shows the disk drive and file name you have chosen next to the word BATCH and, in the far right corner of the screen, a reminder of the name of your current form, QUOTES.

4. Enter a few quotes exactly as you did before and then you will learn how to add them to the main QUOTES file.

   All the same rules apply—you will not be aware that you are entering data into a batch file, except that the QUOTE NUMBER will not be entered.

5. When you press ^E after you have entered some quotes in Batch mode, notice the other items in the menu that relate to batch operation. In addition to **B** for selecting Batch mode, you have **V** for verifying the batch file and **R** for restoring the main file.

   If you are entering quotes at various times during the day, and perhaps other operators are doing the same, then you will wait until the end of the day before going through the verification process.

If you decide to use this technique, each time you call up the QUOTES form you will select Batch mode, enter the name of your batch file, type in the quote, and then exit in the usual way.

If you need to scan the main QUOTES data file while you are using Batch mode, you can press ^E to Exit batch mode and then select **R** from the menu to restore the main QUOTES file. Then you can use any of the Scan modes in the usual way.

Batch Verification

At the end of the day you can verify all the batch files, one after the other, then incorporate them into the main QUOTES file.

Step-by-step procedure

1. To do this, type ^E and select **V** from the menu. In the case of the QUOTES form you have designed there are no fields to be verified by sight or by retyping, so you will simply press ^B as each record appears on the screen. The QUOTE NUMBER will be updated, and the record will be added to the main file.

2. At the end of the process you will see on the screen:

> The batch file has been verified.
> Hit ESC key to enter another batch name.

3. If more than one batch file was entered during the day, then press the **Esc** key and enter the name of the next file to be verified. Continue until you have finished them all.

When you design a form for your own purposes, if you think it would be a good idea for a different person to check each set of batch files, you can specify that at least one item in each record must be *sight verified*. For really vital data, you can demand that a particular field be *retyped*. You enter your selection (either S or R) in FormGen at the prompt Verify field S/R/F.

When you have finished the verification process, press ^E to get back to the menu that enters mode changes, and we will look at another use of batch files.

DATASTAR FILE MAINTENANCE

File maintenance is essential from time to time to keep the operation of the files efficient. By this process records marked for deletion are removed from the file and the remaining records are restored to their correct order. You will learn two different techniques for file maintenance; the first method uses DataStar and is discussed here; another, later in the chapter, uses FormSort, part of the ReportStar program.

During file maintenance two temporary batch files are created (work files); you should ensure before starting that you have enough space for these files in addition to the data and index files on disk. The work files will occupy approximately the same space as the combined size of the existing data and index files.

If by mischance (or bad planning!) you should ever get the message:

```
Disk full.  Replace system disk and hit return.
```

when you press **Return**, you will find yourself back at the prompt.

Step-by-Step Procedure

Take the opportunity of erasing some unwanted files to make more space, or perhaps put a disk in the other drive to use for the work files, which you can then specify when you enter the field name and disk drive for file maintenance. (You lucky hard disk users should never have this experience!)

1. At the prompt, type:

```
DATASTAR B:QUOTES
```

2. Select **F** from the menu and enter the batch file details you are prompted for, as you did previously. It is a good idea to keep the same name for all file maintenance batch files, say FM99. At the end of file maintenance these temporary work files are automatically erased.

3. As file maintenance proceeds you will see the records appear on the screen one after the other. You can suppress this by pressing any key; the last record will stay on the screen until maintenance is complete. This will speed up the process considerably if you are maintaining a large file. If you want to check how far maintenance has progressed, you can press any key again and, after a short delay, the records will appear on the screen once more.

4. At the end of file maintenance you will get the message:

File maintenance is complete. Hit ESC key.

Press the **Esc** key.

You should try out the Select by key mode to test out the renewed efficiency and speed of your file, though this will be more obvious later when you have a larger data file.

SORTING WITH FORMSORT

In the InfoStar tutorial in Part One you learned how to sort names and addresses into order by LAST NAME, the key field for the ADDRESS form, and to produce a simple report using the Quick Report program RGEN.

You will first use FormSort to do file maintenance on your CLIENTS data file. Then you can explore some additional functions of the FormSort routines, which will enable you to prepare new versions of your data files, sorted on different key fields, and with their own index files. For example, if you wished to send out a large mailing, you could sort your client data by ZIP CODE to save on postage. If you were planning to conduct a telephone survey, you could have another version of the same data, this time sorted by telephone area code.

NOTE: There may be a "bug" in your FormSort program if you are using it with MS-DOS 2.11. The symptom of the fault is a message saying File close failure when you try to run FormSort. If you are not getting this error message, ignore what follows on debugging.

MicroPro has published the following patches for the program (if you are not experienced in debugging programs, you may like to ask your friendly dealer to do this for you). This bug has been corrected in InfoStar 1.61.

Step-by-Step Procedure

1. Next to the prompt type:

For FormSort 1.0	For FormSort 1.6
>DEBUG FORMSORT.OVR	>DEBUG FORMSORT.EXE
−F88A3,88A6 90	−F511A,511D 90
−W	−W
−Q	−Q

2. Note that the prompt in Debug is a minus sign; after the last **Return**, the normal system prompt will reappear.
3. Run FormSort; it should function perfectly.

File Maintenance with FormSort

When you used FormSort earlier to sort your ADDRESS file into alphabetical order by the key field in fact you carried out file maintenance at the same time.

Step-by-step procedure

This is all you have to do (assuming programs are on disk in drive A and data files on disk in drive B):

1. At the A> prompt type:

```
FORMSORT B:CLIENTS
```

2. You will see the usual FormSort message on the screen, then one that SuperSort is sorting your data file.
3. When that is complete the message explains that SuperSort is now sorting the index file. For a small file the whole process is completed in half a minute or so.

That's certainly a lot quicker and easier than using the option for file maintenance in Datastar.

Sorting Data by New Key Fields

You can use copies of the CLIENTS form to produce two new forms: MAILSHOT and TELESALE. You will use FormGen to change the key fields. The key fields in the MAILSHOT form will be the STATE and ZIP fields, and in the TELESALE form, the LAST NAME and TEL AREA CODE.

Once you have the two new forms designed, you will use FormSort to produce the appropriate data and index files. You cannot name a new file as an output file in FormSort unless you have a definition file of that name (such as TELESALE.DEF and MAILSHOT.DEF).

Step-by-step procedure

Here's how to do it:

1. At the prompt type **DIR** to make sure that the CLIENTS form is on disk in the current drive (if not, change the logged drive).

2. Then type:

    For CP/M users: `PIP MAILSHOT.DEF=CLIENTS.DEF`
    For MS-DOS users: `COPY CLIENTS.DEF MAILSHOT.DEF`

3. Then do the same to make a copy of CLIENTS called TEL-ESALE:

    `PIP TELESALE.DEF=CLIENTS.DEF`
or   `COPY CLIENTS.DEF TELESALE.DEF`

4. Now you must call up the first of your new forms in FormGen so that you can change the key field. Assume in this exercise that your programs are on disk in drive A and your data on disk in drive B (and that you are logged on to drive B). If necessary, pencil in any changes in drive names to suit your own system. Next to the prompt type:

    `A:FORMGEN MAILSHOT`

    and the form will appear. Since this is an exact copy of the CLIENTS form, you will see the asterisks (indicating key field status) in field 001, the CLIENT NUMBER.

5. You can remove key field status from field 001 by moving the cursor into the field (use ^D) and pressing ^K.

6. Now move (using ^F) to the STATE field and press ^K to make this the new primary key for the MAILSHOT form.

7. To have the zip codes listed in numerical order within each state, move to the ZIP field and press ^K to make this the secondary Key.

8. You should exit from the form by typing ^CB, which will take you back to the **A>** prompt.

9. Now you can modify the other new form. At the prompt type:

A:FORMGEN TELESALE

10. Remove key field status from the CLIENT NUMBER, as before, and make the TEL AREA CODE the primary Key.

11. To make LAST NAME a secondary Key, move to LAST NAME and press ˆK once more.

12. The next stage is to sort the original CLIENTS data to produce two new data files. At the prompt type:

A:FORMSORT MAILSHOT/D CLIENTS

The **/D** causes FormSort to produce a data file only. Since you will be using these CLIENTS sister files only for reports, you do not need index files.

13. When you press **Return** the FormSort sorting message will appear, then various additional messages as the data file is sorted.

14. When the prompt reappears, type **DIR**. You should see the new files MAILSHOT.DEF and MAILSHOT.DTA on the list.

15. Repeat the process for TELESALE; first sort by typing:

A:FORMSORT TELESALE/D CLIENTS

16. Check the directory to see that the new files are listed.

NOTE: In the FormSort command line you put the *output* file name first (TELESALE) and the input file name (CLIENTS) second. You must remember this when you come to do your own file copies.

If you designed an application for this technique that necessitated using the new versions of the files as proper DataStar files, you would have to remember that any updating must be done on the main file, CLIENTS. When updating was complete you would have to repeat the sort routines to produce updated versions of the sister files and then FormSort these to produce updated index files.

FormSort Options

You have just implemented one of the options in FormSort—the **/D**, which produced a data file only. There is the equivalent option for producing index files only— **/N**. You might use this option when, for whatever reason, your data file and index files no longer match, and you need to create a new Index file from the changed data file.

In recent versions of FormSort you can also specify the key or keys by which to sort the file in the command line. These keys for sorting do not have to be key fields in the data file. For example:

```
FORMSORT TELESALE/D CLIENTS KEY=''TEL AREA CODE'',''LAST NAME''
```

will produce the same result as you achieved when you copied the CLIENTS form to create the new TELESALE form with FormGen and then sorted the data by the two new key fields, TEL AREA CODE and LAST NAME.

Although you don't have to actually change the key fields in the copies of your original CLIENTS form, you must still make the copy of the .DEF file, with the name of the new data file you wish to create with FormSort. In this example, you would copy CLIENTS.DEF to produce TELESALE.DEF *before* you typed the FormSort command line (otherwise you would get an error message saying that the TELESALE file could not be found).

You can specify as many Keys as you like in the command line, and you can use either the field numbers or the field names. Don't forget the quotes around the field names.

REPORTSTAR FOR REPORTS AND SUMMARIES

ReportStar is designed to be used with the form definition files and data files you have created with DataStar, giving you considerable control over the format of the output. You can generate anything from a simple list to a complex report, even using data from several different input files. You have already used the built-in sorting routine, FormSort.

In Part 1 you used RGEN to create a Quick Report. Now you will learn how to produce a customized report using REDIT. If you have enough space on your tutorial disk, copy the files REDIT.COM and REMSGS.OVR, otherwise use your ReportStar master working disk, instead of your tutorial disk, to boot up. Hard disk users should copy the files REDIT.COM and RESMSGS.OVR from the master working disk into the tutorial area on the hard disk.

Quick Reports

You will start by producing two quick reports from the new data files you have just created with FormSort. You may remember how you did this in the InfoStar tutorial in Part One.

Step-by-step procedure

1. First you must boot up from the ReportStar working disk in drive A, change logged disk drive to B, and then call up RGEN, the Quick Report program in ReportStar.

2. At the B> prompt type:

```
A:RGEN MAILSHOT
```

3. Now when the screen fills with the quick report program, you will see that you have three .DEF files to choose from. Notice that the cursor is flashing next to the name MAIL-SHOT; just press **Return** to select it.

4. The next screen shows you the field names from the Mail-shot form. To select the headings for the columns on the report you are going to produce, you must identify the fields you want by typing in enough characters to make the selection unique.

    For example, if you want data listed under columns headed TITLE, LAST NAME, STATE, and ZIP CODE, you would have to type **TI** to identify TITLE, **LA** for LAST NAME, **STA** for STATE and **Z** for ZIP CODE. Go ahead and do that now. (You can also use the cursor control keys to move the cursor to the desired field name, if you prefer).

5. When you have selected your four column headings, just press ^**C** to say you have finished, and then **Return** to accept the default to run the report.

6. Then accept defaults (by pressing **Return**) for the next two queries, standard error reporting and disk file output.

7. Make sure your printer is online, either type in the date or press **Return** to bypass each of the three date fields, and the report will print out.

8. Before the report starts printing you will see its format on the screen: if it does not contain the information you had intended you can press **Return**, and you will be asked if

---

FIGURE 10–2   Sample MAILSHOT Report

```
         MAILSHOT REPORT
           10/01/85

     TITLE  LAST NAME      STATE  ZIP
     Mr     Bowman         CO     80224

     Mrs    Jones          CT     06040

     Ms     Smith          CT     06453

     Mrs    James          RI     02906

     Ms     Dyer           VA     22151
```

---

you want to abandon the report. If you do, type **Y**, if not, type **N**.

9. Now try the same kind of thing on your own, using the TELESALE data to produce a report with the headings TITLE, LAST NAME, CITY, TEL AREA CODE, and TEL NUMBER. See Figures 10–2 and 10–3 for comparison.

Summaries

You may find it very useful to produce summaries from the reports you have created with the Reportstar Quick Report program, to show, for example, how many of your clients live in each telephone area code region, or how many in each state. You can do this as an extension of your Quick Report.

Step-by-step procedure

1. To erase the original Quick Reports, type:

FIGURE 10–3   Sample TELESALE Report

```
              TELESALE REPORT
                 10/01/85

 TITLE  LAST NAME    CITY              TEL AREA CODE   TEL NUMBER
 Mrs    Jones        Manchester        203             6493766
 Ms     Smith        New Haven         203             5244455
 Mr     Bowman       Denver            303             9978899
 Mrs    James        Providence        401             2719911
 Ms     Dyer         Springfield       703             2346677
```

> For CP/M users: ERA MAILSHOT.RPT
> For MS-DOS users: DEL MAILSHOT.RPT

2. At the B> prompt type:

A:RGEN MAILSHOT

3. Now select the column headings, as before; Type **TI** and return to select TITLE, then **LA**, **STA**, and **Z** to choose the headings TITLE, LAST NAME, STATE and ZIP. Or, you can use the cursor control keys.

4. So far this is the same as the report you prepared before; now press **^N** to move to the next ReportStar screen and look at the new options listed.

5. The first query asks whether you want a record count by STATE. Type **Y** over the default **N**. Next you will be asked the same for ZIP CODE type **N** to say no.

6. The rest of the options are not required, so type **^C** to say you are finished and accept the default to run the report.

7. Make sure your printer is online, and accept the various defaults; as before, enter or bypass the date fields, and your report will print.

   Now you will have the same kind of list as before, but each time there is a change in STATE you will see a Summary for STATE giving the number of clients in each state (see Figures 10–4 and 10–5). Notice that the list is in ZIP CODE order within each STATE (this is because you made ZIP the secondary key field).

8. Try the same thing now with the TELESALE form (don't forget first to use DEL or ERA on the first TELESALE.RPT). Produce a list under the same headings as last time, with a summary for each telephone area code. You will find that the clients are listed in alphabetical order of LAST NAME, within each telephone area code, because LAST NAME is the secondary key field in the TELESALE form.

REDIT for producing summaries only

Once your list of clients has grown into the hundreds or thousands, you may like to have summaries showing only the number of clients in each state or telephone area code, without the full

---

FIGURE 10–4   Sample MAILSHOT Report with Summaries

```
                    MAILSHOT REPORT
                       10/01/85


STATE = CO

        TITLE  LAST NAME        STATE  ZIP
        Mr     Bowman           CO     80224

Summary for STATE (Count = 1):


STATE = CT

        TITLE  LAST NAME        STATE  ZIP
        Mrs    Jones            CT     06040
        Ms     Smith            CT     06453

Summary for STATE (Count = 2):


STATE = RI

        TITLE  LAST NAME        STATE  ZIP
        Mrs    James            RI     02906

Summary for STATE (Count = 1):


STATE = VA

        TITLE  LAST NAME        STATE  ZIP
        Ms     Dyer             VA     22151

Summary for STATE (Count = 1):
```

---

list of names. You can do this in ReportStar using the custom report program, REDIT.

Step-by-step procedure

1. Next to the B> prompt type:

A:REDIT MAILSHOT

2. When the first screen shows that you are in the MAILSHOT

FIGURE 10–5 Sample TELESALE Report with Summaries

TELESALE REPORT
10/01/85

TEL AREA CODE = 203

LAST NAME	CITY	TEL AREA CODE	TEL NUMBER
Jones	Manchester	203	6493766
Smith	New Haven	203	5244455

Summary for TEL AREA CODE (Count = 2):

TEL AREA CODE = 303

LAST NAME	CITY	TEL AREA CODE	TEL NUMBER
Bowman	Denver	303	9978899

Summary for TEL AREA CODE (Count = 1):

TEL AREA CODE = 401

LAST NAME	CITY	TEL AREA CODE	TEL NUMBER
James	Providence	401	2719911

Summary for TEL AREA CODE (Count = 1):

TEL AREA CODE = 703

LAST NAME	CITY	TEL AREA CODE	TEL NUMBER
Dyer	Springfield	703	2346677

Summary for TEL AREA CODE (Count = 1):

Summary for REPORT (Count = 5):

report, type ^C to say you are ending the definition process (you have already defined the form in RGEN).

3. Now you will see the form as it appeared on the screen when your first report was printing. Type ^S to move the cursor into column 1—the Print Control Column.

4. You will see a new help screen appear. Notice that it has an entry for summaries only—a colon :.

FIGURE 10-6 MAILSHOT Report of
Summaries Only

MAILSHOT REPORT
10/02/85

STATE = CO
Summary for STATE (Count = 1):

STATE = CT
Summary for STATE (Count = 2):

STATE = RI
Summary for STATE (Count = 1):

STATE = VA
Summary for STATE (Count = 1):

Use ^X to move the cursor down column 1 until you reach the line of headings (TITLE, LAST NAME, etc.). Now type a : in column 1.

5. The cursor will now be flashing in the line containing the field positions—the dashed lines—type a :.

6. Now the cursor is in a blank line that was inserted to improve the spacing; you do not need this space for a summaries only report, so press ^Y to delete it.

7. Now type ^C to say you have finished editing, then type **R** to run the report. There will be a few seconds delay; don't panic). Make sure your printer is online, accept the two defaults by pressing **Return**, enter or bypass the date, and your report will print.

Now you will have a list of states, with a summary of the number of clients in each state printed directly underneath, without the list of names. Useful, isn't it?

The colon in column 1 instructs ReportStar not to print that line in the report (which would otherwise be the list of names). You should go ahead and do the same for your telephone area code form, so that you remember the technique; as in all these things, practice makes perfect (see Figures 10–6 and 10–7).

FIGURE 10–7 TELESALE Report of Summaries Only

```
              TELESALE REPORT
                 10/02/85


TEL AREA CODE = 203
Summary for TEL AREA CODE (Count = 2):

TEL AREA CODE = 303
Summary for TEL AREA CODE (Count = 1):

TEL AREA CODE = 401
Summary for TEL AREA CODE (Count = 1):

TEL AREA CODE = 703
Summary for TEL AREA CODE (Count = 1):

Summary for REPORT (Count = 5):
```

Summaries for numeric fields

Look now at the PRICELST form and produce a summary showing the *value of stock* by stock code.

In this exercise you will repeat all the procedures required for copying and changing data files and forms, adding new fields, sorting the new data, and producing the report. First you will copy the three PRICELST files, then go back into FormGen to add a couple of fields to your new form, then sort the new data with FormSort, and finally produce the STOCKLST report.

You will learn some new REDIT techniques in this exercise— how to use the conditional statement INCLUDE IF and how to produce totals of numeric fields.

Step-by-step procedure

1. At the B> prompt type your appropriate copying command (either **PIP** or **COPY**) to make copies of the three PRICELST files (.DEF, .DTA, and .NDX) to create the three new Stocklst files.

2. When the copies are complete, type:

   A:FORMGEN STOCKLST

3. When the STOCKLST form appears on the screen, move

the cursor to a position a few spaces past the PRICE field. Type in a new field name, **QUANTITY**, press the **Space Bar** twice to create spaces, then type ^Q three times to make the field. Then after another two spaces, type the name **VALUE** and press ^Q seven times for the field.

4. Now move the cursor into the field QUANTITY (check the status line to make sure you are in field 005) and press ^R to enter the definition process.

5. You need to specify that QUANTITY should be right justified and padded with blanks; then in the edit mask, under content control, that only numbers may be entered. (If you can't remember how to do this, look back to Chapter 9 at the discussion on FORMGEN). All the rest are defaults.

6. Now type ^F to move into the VALUE field. Press ^R, move through the first few prompts accepting the defaults (by pressing **Return**) and when you reach the prompt Field derived? type **Y**.

7. Then you must type **C** to indicate that the field will be calculated. Enter the following (VALUE is already entered):

VALUE=PRICE*QUANTITY

8. Continue accepting defaults until you reach the edit mask prompt, where you should type **Y**. In entry control, move the cursor with ^D to the fifth position (out of the seven you have allowed) and press the period to indicate that this is where you want a decimal point.

9. Press **Return** to go on to content control, and enter **9** four times followed by a period and **9** twice:

VALUE ____.__   Entry Control
VALUE 9999.99   Content Control

This means that when you enter a dollars and cents amount in this field, the cursor will start at the decimal point for entry of the numeric data.

10. Type ^CB to say the form is finished and to return to the B> prompt.

That finishes the form design. Now you must sort the

STOCKLST data so that it fits the new form, after which you will call up DataStar and enter a few quantity details (and see the values calculated automatically).

11. At the B> prompt type:

A:FORMSORT STOCKLST

12. As soon as the sort is complete, type:

A:DATASTAR STOCKLST

When the form appears, just press the **Space Bar** for Add mode, use **Return** to bypass the first four fields and reach the QUANTITY.

13. Enter **10**, then press ^**B** to say the record is finished. You will see the VALUE field fill in automatically.

14. Press **Return** to file the data and to go on to the next record.

15. Fill in quantities for the first 12 records (all the Finesse design range), pressing ^**B** after each quantity.

16. When you have finished, press ^**EE** to exit back to the B> prompt (or ^**EEC** if you have version 1.0 or earlier).

17. At the B> prompt type:

A:FORMSORT STOCKLST

to sort the updated data.

18. Now you are ready to prepare a quick report with RGEN that you will modify with REDIT (but all in one pass this time). At the B> prompt type:

A:RGEN STOCKLST

At the first screen you will see the cursor flashing next to STOCKLST; just press **Return** to accept it.

19. Now you will have the list of fields to choose from: select CODE, PRICE, QUANTITY, and VALUE. Press ^**N** to go to the next screen.

20. This time you should press **Return** to bypass the prompts for record count by code and page, and enter **Y** for count by report. Then keep pressing **Return** until the cursor is

in the bottom right-hand corner of the block, and enter **T** to say you want a total for value for the report.

21. Press **^C** to end. When the next screen comes up *don't* accept the default to run the report. Instead type **F**, which will save the form and take you straight into REDIT to edit it.

22. Now you will have the first edit screen. Just press **Return** to accept defaults for all the items listed until the next screen appears with the INCLUDE IF prompt.

23. Next to the prompt type:

INCLUDE IF **VALUE>0.00**

thus excluding all records with 0.00 (or nothing) entered in VALUE. When you have done that, press **Return** (if you forget to press **Return**, the INCLUDE IF statement will not be saved).

24. Then type **^C** to end the definition process and **^C** again to accept the form output as it appears on the screen.

25. Now type **R** to run the report, make sure your printer is online, accept the defaults for error reporting etc., enter or bypass the date, and the report will run.

You will see from the report that you have a summary for the report that tells you how many stock lines you have listed, and a total stock value, as requested. If you want to try out this new expertise, erase the report (**DEL** or **ERA** STOCKLST.RPT) and start again. This time you could ask for a total for quantity in stock as well (see Figure 10–8).

You can see that it would be possible to set up a proper inventory system using FormGen, DataStar and ReportStar. You took a short cut by copying the PRICELST form, but you could try working out the format for a real inventory if you have a need for such a program. In the transaction processing discussion in the next chapter, you will see how to update the quantity in stock automatically as orders are processed and invoices produced.

You probably already appreciate the ease of handling the ReportStar program. You should practice preparing further reports, perhaps including data from more than one data file, and you should try using the editing facilities provided to enhance the appearance of the output. You may find it easier to do the editing in WordStar.

FIGURE 10–8   Report Developed with INCLUDE IF Statement

STOCKLST REPORT
10/03/85

CODE	PRICE	QUANTITY	VALUE $
F1/10010	$95.00	1	95.00
F1/10020	$175.00	1	175.00
F1/10030	$75.00	1	75.00
F1/10040	$155.00	1	155.00
F1/10050	$345.00	1	345.00
F2/10010	$120.00	2	240.00
F2/10020	$195.00	2	390.00
F2/10030	$95.00	2	190.00
F2/10040	$190.00	2	380.00
F2/10050	$375.00	1	375.00
F3/10010	$140.00	1	140.00
F3/10020	$225.00	1	225.00
F3/10030	$135.00	1	135.00
F3/10040	$225.00	1	225.00
F4/10010	$175.00	1	175.00
F4/10020	$255.00	1	255.00
F4/10030	$125.00	1	125.00
F4/10040	$235.00	1	235.00

Summary for REPORT (Count = 18):
Total   3935.00

RESTRUCTURING DATABASE

It is quite common to find after you have been using a particular form for a while that you need to add in some extra fields and perhaps eliminate some which have become obsolete. As I mentioned earlier, it is possible (with recent versions of InfoStar) to make such changes in your database even after data has been entered. The Golden Rule is: Keep changes simple.

With earlier versions of InfoStar (or Datastar from pre-InfoStar days) you can achieve the same results, using a combination of MailMerge and FormSort (or SuperSort). You need to be quite experienced with these programs before you attempt it; there are detailed instructions in the MailMerge chapter in Part Two. Since you do not have the necessary programs, you can skip the rest of this chapter.

If you have InfoStar + (including the StarBurst program), you can run the data base restructuring routine from a StarBurst menu by typing **SB ISUTIL** next to the system prompt. The instructions that follow here describe the three steps that make up the database restructure process, and even if you have StarBurst, you should run through this exercise typing the instructions next to the system prompt, as shown. Once you are familiar with the details of the three stages, you will fully understand what is happening, should you decide in the future to restructure from the StarBurst menu.

As an example for this exercise you can modify a form that will be used in Chapter 11.

Stage 1: Modifying the Form in FormGen

You need to modify the CLIENTS form to include some additional fields for entry of the client's purchase order number (PON) and the order date.

Step-by-step procedure

1. First, make copies of the CLIENTS files and use the copies for the modification process:

```
COPY CLIENTS.DEF  CLIENTPO.DEF
COPY CLIENTS.DTA  CLIENTPO.DTA
```

2. There is one additional file you will need for the database restructure exercise: Before you go into FormGen to change the form design, you must make a copy of the .DEF file giving it the extension .OLD. The program uses this later to compare against your new form.

```
COPY CLIENTPO.DEF CLIENTPO.OLD
```

3. Next to the prompt type:

```
FORMGEN CLIENTPO
```

and the copy of the CLIENTS form will appear on the screen.

4. Move the cursor with ˆ**X** until it is outside the existing form, then type in the new fields:

```
CLIENT NUMBER: ****
TITLE: _____  INITS: _____  LAST NAME: _____


STREET: _____ CITY: _____
STATE:  __  ZIP: _____  TEL AREA CODE: _____  TEL NO: _____

CURRENT CLIENT PON: _____        CURRENT DATE: __/__/__
```

5. Note that the PON field is length 15 and that there are 3 date fields, each portion 2 blanks long and separated from each other by slashes.

   Now, with the cursor in the PON field (check the status line to ensure you are in field 011), press ^R and name the field as follows:

011/CLIENT PON

6. Run through the attributes, determing that the field is optional, right-justified, and padded with blanks. After accepting the default for the pad character, press ^C to end the definition of field 011.

7. Press ^F to move to the first of the date fields. Press ^R and enter the field name:

012/PO MONTH

   It is good practice to make all date fields unique. (You are likely to include the date in many different forms and reports and it would be easy to confuse them.) Hence use PO MONTH for the month field associated with the purchase order.

8. Assign the attributes to the field: make it optional, then accept defaults until you reach the edit mask, which you accept. Type **9** for the blanks in content control:

DATE: __/__/__ Entry Control
DATE: 99/__/__ Content Control

   This ensures that no alpha characters can be entered instead of numeric.

9. After accepting the default for record edit characters, move

the cursor with **^F** to the next date field. Enter the field name:

013/PO DAY

10. This time, when you get to the prompt:

Copy attributes of: /

you can enter 012 before the slash, and the field name, PO MONTH, will fill in automatically:

Copy attributes of: **012/PO MONTH**

11. Press **Return**, then **^CFR** to end definition of field 012, move on to the last date field, and start defining field 014.

12. Again, after entering the name, you can copy the attributes of field 012:

Field number/name	**014/PO YEAR**
Processing order	**014**
Copy attributes of:	**012/PO MONTH**

13. Finally, press **^C** to end the definition, then **^CB** to exit back to the operating system prompt.

That is the end of the first stage.

NOTE: There are certain changes that are not allowed in Database Restructure. You cannot add or delete a key field. Since you have always set Record edit characters to **N**, you cannot change the attributes of any field associated with: intermediate fields, derived fields (calculated or file), or allowing operator entry. Apart from these restrictions, you must always ensure that all the fields in the form are named, otherwise you will see an error message during DBR or DBM.

Stage 2: Database Reorganization

The database reorganization program (DBR) is used to update any files that are affected by the changes you have made to your CLIENTPO form in FormGen. So far you have not created any other definition files or report files that reference the CLIENTPO form, so you will not need to implement Stage 2 in this example.

If you have StarBurst, remember this point when you come to run the database restructure program from the StarBurst menu. You will select option 1 from menu 2 to modify your form, then skip option 2, which is for database reorganization, and go straight on to option 3 (described next in stage 3 here).

Stage 3: Database Modification

The form you have modified and the data file associated with it will now be reordered to match the new form design. You have already copied the CLIENTPO datafile, so go ahead and run DBM.

Step-by-step procedure

1. Next to the prompt type:

    DBM CLIENTPO /D

2. Note the /D, which saves the reordered data file on disk (otherwise it would go to the printer, and if your printer is not online, the computer will hang up).
3. After the messages scroll on the screen, showing that the process is proceeding satisfactorily, you will be returned to the prompt.
4. That is the end of your data base restructuring; now you should sort the datafile with FormSort. Next to the prompt type:

    FORMSORT CLIENTPO

and your data will be sorted and a new index file produced.

Finally, call up the new file in DataStar and enter some dates and data in PON. You can use this file as a normal DataStar file or incorporate data into Reports in ReportStar, as discussed in Chapter 11.

Take a break now and look back over the first two InfoStar chapters before tackling Chapter 11. It will call on all the skills you have learned so far, and more!

11

InfoStar III: Transaction Processing

The Transaction Process
Transaction Files
Reference Files
Control Breaks
Designing the Report Files
Running the Reports
Designing Your Own Reports

The term *transaction processing* is specialist computer terminology for online processing as distinct from *batch processing*. There is a very simple example which demonstrates clearly the difference between these two types of data processing. In the old days, if you had $100 in your bank checking account, you could go to three different branches of your bank and withdraw $100 from each without getting caught. The bank records were batch processed, so it was not until the end of the day's business, when the batch was run and the previous day's records were updated, that it was found that you were $200 overdrawn. Today, with the advent of online processing in banks, as soon as you withdraw the first $100 your account record is updated, showing a zero balance, and you would not be allowed to cash any further checks at other bank branches. *Online processing* is just another name for transaction processing.

This tutorial will show you how to build up your own transaction processes, continuing with the forms and files used in the two previous InfoStar tutorials.

Although there is no mention of transaction processing in the manual supplied with version 1.0 of InfoStar, the examples in this tutorial will run under CP/M or MS-DOS, with versions 1.0 or 1.6 of InfoStar (or InfoStar +). I will be giving the instructions for the recent versions of the programs, but you can refer back to Chapter 9 for differences in FormGen prompts, and to your InfoStar manual for differences in Redit or ReportStar prompts or messages. There is one major problem for 1.0 users; you do not have the database restructure program, so it is not a simple matter to modify the various files that you create to run a transaction process (and you can soon build up a suite of six or more files, all interdependent). In addition, there is a "bug" relating to large Index Files: contact your MicroPro dealer for a "patch" to cure this problem.

To work through the tutorial that follows, you need all the InfoStar programs on disk drive A (on a floppy disk system; drive C on the hard disk) and all the forms you created in the last two tutorials on drive B, or equivalent. Since the earlier versions of InfoStar do not have the database restructure feature, those of you with these programs will need to copy the CLIENTS form, and add the extra fields as shown at the end of Chapter 10 to create CLIENTPO files.

THE TRANSACTION PROCESS

Having worked through the first two InfoStar tutorials, you are familiar with the concept of a master form being fed information from slave files. The QUOTES form read in its clients' names and addresses from the CLIENTS file and the details about the furniture items from PRICELST. Once the QUOTES record was complete, it was saved and could be printed directly from DataStar and handed to the client. Now, if this client should decide to purchase the items listed in the quote, he or she would call or send in a purchase order, then you would have to enter the details of the order for your dispatch department, and prepare the invoice for the client; you or a colleague would need to note the codes and quantities of items sold and remember to debit the inventory records accordingly. This is a typical example of a transaction process.

In this tutorial you will learn how to set up the required files in such a way that you need only enter the purchase order details, then run a report that will print your invoices and automatically update your inventory. At the same time as the report is run, you can have other information sent to output files and use these to generate additional reports, for example, to tell you which items' stock levels have fallen below a certain safety level in your inventory, and how many to reorder; or to show your turnover for the period, the total sales tax collected, and a list of invoices sent out, with dates and amounts due.

This chapter explains the central examples in great detail so you will end up with a small working system. Remember, however, that these are training exercises; you should use them to master the design process, then produce the customized forms you need for your own business applications. I will point out any areas that may need some safeguards built in, especially when the person who designed the transaction processing system is not going to be the person running it on a day-to-day basis. Because this is such an interactive process, it is not possible to make changes to the individual forms without, potentially, affecting every other form in the process. This may become obvious to the designer, but not necessarily to the person running the system.

TRANSACTION FILES

The way that the transaction process will work on your example files is shown in Figure 11–1. The central box contains the Transact Report, which is the report you will design to produce the format for the printed invoices. You can see what happens when the report is run: information is read in from the reference databases, CLIENTPOR and INVENTRY, the invoices are printed, the inventory file is updated, and an output datafile (INVDATA) is created to accept information about each invoice.

When you run Transact Report, the vital information that will drive the whole transaction process is the list of current purchase orders—POLIST—so this special reference file is called the transaction file. Note that POLIST also uses STATELST and INVENTRY as slave forms. The individual purchase orders you enter into POLIST are read sequentially from the file when the Transact Report is run; hence the transaction file (POLIST) is said to *drive* the transaction process. As soon as all the POLIST data has been read in and the invoices printed, the report is terminated. When you run the second report, Turnover, the output data file from Transact, INVDATA.DTA, becomes the transaction file which

FIGURE 11-1   Transaction Processing Flowchart

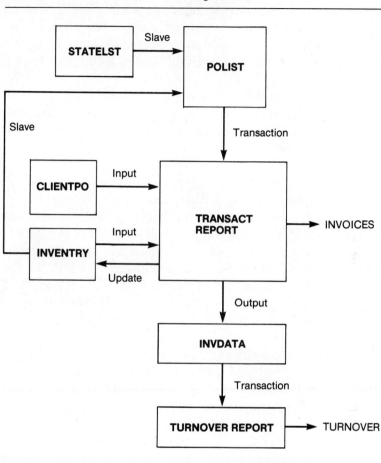

drives the Turnover Report, producing a printed list showing your turnover for the period and the amount of sales tax collected.

In other words, transaction files contain the data read sequentially when the report is run, thus driving the transaction process until the last bit of data has been read. It's a little like the MailMerge process, where merge printing will continue until all the records in the data file have been read and the last letter printed.

REFERENCE FILES

If you refer to Figure 11-1 you can identify the various types of reference files described in detail later (in addition to the transaction files already discussed). Notice that CLIENTPO is used for input to Transact only, while INVENTRY is used for input to the report, receives output data from Transact when updated, and also acts as a DataStar slave file, supplying information on each furniture item to POLIST when the purchase orders are first entered.

The reference files in transaction processing serve a similar purpose to the slave files in DataStar; however, as already mentioned, they can be used for input, output, or both. In the example you will develop, the CLIENTPO file will be used for input only—that is, it will be a reference file that supplies the name and address information for each invoice when you run the report. The Inventory file will be used both for input and output—that is, it will supply inventory information (this time to do with quantities in stock of the furniture items) when the report is run, and it will also receive output data as the inventory records are updated. You will also create the output file, INVDATA, to collect certain information about each invoice. As far as the Transact Report is concerned, this is an output file only, though you know that it will subsequently act as the transaction file to drive the Turnover Report.

The reference files (CLIENTPO, POLIST, and INVENTRY) are designed and created in FormGen and data is entered into them using DataStar. The Report files (Transact and Turnover) are designed in the custom report program, REDIT, and data is read into them during the transaction process. Transact and Turnover produce the Invoices and Turnover Reports, respectively. Sometimes it is convenient to use the Quick Report program, RGEN, to produce printed reports from the output files; you will learn about this at the appropriate point later in the tutorial.

The Scenario

This chapter continues with the furniture scenario developed in the last two chapters. When purchase orders are received from clients who have previously received quotes, you will find their data in the CLIENTPO file (since this was copied from CLIENTS); if the customers don't give you their CLIENT NUMBER (which is the key field) you can use the Edit Scan Mask mode to select them by their LAST NAME, for example. When new clients shop, you must add them to your CLIENTPO file and enter the details of their purchase order number and date. If a client does not give you a purchase order number, you can either leave it out of the form altogether, or invent one. You should at least enter the date for the current order.

The normal sequence each day would be as follows:

1. Update the CLIENTPO file.
2. Enter the purchase orders into POLIST.
3. Run the Transact Report to produce invoices.
4. Run the Turnover Report to see your stock turnover for the day.
5. Have a look at the INVENTRY data to note that it has been updated.

Now that you have an overview of the transaction process, you must work through the design of all the forms. Start with the FormGen designs of the reference files.

The STATELST Form

The STATELST datafile consists of only two fields—STATE and TAX RATE. The advantage of having this information in a slave file is the ease of updating it whenever there is a change in the level of tax for any one state. As soon as you enter the client's state into the STATE field on POLIST, the correct tax rate will be read in automatically.

To work through the exercises in this chapter, you must have a thorough understanding of DataStar: if not, go back to Chapters 9 and 10.

Step-by-step procedure

Go ahead and design this simple form:

1. Next to the prompt type **FORMGEN STATELST** and rotate the help Screen by typing ^J.
2. Enter the two fields and their field names as shown:

STATE: **   TAX RATE % _____

Note that STATE has a length of two and is the key field.

3. After pressing ^K, while the cursor is still in the field, you should press ^R to use the definition procedure: name the field and assign the attributes that say that the field is re-

---

FIGURE 11–2 The INVENTRY Form Design

```
CODE: ********  DESCRIPTION: ------------------------------
SIZE: ----      PRICE: -------

QTY IN STOCK: ----          VALUE OF STOCK: --------

DATE LAST UPDATED: __/__/__ STOCK LEVEL REQUIRED: ----
```

---

quired, and in the content control of edit mask, insert an uppercase **C** in each position to ensure that the entry of STATE details will be in uppercase:

```
            STATE: __          Entry Control
            STATE: CC          Content Control
```

4. Press **^CFR** to end the definition of STATE and move on to the TAX RATE field. Name it, then set the attributes to say the field is required, right-justified, and padded with blanks. In edit mask, set the decimal point in entry control, and the decimal point and a **9** in each blank in content control:

```
        TAX RATE % __.__      Entry Control
        TAX RATE % 99.99      Content Control
```

5. Exit from the form back to the operating system or chain DataStar and enter the details of tax rate for each STATE.

If you had any trouble at all with this very simple form, you had better look back over the tutorial in Chapter 9. In order to succeed with the transaction processing examples, you will need reasonable expertise in FormGen and DataStar, as well as ReportStar. See Appendix B for full FormGen listings.

STATELST is one slave file for POLIST; the other is INVENTRY. Go on now to design INVENTRY.

The INVENTRY Form

Figure 11–2 shows the INVENTRY form design. This is basically the PRICELST form with some extra fields. If you like, you can have some more practice with database restructuring, following the instructions at the end of Chapter 10 to convert PRICELST into INVENTRY. This is especially worthwhile if you are following this tutorial as an exercise and not planning to enter your own inventory data; then you will wish to copy over the PRICELST data file and add the information to the extra fields in DataStar. If you are going to use this tutorial as an outline to enter your own inventory data, you can design a new form from scratch, adjusting field names, lengths, and attributes to suit your own specific needs.

The first four INVENTRY fields provide data to the POLIST form as purchase order details are entered each day. The initial stock details are entered by you in DataStar. When the Transact Report is run, the values are first read into Transact, and then the updated stock values are read back out to INVENTRY, leaving the correct stock levels ready for the next run or for you to use in the meantime. Hence, INVENTRY is a slave file to POLIST, and both an input and an update file to Transact Report.

The last field, STOCK LEVEL REQUIRED, is entered by you in DataStar and can be used to provide the calculation of items to be reordered when the quantity in stock falls below a preset level.

Following are very abbreviated instructions for assigning attributes. If you have any difficulty, read through the appropriate sections in Chapter 9.

Step-by-step procedure

1. Go through each field in turn, naming it and assigning the appropriate attributes, as detailed here.
2. Note that CODE has a length of eight, is the key field, is required, and the content control mask should have an uppercase **C** in the first position.
3. The DESCRIPTION field has a length of 35 and is required.
4. The SIZE field has a length of four, is required, should be right-justified, padded with blanks, and each blank in the content control mask should contain a 9 to ensure numeric entry only.
5. Make PRICE have a length of seven, be required, right-justified, padded with blanks, floating dollar sign, decimal point in entry control, and have a 9 for each blank except the decimal point in content control.

FIGURE 11-3 The INVDATA Form Design

```
DATE: __/__/__     INVOICE NO: ****    TOTAL PRICE: _____

TAX RATE: _____
```

```
        PRICE: ____.__      Entry Control
        PRICE: 9999.99      Content Control
```

6. QTY IN STOCK has a length of three, is required, right-justified, padded with blanks, and should contain numerals only.

7. VALUE OF STOCK has a length of eight, is calculated (enter **VAL OF STOCK=QTY IN STOCK*PRICE**), right-justified, padded with blanks, floating dollar sign and the edit mask should be the same as for PRICE.

8. DATE LAST UPDATED is three fields. Each has a length of two, separated by slashes, as shown. Fields should be named INV MONTH, INV DAY, and INV YEAR, respectively. All are required and should contain numeric data only.

9. STOCK LEVEL REQUIRED has a length of 3, is required, right-justified, padded with blanks, and numeric data only.

That completes the form. Either exit from FormGen back to the operating system or chain DataStar and enter some data. If you have copied the PRICELST data, you will need to use one of the Scan modes to run through the file, entering data into the additional fields as you go. If you are using the form for your own inventory information, enter some items now.

The INVDATA Form

Invdata is an Output file only when the Transact Report is run, but can be used subsequently as the input transaction file to drive one or more additional reports. In this tutorial you will use it later to drive the Turnover Report.

As Figure 11-3 shows, this is another very simple form design.

Step-by-step procedure

1. DATE is defined as usual, but the names should be INVDATA MONTH, INVDATA DAY, and INVDATA YEAR.

2. INVOICE NO has a length of four and is the key field. It should be right-justified and padded with blanks; no other attributes are needed.

3. TOTAL PRICE has a length of eight, right-justified, padded with blanks and decimal points aligned in edit mask, and should contain numeric data only.

4. TAX RATE has a length of five, is right-justified, padded with blanks and decimal points aligned in edit mask, and should contain numeric data only.

5. Exit from the form back to the operating system. The data will be entered as output during the running of the Transact Report, so you do not need to chain DataStar.

You will see later how to specify the correct attributes in RE-DIT to cause data to be output from Transact to an external file, and how this output datafile is used subsequently as input to drive the Turnover Report.

The POLIST Form

Finally, you must design the file which drives the Transact Report—POLIST. It must be set up as a master form, with index fields to its two slave files, STATELST and INVENTRY, and derived fields to hold the data from these slave data files. See Appendix B for full listings of all the reference files.

The POLIST data file is the Transaction file that drives the Transact Report. It contains the data for each day's purchase orders. At the end of each run you would erase its contents, so that you start each day with an empty file.

There is always a problem in designing a form to allow for entry of multiple items when you cannot know in advance whether there will be one item ordered or dozens, as occurs with purchase orders. You can see that if you designed the form allowing many lines for items to be entered (as you did, for example, in the QUOTES form) then you would have an awful lot of blank space when some orders have only one or two items.

By designing the form as shown in Figure 11–4, it doesn't matter whether your client orders one item or a hundred: each item on the purchase order is entered into the form individually and saved. The items are identified as all belonging to one order by PO REF, the primary key field, and are numbered consecutively in the ITEM NO field, the secondary key. So you would number

FIGURE 11–4 The POLIST Form Design

```
PO REF: ***  ITEM NO: **  CODE: _____    QUANTITY: _

DESCRIPTION: _____

UNIT PRICE: _____        TOTAL PRICE: _____

CLIENT NUMBER: ____    STATE: __    TAX RATE % _____
```

the first PO for the day PO REF 1, and number the items ordered in the ITEM NO field for however many items were ordered. The next client's purchase order would be numbered PO REF 2, and the individual items numbered from 1, as before.

Note that the client's name and address are not read into POLIST; they are read directly into Transact when the Transact Report is run. However, you do need to know the CLIENT NUMBER, which you should have written on the actual purchase order when you entered the client's details into the CLIENTPO file.

Note that this form must have two index fields: CODE to link with INVENTRY and STATE to link with STATELST.

Step-by-step procedure

Here are the attributes:

1. Create PO REF with a length of three; it is the first key field, is required, right-justified, padded with blanks, and should contain numeric data only.

2. ITEM NO has a length of 2, is the secondary key, is required, right-justified, padded with blanks, and should contain numeric data only.

3. CODE has a length of eight, is required, verified as a file, the file name is INVENTRY, and in content control the first position should contain a C.

4. QUANTITY has a length of two, is required, right-justified, padded with blanks, and should contain numeric data only.

5. DESCRIPTION has a length of 35, is derived, verified as a file, index field is 003/CODE, and the item number in file (that is in the external file, INVENTRY) is 001. Press ^CFR as no other attributes are needed.

6. UNIT PRICE has a length of seven, is derived, verified as a file, index field 003/CODE, and the item number in file is 003. Press ^**CFR**.

7. TOTAL PRICE has a length of seven, is derived, calculated (**N, TOTAL PRICE = UNIT PRICE*QUANTITY**), is right-justified, padded with blanks, floating dollar sign, decimal point in entry control, decimal point, and 9 in each blank in content control.

8. CLIENT NUMBER has a length of four, is required, right-justified, padded with zeros, and should contain numeric data only.

9. STATE has a length of two, is required, verified as a file, STATELST, and in content control **CC** should be entered to ensure that only uppercase data is stored.

10. TAX RATE % has a length of five, is right-justified, padded with blanks, derived, verified as a file, index field 009/ STATE, and the item number in file 002 (in STATELST). No other attributes required.

11. Now you have finished the form design. Exit from Form-Gen and chain DataStar (assuming you have data in the slave files). Fill in some purchase order details for six or so clients and make sure that the file is functioning correctly.

You will find it quite quick to enter the items after the first entry; the PO REF will remain the same for each client, so you can press ^**C** to copy it from the first entry; you will update the ITEM NO each time you enter another item; the DESCRIPTION and UNIT PRICE fields will fill in automatically from INVENTRY after you have entered the CODE, and the calculated TOTAL PRICE field will also fill in; the last three fields will remain the same after the first entry, so you can use ^**C** to copy the data from one form to the next. The first time you enter the STATE you will see the TAX RATE % fill in automatically from STATELST.

If you are interrupted while entering data and can't remember later where you stopped, you can scan in data order to find out.

Now that you have finished creating all the reference files in FormGen and DataStar, there is one more technical concept you need to understand before you go on to design the Transact and Turnover Reports in REDIT.

CONTROL BREAKS

The term *control break* is another specialist computer term that can best be described by a familiar example. In Chapter 10 you produced two additional forms and sets of data from the CLIENTS form and then produced Quick Reports on them. One listed the clients' names, etc., under the telephone area codes, called TELE-SALE, and the other listed them by state, called MAILSHOT.

Have a good look at the printout of the Reports (Figures 10–4 and 10–5). You are seeing *control breaks* in action. You set up the reports in such a way that all the time the STATE or TEL AREA CODE remained the same, the list of clients in those areas printed out: as soon as there was a *change* in TEL AREA CODE or STATE, the computer stopped printing out names and instead printed out the details of the next area code or state, followed by the appropriate list of clients for the new area. The point at which the computer recognizes that there has been a change in the specified field and interrupts the processing of data, is the control break. Now look at a detailed example on your screen.

Step-by-Step Procedure

1. If you still have MAILSHOT.RPT on disk, look at it now, in REDIT. If you don't have it on disk, run through the instructions in Chapter 10 again to create it from the CLIENTS file. You will examine the Quick Report produced by InfoStar in some detail, and in the process you will learn how to include control breaks in your own custom reports.

2. With MAILSHOT.RPT on disk in your currently logged disk drive, next to the prompt type:

`REDIT MAILSHOT`

3. The first screen just shows the name of the file you are using, Mailshot, so press ^C to display the next screen, which is the report layout.

4. Notice first that the two key fields you specified in Form-Gen (STATE and LAST NAME) have asterisks in them. In REDIT these assume a different meaning—they indicate the fields that define the control breaks.

5. Now look at the column on the extreme left of the screen—the print control column—and you will see that there is a 1 next to STATE and a period next to LAST NAME. The 1 identifies STATE as printing at control break 1 (that is, whenever the data in the STATE field of your data file *changes*); the period ensures that the heading LAST NAME does not print (you did not ask for a summary according to last name).

6. Move the cursor into the print control column by pressing ^S. You will see a new menu at the top of the screen, listing all the print control codes. You may remember that you used a colon (:) when you wished to suppress the printing of the data lines and produce *summaries only* from your files in Chapter 10.

7. Use ^D to move back into the form. Notice the change in the menu again. Now move the cursor into the STATE field and press ^R. You will get a list of field definitions similar to those in FormGen.

8. Run through them by pressing **Return** and notice the attributes that have been assigned. You will see that STATE has a control break status of 001.

9. When you have cycled through the list, use ^F to move into the LAST NAME field and press ^R again; you will notice that LAST NAME has been assigned a control break status of 002. Since this was designated as a nonprinting line, and the LAST NAME was not used for summary purposes, the control break status has no significance for this report. However, it gives you a clue to how the status is assigned.

10. The rest of the form is fairly clear; the headings for the columns, which you selected during the RGEN quick report process, also print at control break 001. If there were a blank in the print control column next to the headings, they would print out every time the data fields were printed. If there were a P, the headings would print only once per page. Using 1 means that the headings will print out at the top of every new list of names under each new state.

The data fields have a blank in the print control column, meaning they should print always. The blank also defines the midpoint of the form. Everything above the midpoint concerns headings, the midpoint itself is where data prints out, and below the midpoint data can accumulate to produce counts, calculations, summaries, and totals.

The midpoint can be defined as nonprinting by using a colon instead of the blank, as you did with the MAIL-SHOT report when you wanted summaries only. By typing : in the print control column of both the datafield headings and the data line, printing of these lines was suppressed.

11. You should move the cursor into the summary for STATE field and look at the attributes that have been assigned. Then look at the Report summary at the bottom of the form. These are simple count routines implemented in the Quick Report when you answer **Y** to the prompt Record count by State?.

12. You will see that the calculation to produce the correct number of records counted at each control break is:

$$\text{C STATE=C STATE+1}$$

13. A control break in a summary field (in this case a count field) is significant because every time there is a change in the data for the STATE, the *counting register* is reset to zero. The very first time the data is filled in, the count starts at zero, so to get the calculation right for the first data item, you have to specify **COUNT=COUNT**+1 (as above for C STATE). When the next control break occurs, the counter is again set to zero. As you work through the other reports, you will use different examples, so this process will become really clear.

14. Press ˆC and **S** to save the form and exit.

You saw in this example that the primary key (assigned in FormGen) becomes control break 001 in REDIT, and that the secondary key becomes control break 002. If you look at the example in the InfoStar manual, you will see an example of three control breaks; you may have up to nine in all.

You have seen, also, that the characters in the print control column define when a line should print (or be nonprinting) and identify the control break levels of headings and datafields. It is clear from this example that the control break status of fields above the midpoint line affects when they print, while below the

TABLE 11–1 Impact of the Control Break Status of Fields

PRINT CONTROL COLUMN	REPORT LAYOUT SCREEN
R	Headings, etc., that should print once per report
P	Headings, etc., that should print once per page
1	
2	
3	
4	Headings, etc., that print at the appropriate control break
5	
6	(1 to 9)
7	
8	
9	
	Midpoint—Blank indicates detail line should always print
:	Midpoint—Colon indicates nonprinting detail line
9	
8	
7	
6	
5	Headings and data field calculations, summaries, and totals
4	
3	at appropriate control breaks (1 to 9)
2	
1	
R	Headings and report level datafield summaries and totals
P	Page footers

midpoint the status is significant in defining how and when counts, calculations, summaries, and totals are generated.

Table 11–1 summarizes these concepts.

From the MAILSHOT example, you will have noticed that, as long as the order shown in the table order is observed, you can have as many of each *type* of line as you like: you may have a report heading (R in the print control column), followed by another R line that inserts a blank line below the heading. Then you may have a page heading, with a blank line below it to improve the format on the printed report. The control break headings will have the appropriate number in the print control column and may have the same number against blank lines above and below, again to improve the final appearance.

You know enough now to go on to design the two reports, Transact and Turnover. By the time you have finished these, you will have covered the essentials of custom report design. Hopefully, you should be able to use these models to design your own custom reports and to produce the kind of transaction processing needed in your own particular business.

DESIGNING THE REPORT FILES

Designing custom reports is rather like designing the master form in FormGen. However, in addition to the assigning of various essential attributes to fields to ensure that forms are linked together correctly and that data from the reference files is read in as required, there is the added complexity of defining control break status.

Keep in mind when designing the custom report that it not only links with all the reference files, but it also becomes the printed report (in the case of your two reports, the invoices and the listing of current turnover figures). This will affect the way you lay out the form.

Remember, also, that although the design of the custom report is vital to the correct running of the transaction process, the process is *driven* by the transaction file—in the case of Transact this is POLIST, and for Turnover it is the Transact output file, INVDATA.

As soon as the report design is complete you want to run the report, so make sure that you have entered data into the three reference files (CLIENTPO, INVENTRY, and POLIST), and that you have *FormSorted the data files*: This is essential to running any report with control break fields. The key fields in each of your forms define the correct sorting order for each file, and these are related, in turn, to the control break status of various fields in your report.

The TRANSACT Report

When you run the Transact Report, it will call in the appropriate information from its reference files, produce the INVDATA output file, and last but not least, the printed invoices. The first phase in the process is to describe all the reference files that are called upon for data, are updated during the run, or receive output data.

The file description screen

Before you start the form design, you must enter the details about your reference files at the file description screen, starting with the transaction file, POLIST.

Step-by-step procedure

1. Call up the **REDIT** program, either by typing REDIT next to the system prompt or, if you have StarBurst, select option **2** from the InfoStar MAIN MENU, then **2** from the REPORTS MENU, to select Custom Report. Now you will see the file description screen.

2. The first line reads

> Enter the number of the next file to define or review.

   The 001 is already entered for you, so just press **Return** to accept it.

3. Next, enter the name of the associated definition (in this case, your transaction file name):

001/POLIST

4. Now there follows a whole set of prompts, for most of which you can accept the defaults.

```
On which disk drive is the definition file located? (-/A/B..)      -
Is the file going to be used for Input or Output? (I/O)            I
Access datafile in Sequence or as Reference file? (S/R)           S
Should the file be read in Index order? (Y/N)                     N
How large should the disk buffer be?                             008
Will the file include more than one volume? (Y/N)                 N
Will the datafile name(s) be entered at run time? (Y/N)          N
Enter the datafile name(s):
Disk drive: (?/-/A/B...) - File name: POLIST___.DTA  Change
disks? (Y/N) N

Enter the condition(s) for record inclusion:
INCLUDE IF
```

5. As soon as you press the last **Return**, the next file description screen displays, with the number 002 ready for you to enter details about the next of your reference files. Before you do that, you should understand a little more about this first file description.

The transaction file is an input file and is always read in sequence, so you should FormSort the data file before each run. You have the option to have the file read in index order, but this slows the process down, particularly if you have a large data file. The optimal figure for size of disk buffer will depend upon the system you are using, but 008 should suffice. If you specify too small a buffer for your system it will slow down the computer; too large a size will use up computer memory. If your system has limited RAM, you can enter 001, 002, or 004 to save memory space (001 is the default value).

The prompt that asks if your file includes more than one volume means is your datafile on more than one disk? or do you have data records in more than one file?. Normally you will accept the default **N** for this; later on, if you need to say Y, you will answer another series of prompts that will allow you to specify the number of volumes and their locations. You will then need to include the change-disk option as well.

Usually you enter the data file name immediately, but you have the option to do so at runtime. At the next prompt, if you accept the dash sign for disk drive it is assumed that the file referred to will be found on the current disk drive at runtime. If you are not sure about this, enter a **?** to indicate that you will enter the drive identifier at runtime.

Finally, you are given the option to include only certain records by using the INCLUDE IF statement. You can be quite specific, for example, INCLUDE IF STATE=CT, or more general, INCLUDE IF CLIENT NO>0005. If you wish to print all the records in POLIST, just press **Return** to bypass this line.

6. Now press **Return** to accept that you are describing file 002 and enter the name of your next reference file:

002/INVENTRY

7. Run through the prompts again, the only difference being that this file is a plain reference file and is not read sequentially, so overtype the S with an **R**. All the rest are defaults.

8. Next enter:

003/CLIENTPO

9. Again, apart from overtyping S with **R**, you can accept all the defaults.

10. Now you come to reference file number 004, INVDATA. Enter:

004/INVDATA

This is an output file, so there will be some new answers to the new prompts.

11. The first prompt you have to change is the input or output query; simply overtype the I with an **O**.

12. Next you will see:

```
Error if old version present, or Add to it? (E/A)                    A
Should an Index file also be written? (Y/N)                          N
```

13. The rest are defaults.

14. Press **^C** to exit from the file description screen to the report layout screen.

If you had selected **E** (for Error if old version present) then each time the report was run you would have to erase INVDATA.DTA beforehand or give a new file name for the output. When you say **A** you are asking for the new output to be added to the old in the existing file INVDATA.DTA.

If you respond to the query about writing an index file, it means that as well as creating or updating your data file, a matching index file will be created also. It is better to say no and make the index file later with FormSort, which is quicker.

That completes the file description phase. You have described your three input files (note that although INVENTRY is updated during the run, it still counts as an input file), and your one output file. Now you are ready to design your report layout.

Headings and data fields

Have a look at the design of the Transact Report in Figure 11–5 before you begin. You will start by laying out the whole report with headings and field lengths, then go on to assign attributes, and finally fill in the print controls for each line.

The first thing to notice is that the main heading, INVOICE, appears twice, as does the DATE. There is method in this apparent madness! When you come to assign the print controls, you will find that the first set of invoice and date fields print only at the report start (R in the print control column). The second set appears on each page (that is, on each invoice after the first).

FIGURE 11-5 Transact Report Listing with Field and File Attribute Definitions

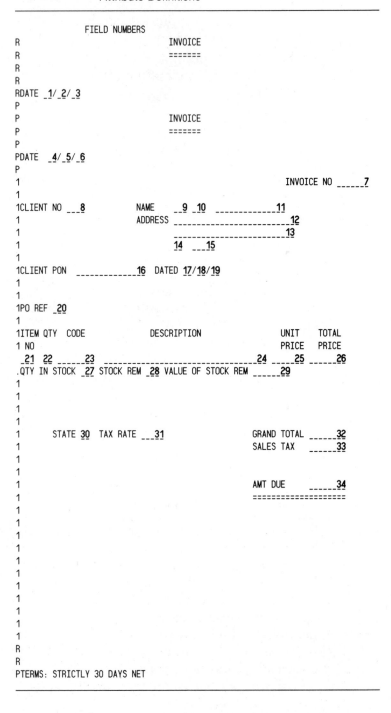

```
            FIELD NUMBERS
R                               INVOICE
R                               =======
R
R
RDATE _1/_2/_3
P
P                               INVOICE
P                               =======
P
PDATE _4/_5/_6
P
1                                                  INVOICE NO _____7
1
1CLIENT NO ___8        NAME   __9 _10 _____11
1                      ADDRESS _____12
1                             _____13
1                                    14   ___15
1
1CLIENT PON _____16  DATED 17/18/19
1
1
1PO REF _20
1
1ITEM QTY  CODE           DESCRIPTION           UNIT   TOTAL
1 NO                                            PRICE  PRICE
 _21 22 _____23 _____24 ____25 _____26
.QTY IN STOCK _27 STOCK REM _28 VALUE OF STOCK REM _____29
1
1
1
1
1     STATE 30  TAX RATE ___31        GRAND TOTAL _____32
1                                     SALES TAX   _____33
1
1
1                                     AMT DUE     _____34
1                                     ==================
1
1
1
1
1
1
1
1
1
1
1
R
R
PTERMS: STRICTLY 30 DAYS NET
```

Step-by-step procedure

1. Start entering the headings, field names, and field lengths. You will name the fields during the assignment of attributes. Use the **Space Bar** to reach the center of the top line and type **INVOICE**. Press **Return**, space across and underline the heading.

2. Press **Return** a couple of times to create some blank lines. Then type **DATE** followed by a space, then type **^Q**, twice followed by a / and **^Q** twice more. Then type / again and **^Q** twice more to make the three date fields.

3. Leave a blank line, then make the page heading, **INVOICE**, and underline it as before. Insert two more blank lines and enter the title and three fields for P DATE. After another couple of blank lines, space well across the screen to enter the INVOICE NO and fill its field length with **^Q** six times.

4. Continue like this, entering the headings, field names, and field lengths, following the form design in Figure 11–5, with the following field lengths:

   CLIENT NO: 4
   NAME: make 3 fields for title, initals, and last name:
      3, 3, and 15
   ADDRESS: allow 4 fields, 27, 26, 2, and 5
   CLIENT PON: 15
   PO REF: 3
   ITEM NO: 3 QTY: 2 CODE: 8 DESCRIPTION: 35 UNIT
      PRICE: 7
   TOTAL PRICE: 8
   QTY IN STOCK: 3 STOCK REM: 3 VALUE OF STOCK REM:
      8
   STATE: 2 TAX RATE: 5 GRAND TOTAL: 8 SALES TAX:
      8
   AMT DUE: 8

5. Now, make several blank lines, and at about line 50 type in the TERMS line.

Once you have entered the form you may decide to adjust the line spacing: to delete a whole line you just use **^Y**; to add a blank line you use **^N** (but remember *always* to first fill the line buffer by pressing **^P** in a blank line otherwise you will insert a line containing any headings and fields that happened to be in the

Line Buffer at that time). If you need to delete a whole field from your form, use ^Z.

That completes the design of your form's headings and general layout. Now you can return to the first set of date fields and start the field definitions. You will notice some similarities between this and FormGen, but there are many differences, too. This is quite a lengthy process so perhaps you feel like taking a break now; while you have your cup of coffee look back over the process so far and ahead to see what's coming.

The field definitions

Every field on the form must be defined, even if you only give it a name. If it is to be filled with data from a reference file, or if any data is to be output to a file, you will have to give the appropriate details.

Step-by-step procedure

1. Move the cursor into the first date field and press **^R**.
2. Name the field **RR MONTH**. Press **Return** until you reach the prompt:

    ```
    Field source: (File/Calc/Input)                                    I
    ```

    and overtype the F with an **I** as shown. You will be asked for the prompt; type **ENTER MONTH (MM)**.
3. Press **Return** to accept the next few defaults until prompted:

    ```
    Enter load condition ( /R/P/n/*):                                  R
    ```

    Type **R** as shown to specify that the month should be loaded at the start of report (that is, that you will type it in when prompted).
4. Press **Return** a few more times until you reach the prompt:

    ```
    Output field to file (Y/N)                                        Y
       File number/name:                                      004/INVDATA
       Field number/name:                               001/INVDATA MONTH
    ```

5. When you type **Y** as shown to say that the field data should be output to a file, you have to give the number of that

file (as you specified earlier in the file description process) and its destination field in that file, as detailed here for RR MONTH.

6. To summarize this first field:

```
Field number/name                              001/RR MONTH
Equivalent to field:                                /
Copy attributes of field:                           /
Field source (File/Calc/Input)                      I
  Enter input prompt:
    ENTER MONTH (MM)
Enter pad character:
Right justified? (Y/N)                              N
Edit mask? (Y/N)                                    N
Enter load condition: ( R/P/n/*)                    R
Output field to file? (Y/N)                         Y
  File number/name:                          004/INVDATA
  Field number/name:                       001/INVDATA MONTH
Enter field clear condition: ( /./P/n/*)
```

7. Each field name must be unique, so this first MONTH field is named RR MONTH to distinguish it from R MONTH in field 004. You have specified that it will be input (I) at the start of the report (R), so you will enter the current month when prompted ENTER MONTH (MM) at run time. The content of the field is to be output to the first field of the INVDATA data file. When you come to field 004 you will see that it, also, is output to a file. This is another reason for having two current date fields on the report—you can only output each field to one file.

8. Now press ˆF to move to the next field and ˆR to start defining it. All your responses will be the same except that the field name is RR DAY and it is output to field number 002 in INVDATA. Go straight on to RR YEAR and define that in the same way: It will be field 003 in the output file.

9. Fields 004, 005, and 006 are also date fields—R MONTH, R DAY, and R YEAR, respectively. To save typing the date twice when the report is run, you can simply copy the data from the first three date fields. To do this you must specify that the source is **C** and then enter the following:

```
Field source: (File/Calc/Input)                     C
  Numeric/String                                    S
Enter string expression:
  $R MONTH=$RR MONTH
```

Although the data in RR MONTH is numeric, this is not a mathematical calculation—you simply want the *content* of the first field to be read in to the fourth field. It is called a *string* (in computing, a *string* is a set of alphanumeric characters, or letters, which may or may not form an intelligible phrase). The dollar sign indicates that what follows is a string, so the whole *string expression* means: ''Set the contents of RR MONTH equal to the contents of R MONTH.''

10. When you reach the prompt about load condition, press **Return** to leave it blank. Then type **Y** to say you want the field output to file 002/INVENTRY, field 007/INV MONTH. Finally, press **Return** to bypass the field clear condition prompt.

11. Carry on with the next two date fields, just updating the string expression for $R DAY and $R YEAR. Don't forget to update the output field information (008 and 009).

12. The next field is 007/INVOICE NO, which is a self-referenced calculated field (like you used for QUOTE NO in Chapter 9). Its attributes can be summarized as follows:

```
Field number/name                                    007/INVOICE NO
Equivalent to field:                                      /
Copy attributes of field:                                 /
Field source: (File/Calc/Input)                           C
  Numeric/String                                          N
  Enter algebraic expression:
    INVOICE NO=INVOICE NO+1
Enter pad character:
Right justified? (Y/N)                                    Y
Edit mask? (Y/N)                                          N
Enter load condition: ( R/P/n/*)                          P
Output field to file? (Y/N)                               Y
  File number/name:                                004/INVDATA
  Field number/name:                             004/INVOICE NO
Enter field clear condition: ( /./P/n/*)
```

13. This time the calculation is numeric, so you are asked for an algebraic expression. The INVOICE NO will now update by 1 as each new invoice is created during the report run (hence, it is loaded once per page). This field also is output to Invdata.

14. Nearly all the remaining fields are read in from reference files; I will run through the first in detail:

```
Field number/name                                    008/CLIENT NO
Equivalent to field:                                      /
```

```
Copy attributes of field:                            /
Field source: (File/Calc/Input)                      F
   File number/name                           001/POLIST
   Field number/Name                          008/CLIENT NO
Enter pad character:
Right justified? (Y/N)                               Y
Edit mask? (Y/N)                                     N
Enter load condition: ( R/P/n/*)
Output field to file? (Y/N)                          N
Enter field clear condition: ( /./P/n/*)             .
```

The CLIENT NO is to be read in from POLIST, the transaction file (the link with POLIST is PO REF, which you will define when you get to it); since the field is derived from the transaction file, which is to be read in sequence, you must not specify any load or clear conditions.

15. Fields 009 to 015, the name and address details, are all read in from the CLIENTPO file. I will run through the first one for you in detail. Because the CLIENT NO is the key field in the CLIENTPO file, it will be the index field for all the name and address details for each invoice.

```
Field number/name                            009/TITLE
Equivalent to field:                                 /
Copy attributes of field:                            /
Field source: (File/Calc/Input)                      F
   File number/name                          003/CLIENTPO
   Field number/Name                          002/TITLE
   Index field number                         008/CLIENT NO
Enter pad character:
Right justified? (Y/N)                               N
Edit mask? (Y/N)                                     N
Enter load condition: ( R/P/n/*)                     P
Output field to file? (Y/N)                          N
Enter field clear condition: ( /./P/n/*)             .
```

Because the field is derived from a plain reference file, you need to enter the field in the report that will act as the index field (it is 008/CLIENT NO); note, also, that it is loaded at each new page (P) and never cleared (.).

16. Continue with the rest of the fields (up to 019), just changing the reference file field number and name as appropriate.

17. With field 020, PO REF, the first thing you must do is to make it a control break field by pressing ^K while the cursor is in the field (remember that the asterisks in a report field indicate control break status).

```
Field number/name                           020/PO REF
Equivalent to field:                                /
Control break level:                              001
Copy attributes of field:                           /
Field source: (File/Calc/Input)                     F
    File number/name                        001/POLIST
    Field number/Name                       001/PO REF
Enter pad character:
Right justified? (Y/N)                              N
Edit mask? (Y/N)                                    N
Enter load condition: ( R/P/n/*)
Output field to file? (Y/N)                         N
Enter field clear condition: ( /./P/n/*)            .
```

Note the extra line giving the control break level—in this form you only have one control break.

18. Fields 021 to 026 are derived from POLIST and are very straightforward. You will have to give the file number and name for each and update the field number and name in the reference file for each, starting with 002 for ITEM NO. Following are definitions of UNIT PRICE in more detail, since this field has some additional features:

```
Field number/name                        025/UNIT PRICE
Equivalent to field:                                /
Copy attributes of field:                           /
Field source: (File/Calc/Input)                     F
    File number/name                        001/POLIST
    Field number/Name                     006/UNIT PRICE
Enter pad character:
Right justified? (Y/N)                              Y
Edit mask? (Y/N)                                    Y
Enter load condition: ( R/P/n/*)
Output field to file? (Y/N)                         N
Enter field clear condition: ( /./P/n/*)
```

19. In response to the request for an edit mask, you will be given a list of choices. You want a floating dollar sign and a decimal point aligned.

20. Enter the edit mask condition codes:

$$\text{UNIT}$$
$$\text{PRICE}$$
$$\text{F\_\_\_.\_\_}$$

21. Note that you can put the F in every position up to the decimal point; then when data occupies any of these po-

sitions it overrules the F, so you end up with data; either
one, two, three, or four digits; and a dollar sign to the left
of the data.

If you use the single F as shown here, the dollar signs
will line up in the output (the printed invoice).

22. Next, you must enter the character you wish to float; if
you entered F four times, you must now enter four dollar
signs.

UNIT

PRICE

$___.__

23. The next field, TOTAL PRICE, has all the same attributes
as UNIT PRICE, including the edit mask, but is also an
output field to INVDATA:

Output field to file? (Y/N)	**Y**
File number/name:	**004/INVDATA**
Field number/name	**005/TOTAL PRICE**

This completes the line of items that will print out on each
invoice, called the detail line.

24. The next three items are related to the INVENTRY file
and will not print out on the invoice, but you need to enter
them in this position, then specify later that this is a nonprinting line when you assign the Print Control characters.

Field 027/QTY IN STOCK is derived from INVENTRY:

Field source: (File/Calc/Input)	**F**
File number/name:	**002/INVENTRY**
Field number/name:	**005/QTY IN STOCK**
Index field:	**023/CODE**

25. Field 028/STOCK REM is a calculated field, and the value
is used to update the INVENTRY file. So, as you fill out
your invoices, the initial quantity of each item is read in
from the INVENTRY file, then the final quantity is read
back to update the quantity in stock. In this way, your
inventory will always be up to date.

Field source: (File/Calc/Input)	**C**
Numeric/String? (N/S)	**N**
Enter algebraic expression:	
STOCK REM=**QTY IN STOCK-QTY**	

26. Read this back out to Inventry to update the QTY IN STOCK:

```
Output field to file? (Y/N)                              Y
    File number/name:                          002/INVENTRY
    Field number/name:                        005/QTY IN STOCK
    Index field number/name:                      023/CODE
```

27. Field 029/VAL OF STOCK REM (value of stock remaining) is a calculated field and is also used to update the IN-VENTRY file. Remember that the VALUE OF STOCK field in INVENTRY was derived from a calculation; however, when you update the QTY IN STOCK field in INVENTRY, the calculation is not performed again. So you have to do the calculation in the Report, then write the new value back to the INVENTRY file):

```
Field source (File/Calc/Input)                           C
    Numeric/String? (N/S)                                N
    Enter algebraic expression:
    VAL OF STOCK REM=STOCK REM*UNIT PRICE
```

28. Then, to update INVENTRY:

```
Output field to file? (Y/N)                              Y
    File number/name:                          002/INVENTRY
    Field number/name:                        006/VAL OF STOCK
    Index field:                                  023/CODE
```

29. Now you encounter the first totaling line: field 030/STAT. Since this is the second occurrence of the STATE field in this report, STATE is abbreviated to STAT to make the name unique. This is the first field that involves a control break, so I will explain the items in parentheses after the *LOAD IF* and *CLEAR IF* condition prompts.

30. So far you have seen the blank load condition (which means *load always*), the **R** for *load at start of Report*, and the **P** for *load at each new page*: the lowercase **n** represents any control break number from 1 to 9, and the asterisk prompts you to specify your own particular *LOAD WHEN* condition (in the form of a *logical expression*).

    The field is derived from POLIST:

```
Field number/name                                     030/STAT
Equivalent to field:                                     /
```

```
Copy attributes of field:                                    /
Field source: (File/Calc/Input)                              F
    File number/name                                   001/POLIST
    Field number/Name                                  009/STATE
Enter pad character:
Right justified? (Y/N)                                       N
Edit mask? (Y/N)                                             N
Enter load condition: ( R/P/n/*)
Output field to file? (Y/N)                                  N
Enter field clear condition: ( /./P/n/*)                     1
```

31. Now we are below the mid-point of the form. It is necessary to specify that the field should be cleared *every time a new invoice is started* (that is, at control break 001), so you enter 1 as the field clear condition.

32. The same applies to 031/TAX RATE, which is also read in from POLIST; in addition, this field should be right-justified and then output to file 004/INVDATA, field 006/TAX RATE (in INVDATA.DTA) and, finally, cleared at control break 1.

33. Field 032/GRAND TOTAL is calculated:

GRAND TOTAL=GRAND TOTAL+TOTAL PRICE

It should be right-justified, needs an edit mask like TOTAL PRICE (with floating dollar sign and decimal point alignment).

34. Now you need to understand how these totaling fields work in InfoStar custom reports. When the first item in the first purchase order is read into Transact Report, the TOTAL PRICE data will be added to GRAND TOTAL (which starts at zero); then as subsequent items are read in, each TOTAL PRICE in turn is added to GRAND TOTAL. If you forgot to specify that the field should be cleared at control break 1, data would go on being added all the way through the report.

    By specifying the clear condition, you ensure that at the end of each invoice (identified by the computer as the point where new purchase order data is received) the GRAND TOTAL stops accumulating and prints out the correct amount.

35. You need the same attributes for 033/SALES TAX. The calculation is:

SALES TAX=TAX RATE*GRAND TOTAL/100

36. Don't forget the clear condition for control break 1.

37. The same again for 034/AMT DUE:

AMT DUE=GRAND TOTAL+SALES TAX

38. All three fields have the same justification and edit mask.

If you like you can also have headings in boldface or underlined; move the cursor in front of the heading INVOICE and press ^V : a new help screen will appear. Decide on the correct control characters and insert them before and after the heading (as in WordStar). You can look at the screen layout without seeing the control characters by pressing ^O. This will also suppress the nonprinting lines.

That completes the form layout and field definitions. I am sure you need a break! After that, you will finish off the report by filling in the print control column. Then you can save it and try running it. Reports are normally run and printed at the same time, but you have the option of "printing" the report to a disk file (which will be given the extension .PRN). Then you can look at it on the screen to make sure that it has run correctly. This is fine for the training examples, but once you are running real-life reports, you need to ensure that they are thoroughly tested in advance: each time you run the report, you update the various files. So if you repeat a run, you will, for example, debit your inventory twice with the same purchase orders.

After running Transact you should continue with the design of the Turnover Report. Then there is a final overview of what you have achieved with this transaction process and some advice on designing your own reports.

The print control column

Look back at Figure 11–5, which shows the whole Transact Report layout, including the characters in the print control column.

Step-by-step procedure

1. Move the cursor into the first column of the top line of the form, using ^S.

2. Start from the top. Report headers have an R in the print control column (PCC), so type **R** in the first line; note that the cursor goes automatically to the line below, so type **R** four more times (the last one should be level with the first DATE field).

3. Page headers have a P in the PCC, so type **P** six times; the last should be in line with INVOICE NO.

4. Type **1** in each field of all the rest of the lines, down to the detail line—the line containing the items that will print out on the invoices. In this example, there are 14 repeats of 1, the last one level with the NO of ITEM NO.

5. The detail line has a blank in the PCC; just press the **Space Bar** to produce it.

6. The next line must be nonprinting; you achieve this by typing a **.** in the PCC.

7. Now all the rest contain a series of **1**—down to the footer regarding TERMS. On the sample form there are entered 21 of 1.

8. Because there should be a page footer comment, and because it is essential to maintain the correct order (RP123 :321RP), there has to be an R line before the P for the TERMS, as shown in Figure 11–6.

That really is the end of the Transact Report; now you can save it and then try running it.

Running the transact report

When you press ^C to save the report you will be prompted to answer a few questions, assuming you have made no mistakes. If there are any errors in the form layout, you will be told as much as soon as you press ^C to save the form. If you do get an error message, read what it says and try to establish what you have done wrong (this example has been tried and tested—if you get an error message, it is because you have made a mistake in copying it). There is a summary of error messages in the InfoStar Reference Manual, in case you have any difficulty understanding the screen's shorthand version.

If all is well, you can choose option **R** to run the report. Make sure your printer is powered on and online, enter the three date fields when prompted, and the report will run. You will see the invoices printing out, and know that at the same time your IN-

FIGURE 11-6 Sample Invoice

```
                         INVOICE
                         =======


DATE 10/03/85
                                         INVOICE NO      1


CLIENT NO 0001           NAME    Ms  J M  Smith
                      *  ADDRESS 1 Main Street
                                 New Haven
                                 CT  06453


CLIENT PON A/100185      DATED 10/01/85


PO REF 1

ITEM QTY  CODE            DESCRIPTION          UNIT    TOTAL
NO                                             PRICE   PRICE
1    1  U1/10010  Dressing table, mirror and lights $125.00 $ 125.00


2    2  U1/10020  Master wardrobe, fitted       $225.00 $ 450.00


3    2  U1/10030  Matching top cupboard         $ 95.00 $ 190.00




         STATE CT  TAX RATE  5.50         GRAND TOTAL $ 765.00
                                          SALES TAX   $  42.07


                                          AMT DUE     $ 807.07
                                          ====================



TERMS: STRICTLY 30 DAYS NET
```

FIGURE 11-7   Turnover Report Listing with Field and File
Attribute Definitions

```
          FIELD NUMBERS

R                              TURNOVER
R                              ========
R
R TURNOVER REPORT DATE _1/_2/_3
R
. INVOICE NO ___4     TAX RATE ____5
: TOTAL PRICE _____6 SALES TAX _____7 AMT DUE _____8
R TURNOVER _____9 TOTAL SALES TAX _____10 TOTAL AMT DUE _____11
```

VENTRY file is being updated and data is being written out to
INVDATA, your specified output file.

Compare your Report with Figure 11-6. If all is well, congratulations! You have achieved your first InfoStar transaction
process. Have a look at the INVENTRY and INVDATA files to
check the updating and output processes. While you are still
flushed with success, go on to design the Turnover Report.

There are full listings of the Reports' attributes, etc., in Appendix C.

The Turnover Report

This second report is much shorter and should seem very straightforward now that you have worked through Transact. There is
not so much detailed instruction in this example, so if you are
unsure at any stage, look back over the Transact form, or read
through the appropriate sections in the InfoStar Training Manual.
You may find now that you would benefit from reading through
the pages in the InfoStar Reference Manual relating to custom
reports. It is extremely detailed and covers all aspects of report
design, layout, and definitions.

Report layout

Look at Figure 11-7 to see what you are aiming for. The Turnover
Report will be driven by the output file from Transact:INVDATA.
This transaction file is the only reference file for Turnover, in
fact, so there are no preliminary FormGen forms to create, or data
to enter in DataStar.

Step-by-step procedure

Let's start then:

1. Next to the prompt type:

REDIT TURNOVER

and press **Return**.
2. The first screen is the file description screen. Press **Return** to accept the default 001/and next to it enter the name of the transaction file, INVDATA.
3. Go through the prompts, accepting the defaults by pressing **Return**, until you reach the buffer size. Enter 008 if that worked for Transact. You can accept all the other defaults.
4. Press ^C to go on to the report layout screen.
5. Start with the headings, field labels, and field lengths, as before, beginning with the report heading TURNOVER. Press **Return** and move the cursor across with the **Space Bar** to underline the heading.
6. Move down a few lines and type **TURNOVER REPORT DATE** followed by the usual format for the three date fields.
7. Move down another couple of lines and enter INVOICE NO and the ^Q four times to make the field. Space across and type TAX RATE, field length 5.
8. On the next line type **TOTAL PRICE**, give it a length of 8, then SALES TAX, with a length of 8, and AMT DUE, with a length of 8.
9. Leave one line space, then on the bottom line of the form type **TURNOVER**, length of 9, then **TOTAL SALES TAX**, length of 8, and finally **TOTAL AMT DUE**, with a length of 9.

Field definitions

Go back to the top of the form, move the cursor into the first field, and press ^R.

Step-by-step procedure

1. Name the first field, 001/REPORT MONTH. Move through the prompts; type **I** to say that the month data will be Input

at the prompt ENTER MONTH (MM), and later type **R** to load the data at the start of the report.

2. Continue with the definitions of REPORT DAY and RE-PORT YEAR.

3. The fourth field 004/INVOICE NO is the control break field (as INVOICE NO is the key field in the INVDATA form). With the cursor in the field, press ^K. Then press ^R and work through the definitions, saying the source of your INVOICE NO data will be the file 001/INVDATA, field 004/INVOICE NO.

4. The next two fields, 005 TAX RATE and 006 TOTAL PRICE, are both read in from 001/INVDATA, fields 006 and 005, respectively. In addition, TOTAL PRICE needs the edit mask to enter a floating dollar sign and decimal point alignment (as you did earlier in Transact).

All the remaining five fields are calculated and need floating dollar signs and decimal point alignment. I will give you the calculations for each field:

007/SALES TAX:

SALES TAX=TOTAL PRICE*TAX RATE/100

008/AMT DUE:

AMT DUE=TOTAL PRICE+SALES TAX

009/TURNOVER:

TURNOVER=TURNOVER+TOTAL PRICE

010/TOTAL SALES TAX:

TOTAL SALES TAX=TOTAL SALES TAX+SALES TAX

011/TOTAL AMT DUE:

TOTAL AMT DUE=TOTAL AMT DUE+AMT DUE

That is the end of field definitions; now on to the print control characters.

Print control column

Move the cursor back up to the top of your form and press ^S to move it into the PCC.

FIGURE 11–8 Sample Final Turnover Report

TURNOVER

========

TURNOVER REPORT DATE 10/03/85

TURNOVER $ 7590.00 TOTAL SALES TAX $432.11 TOTAL AMT DUE $ 8022.11

Look again at Figure 11–7 and copy the entries from the PCC.

You will need to press **R** for the first five lines to indicate that these are report headings and the report date. The fifth **R** ensures that a blank line will be inserted between the heading and the line of data.

The line containing the Invoice No and Tax Rate must be non-printing, so enter a dot (period).

The next line is the detail line at the mid-point of the form, but you don't want this to print either; in this case enter a colon. Remember, at the mid-point you must have either a space (to print the detail line) or a colon (to make it non-printing).

The last line must be an **R** to produce the correct kind of Report summaries.

That completes the Turnover form: I hope you were able to cope with the abbreviated instructions, and that you are beginning to have a feel for what we are doing.

Since you ran the Transact Report at the end of the last section, your input file for Turnover—Invdata—has some data in it; so let's run Turnover and look at the printed Turnover Report.

Running the Turnover Report

Make sure that your printer is powered on and online; press ^C to save the completed form and **R** to run the report (you shouldn't get any error messages). Accept the default to print the report, enter the three date fields when prompted, and the report will print. It is only a one-liner, so don't think there is something wrong; have a look at Figure 11–8 for comparison.

Printed on that one line, you have the TURNOVER for the day, with the date of the run, the TOTAL SALES TAX collected, and the TOTAL AMOUNT DUE. Next time you generate the report (after another transaction run) you will update the line with the new run date and the updated data (the cumulative turnover).

RUNNING THE REPORTS

Once you have all the reference files full of data, have sorted them, and the reports designed and defined to your own satisfaction, you can run reports very easily. To run Transact, you just type **REPORT TRANSACT** next to the prompt (having made sure that the printer is powered on and online). Then enter the date fields next to the prompts, and the invoices will print. After each run you must delete the POLIST data file; since this is the file that drives the whole transaction process, it must contain only the current purchase order information.

After each run you should check the INVENTRY file (either look at it in a non-document file in WordStar, or **TYPE** it to the screen with a system command) to make sure that the QTY IN STOCK, etc., has been updated: also check INVDATA.DTA to make sure that the appropriate fields have been output.

DESIGNING YOUR OWN REPORTS

You have now completed the design and entry of two full custom reports; in the process, you have covered many of the attributes in field and file definition and gained an overview of how a transaction process works. You may be able to modify the designs of these forms and use them in your own business (the listings in Appendix C will help). With recent versions of InfoStar (or InfoStar +) it is relatively easy to make changes in the forms and then to run the database restructuring programs (DBR and DBM) to adjust all the files that are affected by the changes (any related .DEF or .RPT files).

With the earlier versions of the software, under MS-DOS or CP/M, these examples of transaction processing run perfectly. But if you need to make any modifications, you do not have the DBR and DBM programs. This means that any changes you made in one form which affected other related definition forms or reports, may mean that you would have to run through your report, modifying the file descriptions, and then redefining any affected fields. This can certainly be done, but it may prove to be a long and tedious business. Of course, once you have the design right, everything will run. Beware of a "bug" in InfoStar 1.0 relating to large index files. In this example it could be the INVENTRY file: since this is a reference file which is updated during a report run, the .NDX file increases in size. Contact your MicroPro dealer for a "patch" to cure this problem.

When you are entering a form design of your own from scratch, you will need to have a clear outline prepared in advance, detailing any calculations, totals and summaries, and any associated control breaks. You will probably find it necessary to fill in the PCC as you go along, rather than at the end as you did in the exercises above. If you have any difficulty in assigning the correct control breaks or in getting totals or summaries to add up correctly, try running a Quick Report (RGEN) on your data and look at the result with REDIT. The format may not be pretty, but you will be able to look at the control break assignments and use **^R** to check the field definitions. This can be very instructive.

You can begin your own design efforts by extending the model outlined in this chapter. You could create a report that would print a list of invoice numbers, with the date, tax rate, sales tax total, and grand total using INVDATA.DTA as the transaction file. Then you could make use of the stock data produced by the transact report to drive a new report; this would note when stock of any item (code) fell below some preset level (remember, you included a field for entry of the stock level that was required). You would need to design a form in FormGen to collect the output stock data from Transact, then use this data file to drive your Reorder Report. As you extend your main report (in this example TRANSACT), you will inevitably increase its complexity and add more reference and output files. You should keep the total number of fields in your main report below 120 to be sure of error-free running.

You will find it easier to check how well your reports run by printing them to a disk file (.PRN) first. You can **TYPE** this to the screen with the system command to make sure your fields are in the right places and totals are calculating correctly. It has the added advantage that lines you have designated as nonprinting will, in fact, appear on the screen listing (with a dot in the first column to show that they would not print on the printer). This preview is very helpful when you are developing your own applications.

As discussed at the beginning of this chapter, there are some pitfalls when running reports that you must try to prevent. This is not such a problem if you are designing and running reports yourself—you know precisely how the transaction has been set up. When other people run the process, you must make it almost impossible for them to do the wrong thing or do it at the wrong time. For example, since there is an intimate link between key fields in data files and control breaks in reports, the data files must be sorted before every run. If you have files that are updated during a run (such as INVENTRY in this example) you must ensure that a copy of the files is made (preferably by writing a batch file to do this automatically or by using StarBurst, if you have InfoStar +) before the report is run. Then, if something goes wrong and the report needs to be run again, you don't update the inventory twice with the same purchase orders.

Work out all the likely failure points in your transaction process and try to build in the safeguards. By this time you would benefit significantly by reading the InfoStar manuals: try the training manual first. There are some interesting extensions of the purchase order model that you could possibly adapt to use with Transact. Then read the section on custom reports in the Reference Manual; it is packed with information, though rather too dense in style for a complete beginner.

Do you feel inspired to carry on with transaction processing? Although it is not the easiest of techniques, it is very rewarding. And it will really help to improve the efficiency of many essential tasks in your business. After completing these three lengthy tutorials on InfoStar, you can really appreciate the great flexibility of the programs and will see many new uses as you become more proficient in handling them.

Chapter 12 describes SuperSort. It will seem very easy after all this! If you don't have the SuperSort program, go straight to Chapter 13 on MailMerge.

12

SuperSort Tutorial

Sorting DataStar and CalcStar Files
Select and Exclude Features
Formatting the Output from SuperSort
Sorting Large Files
Creating New Index Files
SuperSort for DataStar File Maintenance
Conclusion

If you own InfoStar, you will probably use the built-in FormSort program for most of your data file sorting needs. However, there are many additional functions available in SuperSort, so if you think you may need such routines, read on. If you are not an InfoStar user, then you will need to know how to operate SuperSort.

When you use FormSort, the sorting routine in InfoStar, you may notice that it is actually making use of SuperSort routines—you will see the message SuperSort is sorting your datafile, for example. If you should ever have a need for a program with the flexibility and wide range of uses of SuperSort, you will find this chapter very helpful. SuperSort can sort files into almost any order you can imagine. Generally you use it to sort your DataStar and CalcStar files, but it can be used for sorting files in almost any format. While you would be using it primarily as a tool in conjunction with your MicroPro programs, its functions (in the original CP/M version) could be incorporated into custom built programs written in BASIC, FORTRAN, or COBOL, for example. The recent MS-DOS versions cannot be incorporated into other programs.

276

Like FormSort, you can use SuperSort for file maintenance of large DataStar files; it is much quicker and safer than using the built-in file maintenance function in DataStar. You can also create new index files from your data files after file maintenance, if you have lost or corrupted the originals, or simply because you need to make new index files from sorted subsections of the original data file.

SORTING DATASTAR AND CALCSTAR FILES

With your tutorial disk in drive A type:

SORT

and press **Return**.

You will see the usual sign on message about SuperSort and then see an asterisk prompt.

Remember that a *data file* contains all the individual *records* you have entered and that each of these records consists of a number of *datafields*. DataStar records are of variable length and are termed *carriage return delimited records*, that is, each record is separated from the next by a carriage return.

By now you probably have some data files of your own creation to use as examples in the sorting routines that follow. You can simply enter the name for your own file in place of the examples used here. Remember that you can sort a CalcStar file that has been converted to DataStar format, if you wish. You need the same information about the field names and lengths, so make sure you have this handy.

Before you start it would be helpful if you had the printout of your various datafield definitions showing the lengths of each datafield, since you will need to know the maximum length of records in each file and the lengths of any fields you may wish to use as keys in the sorting process.

Sorting in Alphabetical Order

The simplest sort procedure converts your data file entries from input order to alphabetical order. The information the program needs in order to do this for you is listed here with a brief explanation of each command. ADDRESS.DTA is the example file for sorting, but if you choose to use your own data file, you must use the appropriate numbers for record length and field lengths where necessary.

Type in the command lines next to the asterisk prompt, pressing **Return** after each. There is a summary of what should appear on your screen at the end of the first section. In SuperSort commands you use a hyphen between words, as you will see.

Step-by-step procedure

1. First type the INPUT-ATTRIBUTES. That is, describe the type of file you are submitting and the maximum length of any one record.

> INPUT-ATTRIBUTES=100,CR

As far as the length is concerned, you can total the field lengths on the DataStar form for the file you are planning to sort, then that number will represent the maximum length for any individual record. The only other attribute you must specify for this first sort is that the records are *carriage return delimited*, which can be abbreviated to **CR** in SuperSort.

2. Next type the SORT-FILE. You must enter the name of the file which you are submitting to be sorted, taking care to specify the drive on which the file is stored:

> SORT-FILE=A:ADDRESS.DTA

3. Next identify the OUTPUT-FILE. Here you must give the name of the new file that you wish to be created to hold the sorted data:

> OUTPUT-FILE=ADDRESS.SRT

Later in the tutorial you will learn to specify further details about the output file at this point, but for this first sort procedure the name alone will do. Again, you can specify a different drive if necessary.

4. Next label the **KEY.** You must specify which field in the record is to be used for the sort procedure. You may have up to 32 different keys, but for this first run just select one, perhaps the LAST NAME field. You must enter the *field*

number and *length*; note the pound sign before the field number:

KEY=#1,25

This command tells SuperSort that you wish to have the file sorted using the LAST NAME field (#1) as the *key* for the sort. Note that in SuperSort you can use *any field* as the key for sorting, not just the particular fields you specified as *key fields* in DataStar.

Since the LAST NAME field contains *alpha characters* rather than numbers, the file will be sorted in alphabetical order.

5. If you wish to start at A and end at Z, you need add no further attributes to the key command, since *ascending order* is the default. If you would like to sort in reverse order, you simply add DESCENDING as follows:

KEY=#1,25,DESCENDING

6. The final command to start the sort is **GO**. If you have chosen to sort the ADDRESS.DTA file, the screen will now look like this:

```
*INPUT-ATTRIBUTES=100,CR
*SORT-FILE=ADDRESS.DTA
*OUTPUT-FILE=ADDRESS.SRT
*KEY=#1,25
*GO
```

7. If you made any errors when typing in these commands, you will have found how good SuperSort is at telling you where you have made the error. To correct a line, simply type it in again.

In SuperSort, the *last entry* of any particular command is the one that will be implemented by the program. So, if you had typed all the commands except **GO**, you could change any of the other commands simply by entering that command line again. For example, you could change the data file to be sorted by typing:

```
*SORT-FILE=ADDR-2.DTA
```

and that command would cancel the previous one that stated that ADDRESS.DTA was to be the sort file.

Note that you cannot leave spaces between words in SuperSort commands; you must put in hyphens to separate any two-word commands. In practice, once you are familiar with the terminology you can use abbreviations for all the commands. This has the added advantage that you may then be able to fit all the commands on one line, as you will learn later in this tutorial.

8. After typing **GO** you just press **Return** and the sort procedure is performed. At the end of sorting, which in the case of small files takes only seconds, you will be given information relating to your files. First, you will see the number of records that have been sorted and then the size of the output file measured in K.

9. You can check that your file has been sorted correctly by listing it on the screen using the system TYPE command, or by calling up WordStar and looking at it as a non-document file.

Now that you have a *sorted* data file, it is quite permissible to make deletions or corrections to the file in WordStar—something you can never do to an actual DataStar file. So if you wish, you can delete whole records or make other corrections at this stage before you go on to use the sorted file for merge printing, for example.

Sorting in Numerical Order

This time use the QUOTES data as an example. If you total up the maximum number of characters in one whole record, you will find it is 545, so this is the figure you will need for the **INPUT-ATTRIBUTES** command.

Try sorting the file in QUOTE NUMBER order. Ideally, to demonstrate the points I wish to make in this exercise, you need to have at least 20 or so quotes entered in your file.

Step-by-step procedure

1. Try entering the following:

```
*INPUT-ATTRIBUTES=545,CR
```

```
*SORT-FILE=QUOTES.DTA
*OUTPUT-FILE=QUOTES12.SRT
*KEY=#1,6
*GO
```

2. Now look at the result using the **TYPE** command.

 If you have more than one screen of data and you are using the **TYPE** command, you can press ^S to stop the screen at any point and then restart it by pressing any key.

 It is not actually in numerical order, is it The quote numbers go in sequence:

1, 10, 11, 12, 13, 14, 15, 16, 17, 18, 19, 2, 20, 21, etc.

This is because you must specify that numeric fields be right-justified for sorting. If you do not specify, the *default* of left-justified is assumed.

3. Run the sort again; if you use the same name for the output file, the previous file will simply be overwritten.

```
*INPUT-ATTRIBUTES=545,CR
*SORT-FILE=QUOTES.DTA
*OUTPUT-FILE=QUOTES12.SRT
*KEY=#1,6,RIGHT-JUSTIFY
*GO
```

4. Now when you **TYPE** the QUOTES12.SRT file, you will find that the quote numbers are in correct numerical order.

Sorting by More than One Key

Next look at sorting in date order, when the user specifies in addition that the records should be in numerical order on any one date:

```
*INPUT=545,CR
*SORT=QUOTES.DTA
*OUTPUT=QUOTESD1.SRT
*KEY=#45,8,#1,6,RIGHT
*GO
```

Note the use of abbreviations (later you will learn to shorten these even further) and the introduction of a second **key** to sort by.

If you look at the file QUOTESD1.SRT you will find the list is in DATE (field 045) order, and if you look at all the records for one date, they will be in order of QUOTE NUMBER (field 001).

The file could be sorted again, this time specifying that on any one date the records should be in alphabetical order by LAST NAME (field 005). You must be careful not to give conflicting instructions; for example, it would not be possible for the file to be sorted so that both the LAST NAME and the QUOTE NUMBER were in order!

To sort in date and name order:

```
*INPUT=545,CR
*SORT=QUOTES.DTA
*OUTPUT=QUOTESDN.SRT
*KEY=#1,6,RIGHT,#5,15
*GO
```

Try out some sort procedures of your own until you feel happy with all the commands you have learned so far.

SELECT AND EXCLUDE FEATURES

The next stage, now that you have had some practice with straightforward sorting, is to try to SELECT some records and to EXCLUDE others.

You can probably think of many useful examples, using the QUOTES file. For instance, you could pick out the clients whose QUOTES were for amounts greater than $1000 but less than $1200, for the Ultima range of furniture.

It is best to start with something simple and then build up to the more complex sorts.

Record Selection

First, how would you try selecting all the items in the Ultima range from your Price list file (PRICELST.DTA)?

```
*INPUT=200,CR
*SORT=PRICELST.DTA
*OUTPUT=PRICEULT.SRT
```

```
*KEY=#1,8
*SELECT=#1>=''U''
*GO
```

Note that you must specify as a KEY the field you wish to use in the **SELECT** command. Also, that in the SELECT command you have to use precisely the format shown here. These two commands say: I wish to sort by the code number and I wish to select only code numbers beginning with a **U** or greater.

You may remember that the Code Numbers started with the letter F, S, or U so when you use the format >= you are saying, select codes starting with a U or with V, W, X, Y, or Z. But there are no records in your file starting with a letter greater than U, so this command is correct in these circumstances.

If you turn to the QUOTES file now, you could sort all records that were quotes for the Finesse range, price code 2:

```
*INPUT=545,CR
*SORT=QUOTES.DTA
*OUTPUT=FIN-2.SRT
*KEY=#12,10,#13,1
*SELECT=#12=''FINESSE''
*SELECT+#13=''2''
*GO
```

Note that when you wish to specify more than one **SELECT** feature—only those records that satisfy *both* the criteria given here—then the second and subsequent **SELECT** commands must read **SELECT**+. If you typed **SELECT**= again by mistake, this command line then *cancels* the previous **SELECT** command, and you will have a file containing *all* the records that had price code 2 in field 013.

Note also that you must *enclose in quotes* the contents of the field you wish to **SELECT** and you *must* have an exact match in terms of all uppercase or mixed upper and lowercase letters.

You can have up to 15 different **SELECT** parameters, so in theory you could specify that you wished to choose only those records for clients with names beginning with J, which had PA in the STATE field, had a ZIP code beginning 194, were on the telephone, Finesse for the design, PRICE CODE 3, TOTAL PRICE exceeding $1000,and whose quote was issued in June (plus a few more if you could think of any!).

Excluding Records

The **EXCLUDE** function is used in precisely the same way. One way to end up with a set of records for all the clients interested in the Supreme range would be to **EXCLUDE** those who chose Finesse or Ultima:

```
*INPUT=545,CR
*SORT=QUOTES.DTA
*OUTPUT=SUPREME.SRT
*KEY=#12,10
*EXCLUDE=#12=''FINESSE''
*EXCLUDE+#12=''ULTIMA''
*GO
```

Having excluded Finesse and Ultima, you will be left with a list of the Supreme quotes. This is an example—obviously you could achieve exactly the same result by using **SELECT "SUPREME"**.

SELECT and EXCLUDE Used Together

You can extend the usefulness of these commands by using them in combination. Note that after the first **SELECT** or **EXCLUDE** command, any subsequent **SELECT** or EXCLUDE commands must be followed by a PLUS sign instead of an EQUALS sign.

In this example, you will select all quotes for Ultima, excluding those for less than $1000 (<**$1000**) or more than $1200 (>**$1200**). Enter:

```
*INPUT=545,CR
*SORT=QUOTES.DTA
*OUTPUT=FINMID.SRT
*KEY=#12,10,#44,9
*SELECT=#12=''ULTIMA''
*EXCLUDE=#44<''$1000''
*EXCLUDE+#44>''$1200''
*GO
```

You should try out lots of these select and exclude exercises until you feel really confident that you can select or exclude by any field, or combination of fields, at will.

FORMATTING THE OUTPUT FROM SUPERSORT

You can add extra attributes to the commands you have learned so far and produce well laid out lists or tables.

Creating a Price List

You can start with something quite simple. Using the file sorted earlier, PRICEULT.SRT, you can produce a file containing just the code number and the unit price.

You will specify that you want **K-OUTPUT**, that is, only the key fields that you list next to **KEY** will be present in the output file. Remember that in SuperSort *any* field can be specified as a key for sorting; you are not tied to the key fields you assigned in DataStar.

```
*INPUT=200,CR
*SORT=A:PRICEULT.SRT
*OUTPUT=B:ULTDATA.SRT,K-OUTPUT
*KEY=#1,8,#4.8,RIGHT
*GO
```

Use the system **TYPE** command and **^P** to list the file on your printer; you will have quite a reasonable looking price list that you will find quite adequate for most purposes. If you want the DESCRIPTION as well, then you can simply add the extra key. If you prefer, you could use WordStar and MailMerge to produce a printed Price List, which could be easily updated and run off whenever new prices came into effect.

A reasonable abbreviation of the above commands would easily fit on one line:

```
I=200,CR; S=PRICEULT.SRT; O=ULTDTA.SRT,K-OUT; K=#1,8,#4,8,RIGHT; GO
```

Once you are familiar with the commands, you will find it very tedious to enter them in full every time so it is well worth getting to know the abbreviations.

Command Files

There is yet another alternative to entering the same SuperSort commands over and over again. For example, you may need to update your file of price lists quite frequently and, of course, every time you make additions or deletions you have to re-sort the file. The solution is to set up a command file.

Step-by-step procedure

You simply open a non-document file in WordStar and enter the commands.

1. Call your file by a name that will tell you what you use it for, such as LISTSORT.CF (if you give the extension .CF to all the command files you set up, you will easily be able to identify the specific file you need by typing **DIR *.CF**).

2. Start typing immediately below the ruler line—you must enter *only* the following:

```
LIST
I=200,CR;S=PRICEULT.SRT;O=ULTDATA.SRT,K-OUT;K=#1,8,#4,8,RIGHT;G
```

LIST ensures that your SuperSort command line will appear on the screen when you use the file.

3. Save the file with a **^KD**, exit from WordStar, and call up the SuperSort program by typing **SORT** next to the A> prompt.

4. To implement the command file, type the following next to the asterisk prompt:

```
CFILE=LISTSORT.CF
```

As soon as you press **Return** the sort procedure will be performed.

5. If you wish, you can include most of the SuperSort commands but leave some to be entered from the keyboard; you may find it convenient to leave out the **GO** command, for example, or the input filename.

If you are going to be doing a lot of sorting, I think you will find this a very useful routine to adopt.

More Complex Formatting

You could sort the QUOTES.DTA file to give you a list of quotes in date order, with the quote number, last name, and total amount.

If you used the method described previously, you would find that the fields are too close together, you need to introduce some extra spaces to improve the appearance and make the list easier to read.

This can be achieved in two stages. First, you must produce an output file that has *fixed length* fields (instead of *carriage return delimited*), and you will make the total record length longer than the existing maximum of **545**.

In the second stage, you will allot some of these extra spaces to positions *between* fields to produce a better formatted output file.

The first stage would be:

```
*INPUT=545,CR
*SORT=QUOTES.DTA
*OUTPUT=QUOTES.INT,555,FIXED-LENGTH
*KEY=#45,8
*GO
```

In this first stage you took the QUOTES file, sorted in date order, converted the file from *carriage return delimited* to *fixed-length*, and added an extra **10** spaces to the end of the file (by specifying 555).

Now for the second stage:

```
*INPUT=555,FIXED-LENGTH
*MERGE-FILE=QUOTES.INT
*OUTPUT=QUOTES.OPT,CR,K-OUTPUT
*KEY=#45,8,546,548,#1,6,RIGHT,549,552,#5,15,553,555,#44,9
*GO
```

In this stage, you took the sorted fixed length QUOTES file, QUOTES.INT (for interim), merged it (since it was already sorted), converted the output file (QUOTES.OPT) back to carriage return delimited, then took some of the spaces you have added, putting three of them between the date and the quote number, four between the quote number and the last name and the remaining three between the last name and the amount.

When you use the **TYPE** command for this on your screen you will see four neatly spaced columns of easy-to-read data.

You should go through some more formatting routines so that you really understand what you are doing. Also, it may help at this stage to read through the section in the SuperSort manual called the *Operator's Handbook*. You will find full details of the sorting routines described, and you should read, when you are a little more experienced, "Utilization Hints".

SORTING LARGE FILES

You should not have had too much trouble so far sorting these relatively small data files. Once you have large files to sort, particularly if you do not have a hard disk or high capacity floppy disks, you will have to be aware constantly of how much space is required by SuperSort whenever it performs a sort routine.

Space Requirements

SuperSort itself (SORT.COM), occupies 32K of disk space.

When a file is sorted, a separate work file is created that occupies about the same amount of space as the data file being sorted.

After sorting, the output file will need its own space.

Getting Around the Space Problem

There are several ways of organizing your files and disks to minimize the space problem.

You could have three SORT disks—SORTPROG, SORTWORK, and SORT-OUT.

The first, SORTPROG, could have just the SuperSort program on it—SORT.COM—and the input file (the file to be sorted).

The second, SORTWORK, would be used for the work file.

The third, SORT-OUT, would be used for the output file.

Using this system you should be able to sort files of a size just below the maximum storage area of your floppy disks.

Sorting Routine for Large Files

The following summarizes each step to use when you sort large files.

Step-by-step procedure

1. Place SORTPROG in drive A and SORTWORK in drive B.
2. Type **SORT** and and press **Return** to get the asterisk prompt, then enter the file details, making the sort file **A:filename**

and the output file **B:filename/C**.

The **/C** means change disks before writing output file.

3. Type **W=B:**, then **GO** and then press **Return**.

The **W** indicates the drive where you want the work file to be located.

4. When prompted, replace the SORTWORK disk with SORT-OUT and the output file will write to it.

To recap: The data file to be input for the sort was located on disk SORTPROG. The input file in drive A was sorted using the disk in drive B, SORTWORK, as the working disk. Finally, the disk in drive B was changed for SORT-OUT and the output file was written to it.

You will find that you can manage with two disks most of the time—using the one in drive A for the program and the data file and the one in drive B for the work file and output.

CREATING NEW INDEX FILES

A very useful function in SuperSort is the ability to create new index files for DataStar data files. You will use this facility routinely if you perform file maintenance using SuperSort.

In addition, you may need this facility if at any time you should accidentally erase or corrupt the index file, or if you have sorted a subset of your data file and need an index file to match.

Remember that your DataStar data file will only work if you have an index file that matches it exactly.

Method

You will use the data file as the input file and specify that the output file must be fixed length and contain only the keys and pointers (in this instance, the key or keys are the *actual* DataStar key field or fields). The pointers are part of the essential internal workings of the index file that facilitate the data retrieval process in DataStar.

Step-by-step procedure

For the data file you can rename the file you sorted earlier, PRICEULT.SRT.

1. You can use the appropriate CP/M or MS-DOS command as follows:

   CP/M: `REN PRICEULT.DTA=PRICEULT.SRT`
   MS-DOS: `REN PRICEULT.SRT PRICEULT.DTA`

   The **REN** command requires that you enter the *new name first* and the *existing name* after the equals sign. In MS-DOS the order is reversed, and there is a blank instead of an equals sign.

2. Now you have a data file which needs a matching Index file, type:

   ```
   *INPUT=200,CR
   *SORT=PRICEULT.DTA
   *OUTPUT=PRICEULT.NDX,FIXED,KP
   *KEY=#1,6,#1,2
   *GO
   ```

   Note the output attributes specifying fixed length and keys and pointers. Note also the *extra Key*—the use of #1 a second time ensures that *two extra bytes* are added to each record for DataStar to use later.

3. Finally, now you have the data and index files, you must use a program made available with DataStar version 1.4 or later—PUTEOF (this means Put End of File).

   You simply enter the following next to the A> prompt:

   ```
   PUTEOF PRICEULT.NDX
   ```

4. Press **Return** and the index file will have an end-of-file marker added.

   You do not need to understand the technicalities of what you have just done—but you must remember how to do it!

SUPERSORT FOR DATASTAR FILE MAINTENANCE

This section lists the routine that allows you to sort very large files, in the process obviating the need to use the file maintenance system from DataStar (which is perfectly fine for small files but very slow and tedious for anything larger than about 15K).

Once you have used this method, I don't suppose you will bother with file maintenance again:

```
*INPUT=545,CR
*SORT=A:QUOTES.DTA
*OUTPUT=B:QUOTES.SRT
*KEY=#2,4
*EXCLUDE=FIELD 1,1=0FFH (note this is a zero)
*WORK=B:
*GO
```

Note that the work drive is B and the output file will be written to drive B as well. If the files get very big, you will have to operate the three disk system described earlier in this chapter.

The **EXCLUDE** line means "exclude any records that have been marked for deletion in Field 1 (1,1)." The **0FFH** is the HEX CODE for the marker.

Again, you do not really need to understand these technical details—just follow the instructions.

Completing the file maintenance procedure

Having sorted QUOTES.DTA and excluded marked records (records that have been edited or deleted in DataStar), you must rename the QUOTES.SRT to QUOTES.DTA. Then you must run the sort routine that creates the new index file, using the new QUOTES.DTA as the input file.

Make sure you delete any old copies of the QUOTES data and index files.

Finally, don't forget to use PUTEOF to add an end-of-file marker to your new index File.

CONCLUSION

That is the end of the SuperSort chapter. It covered only the parts of this program that you are most likely to need. However it is a very extensive program and you should read through the manual now that you know some of the terminology to see if there are any other routines that would be useful for your particular applications.

13

MailMerge in Depth

In this last chapter you will discover the power of the MailMerge program. You will use its great flexibility to manipulate your data and text files, to produce mailing lists and labels, and (with conditional printing) to print only selected text and send it to selected clients.

You will start by extending your knowledge of merge printing letters and data; then you can try the various label formats, for label sheets that contain one-, two-, and three-across labels. You will see how to use conditional print commands to select the targets for your mailshots and to choose what you wish to say to whom by selecting the appropriate text for your form letters. Finally, I will run through some common merge printing problems and some miscellaneous tips to help you master the techniques.

PREPARING MATRIX DOCUMENTS

This section describes how you would go about sending a letter to all the clients who asked for quotes last month, telling them that there are special discounts during the Spring Sale and suggesting that the clients come into the store to check the details.

Using the QUOTES data file as an example, you will see how to use Mailmerge to extract only the data fields you require for this mailing. There were 47 fields in the original QUOTES file; you will pick out the 10 fields you need for this letter. By now you may have your own data files prepared that you could use instead of QUOTES.DTA as in these exercises. You should be able to adjust the matrix letter and dot commands to suit your own purposes.

If you have WordStar and MailMerge only, use the name and address file you created in Part One, though by now you will have entered some new data files in WordStar. Look ahead a couple of pages to see the kind of letter you will write and then go back to your non-document file and add some extra data to represent the DESIGN, SIGNED, and POSITION fields (have a look at the QUOTES file in Chapter 10 to see what data these fields contained). You can name your completed file MAILMRG.DTA and bypass the next section on the creation of the data file from the Q.MRG file. Go to the section entitled The Matrix letter and enter the form letter for your mailshot.

MailMerge for Datafield Selection

This discussion applies to you if you have all the MicroPro programs.

Step-by-step procedure

1. Boot up your system. Next to the prompt type **WS** to call up WordStar.
2. Select **L** to change the logged disk drive. You will be asked for the *new disk drive*; just enter **B** and press **Return**.
3. Now select **D** and open a new file called Q.MRG.
4. Next, you will need to enter the dot commands that define the way the letter is formatted when printed, followed by those that give the name of the data file to be called upon and the list of *variables* that it contains. Then you will type in the text of the matrix letter, defining the positions in the text where variables will be filled in from the data file.

First, make the selection of fields from QUOTES.DTA: Directly below the ruler line in your new file Q.MRG enter the following dot commands that omit page numbers, make the top and bottom margins zero, give a zero left margin, and turn off print-time line forming. Remember that the dot *must* be entered in column 1 to take effect:

```
.OP
.MT 0
.MB 0
.PO 0
.PF OFF
```

Normally in MailMerge, lines of text that contain your selected variables between ampersands—for example, &LAST&—will be automatically reformed to the margins you have preset. Obviously this is essential in most cases, because the actual data for the LAST NAME that will replace &LAST& could be anywhere from 2 characters to 20 characters long.

When, under special circumstances, you do not want a line containing variables to be reformed when printed, you can use the dot command **.PF OFF**, as you have here. You must use it in this case, because you are creating a data file of selected fields from the QUOTES.DTA file, and you want the new file to be in *precisely* the same format as an original DataStar file, so that MailMerge will handle it correctly. The .PF stands for print-time line forming.

5. Now you can add the dot commands that identify the data file and variables. As there are 47 fields in the data file, call them F1 to F47:

```
.OP
.MT 0
.MB 0
.PO 0
.PF OFF
.DF B:QUOTES.DTA
.RV F1,F2,F3,F4,F5,F6,F7,F8,F9,F10,F11,F12,F13,F14,F15,F16,F17
.RV F18,F19,F20,F21,F22,F23,F24,F25,F26,F27,F28,F29,F30,F31,F32
.RV F33,F34,F35,F36,F37,F38,F39,F40,F41,F42,F43,F44,F45,F46,F47
```

Note that you can use any unique symbols to represent the field names next to the **.RV**—the actual names do not have to be used. Note also that if the list of variables is too long to fit on one line, you simply end the line between two variables, (you do not need a comma after the last variable on the line), put another **.RV** on the next line, and continue the list where you left off. You can have as many lines starting **.RV** as necessary to complete the list.

6. Now you need to select the name and address fields, F3 to F9, the design field, F12, and the manager's name and position, F46 and F47. Since this must end up looking like a DataStar file, you have to put the variables between ampersands in data file order, with a comma between each variable, like this:

```
.OP
.MT 0
.MB 0
.PO 0
.PF OFF
.DF B:QUOTES.DTA
.RV F1,F2,F3,F4,F5,F6,F7,F8,F9,F10,F11,F12,F13,F14,F15,F16,F17
.RV F18,F19,F20,F21,F22,F23,F24,F25,F26,F27,F28,F29,F30,F31,F32
.RV F33,F34,F35,F36,F37,F38,F39,F40,F41,F42,F43,F44,F45,F46,F47
&F3&,&F4&,&F5&,&F6&,&F7&,&F8&,&F9&,&F12&,&F46&,&F47&
```

7. Press **Return** after the last ampersand. Note that your line of variables must look *exactly* like this—with no excess spaces: no line between the last **.RV** line and the beginning of your variables list and no line below the list. To be certain of this, place the cursor on the line directly below your first ampersand and press **^T** several times, until a dot appears in the flag column.

8. Now all you need to do is to merge print this file and you will have a useful data file to use for the mailing you will prepare in the next section.

9. Save Q.MRG by typing **^KD**.

10. Select **M** from the WordStar OPENING MENU and when asked for the Name of file to Merge, type **Q.MRG** and press **Return**.

11. The first prompt is:

```
                    Disk file output? Y/N
```

Type **Y** to say Yes.

12. The next prompt will be:

```
                    Disk file name?
```

13. Type **MAILMRG.DTA** then press the **ESC** key to start the merge printing process.

Remember that you must have data in the last field of your datafile records for MailMerge to function correctly.

Now your new data file, MAILMRG.DTA, is being created on drive B. When the merge is completed you will be returned to the WordStar OPENING MENU; select **N** to open a non-document file, and type **MAILMRG.DTA** to look at your file. You should see your list of name and address fields, plus the DESIGN, SIGNED, and POSITION fields, for all the clients' quotes you filled in during the DataStar tutorial.

Remember from the ReportStar tutorial that you could easily turn this data into a proper DataStar file now. You would use FormGen to design a form, MAILMRG.DEF, to match the data fields you have selected, then you would type FORMSORT MAILMRG to produce a sorted data file and an index file.

This is the way to restructure your database files, if you have version 1.0 or earlier of InfoStar (in later versions there is a data base restructuring program provided). You would use precisely the same technique, including the variable references (between ampersands) of all the existing fields you wished to keep, in any order you cared to specify. If you wished to allow for the inclusion of additional datafields, you would simply insert a comma between existing field references to indicate the position of each new field. There is a detailed example later on in this tutorial, under the heading Restructuring Data Files Using MailMerge.

The Matrix Letter

Now you have your data file organized, you can go ahead and type your matrix letter—the form letter you are going to merge with the data file.

Step-by-step procedure

1. If you are at the WordStar OPENING MENU, select **D** and open a file called **MAILSHOT.TXT**.

2. Directly below the WordStar ruler line, enter the following dot commands you need to define the *page offset*, the *top margin*, the *omit page numbers*, the name of the *data file*, and the list of *variables*.

```
.PO 15
.MT 0
.OP
.DF MAILMRG.DTA
.RV TITLE,INIT,LAST,STR,CITY,STATE,ZIP,DESIGN,SIGNED,POSITION
```

These commands say:

`.MT 0`	Printing should start where you position the print head on the paper (there is no top margin).
`.PO 15`	Leave a wide left margin.
`.OP`	Do not print page numbers.
`.DF`	Data file—use MAILMRG.DTA.
`.RV`	Read variables, as listed.

3. Now you must enter the text of the mail shot letter, inserting the variable names between ampersands wherever you want them to appear in the text.

Here is how your completed matrix letter should look:

```
. .                                                                   -
L------!-----------------------------------------------!------R       <
.PO 15                                                                <
.MT 0                                                                 <
.OP                                                                   <
.DF B:MAILMRG.DTA                                                     <
.RV TITLE,INIT,LAST,STR,CITY,STATE,ZIP,DESIGN,SIGNED,POSITION         <
&TITLE& &INIT& &LAST&                                                 <
&STR&                                                                 <
&CITY& &STATE& &ZIP&                                                  <
                                              5th March 1985          <
                                                                      <
Dear &TITLE& &LAST&,                                                  <
                                                                      <
```

```
You may remember that you visited our showrooms a  few  weeks
ago  and asked for a quotation on the &DESIGN& range of fitted
bedroom furniture.                                                <
                                                                 <
We  have some very good news for you - that price we gave  you
will be slashed by 25% in our Spring Sale!                       <
                                                                 <
This fantastic offer can only last UNTIL THE END OF MARCH - so
come in NOW and place your firm order to get your new  bedroom
furniture  at these unrepeatable prices.  I promise you,  you
won't regret it!                                                 <
                                                                 <
I look forward to seeing you in the store very soon.             <
                                                                 <
Sincerely,                                                       <
                                                                 <
                                                                 <
                                                                 <
                                                                 <
                                                                 <
&SIGNED&                                                         <
&POSITION&                                                       <
.PA                                                              .
```

The **.PA** at the end of the letter ensures that, when you merge print the letters, each one will start on a new page.

4. Again, there should be no excess spaces in your letter. With the cursor next to the .PA command, press **^T** several times. In the example notice the flag column on your screen, showing the hard returns (which you remember look like this <) after the SIGNED and POSITION lines, and the period in the flag column after the **.PA** to show that there is no hard return and, therefore, no lines following it.

Your screen should look the same.

MERGE PRINTING LETTERS AND ENVELOPES

Merge Printing the MAILSHOT Letters

Before printing save your file, MAILSHOT.TXT, by typing **^KD**.

Step-by-step procedure

1. Press **M** to select the MailMerge option from the WordStar OPENING MENU.

2. Enter the name of the file when prompted. Make sure your printer is powered on and online.
3. Then press **ESC** to start merge printing (if you have continuous stationery or a single sheet feeder) or press **Return** and accept all defaults until you reach:

```
Pause for paper change between pages? Y/N
```

4. If you have to insert single sheets one at a time, type **Y** to cause the printer to pause after each page is completed. When the first form letter has been printed, the printer will stop and the screen will display the message:

```
PRINT PAUSED merge printing B:MAILSHOT.TXT
```

5. When you have the next sheet in place, press **P** to restart the printer.
6. If you are going to merge print mailshots regularly, particularly if you are preparing more than 25 or so letters at one time, you should investigate the possibility of having a single sheet feeder attached to your printer.

If you have carefully followed the layout above, you should see the letters appearing, one by one, with all the information slotted into the appropriate places. Remember, you can interrupt the printing process at any time by pressing **P** to STOP PRINT, so as soon as you are satisfied that the merge is successful (unless you are printing your own letters and want them all) you can press **P** and then **Y** to abandon the run.

If the Merge is not correct, check through your file carefully and see if you can spot the error. If necessary, look back at the last page of Chapter 5 in Part One and run through the checklist for failed merge print runs.

Saving the MAILSHOT Header

It is worthwhile writing the details of the MAILSHOT header to a separate file for future use. You may well need the same or similar details for another letter, and it would be a waste of time to have to work the details out again—especially now that you have them functioning correctly.

Step-by-step procedure

1. Call up the MAILSHOT.TXT file in WordStar and mark the beginning of the file with a **^KB**. Move the cursor down to the line below the last line of the address and type **^KK** to mark the end of the block you wish to move.

2. Your file should look like this:

```
<B>.PO 15
.MT 0
.OP
.DF MAILMRG.DTA
.RV TITLE,INIT,LAST,STR,CITY,STATE,ZIP,DESIGN,SIGNED,POSITION
&TITLE& &INIT& &LAST&
&STR&
&CITY& &STATE& &ZIP&
<K>
```

(You will see the remaining letter text on your screen below the marker).

3. As soon as you press **Return**, the whole block will be highlighted and the <B> and <K> markers will disappear.

4. Now, type **^KW** and when prompted:

Name of file to write marked text to:

enter MAIL-HDR.FMT (for format) or some name that you will remember when you need it later. Save the original file using **^KQ**, since you have not actually edited it (you don't even have to turn off the highlighting with a **^KH**).

5. Should you need to use MAIL-HDR.FMT for another document, you simply open your new file in the usual way and then *read in* the header file using **^KR**. If necessary, you can then adjust the details of dot commands, ruler lines, and so on to suit the new purpose.

6. If subsequently you use the same details for a different mailing, you may need to include additional variables and perhaps also change the name of the data file.

Merge Printing the MAILSHOT Envelopes

You should complete this merge printing exercise by merging the envelopes to go with your letters. If you are only sending out small numbers of documents each day, you may feel that it is just as quick to type the envelopes. However, if you should need to send out large numbers of mailings, you will find it much quicker to use continuous envelopes (envelopes attached to continuous paper) and merge printing.

Step-by-step procedure

1. Open a new WordStar file called **MAIL-1.ENV** for your first mailshot and read in the header you have just created using **^KR**.

2. You will need to change some of the print formatting dot commands as follows (the additions and changes are in bold type):

```
.PL 40
.PO 33
.MT 0
.MB 0
.OP
.DF MAILMRG.DTA
.RV TITLE,INIT,LAST,STR,CITY,STATE,ZIP,DESIGN,SIGNED,POSITION
&TITLE& &INIT& &LAST&
&STR&
&CITY& &STATE& &ZIP&
.PA
```

3. You merge printed envelopes in Part One, so this is not completely unfamiliar to you. Remember that the **.PO 33** will cause the address to be printed from column 33, roughly half way across a standard business envelope. You may have to adjust this number to suit the format of the envelopes you are using.

4. Using a **.MT** of zero ensures that printing will start at the position you set the envelope in relation to the print head in the printer. This should be about midway between top and bottom. If you have continuous envelopes, the **.PA** ensures that the next envelope is fed to the same starting position, whether the previous address consisted of 3, 4, 5, or 6 lines.

5. The Page Length, **.PL 40**, ensures that the envelope will be ejected after printing. When you insert the next envelope,

you will need to press **P** to continue to print. If you are using continuous envelopes, you will have to adjust the page length to something between 15 and 25, according to the depth of the envelope. Trial and error will determine the exact figure.

6. Save your file with a **^KD** and try merge printing the envelopes. If you like, try this out first on ordinary printer paper, just to check that everything is correct before you risk wasting envelopes.

Sometimes it is not convenient to merge print envelopes. If you have very large numbers to merge print or if you are trying to print on extra large sized envelopes, it may be much quicker and simpler to use adhesive labels.

MERGE PRINTING LABELS

Labels for computer printing come in all sorts of shapes and sizes. Usually they are attached to sheets of rather heavy, coated paper and are designed to be used in a printer with a tractor feed. If you do not have such a feed, you may well have problems—the sheets of labels will tend to slide around if you try to use them with a friction roller only.

If you are planning to merge print large numbers of labels on a regular basis, you should talk to your dealer about having a tractor feed fitted to your existing printer. An alternative is to buy a cheaper, often faster, dot matrix printer to keep for labels and perhaps also for printing drafts of documents.

The most common label formats are those with the labels one-, two-, or three-across. Once you have mastered printing on these, you will be able to cope with any other format you may encounter. Also, the technique you must learn for producing labels will be used again later when you come to formatting the output from data files.

This chapter will cover each label format in turn, using the same header file as you used for envelopes. It's a good idea for you to work through all three exercises.

One-across Format

One-across labels are usually mounted on narrow paper, so to use these you will need an *adjustable tractor*.

Step-by-step procedure

1. Open a new file in WordStar called **LABEL-1.FMT** and read in the header file, **MAIL-1.ENV**, with a **^KR**.

2. Change the values for the dot commands as shown below, but notice that one-across labels use an almost identical format to envelopes.

3. Before you save this file, *make absolutely certain that you have no extra lines inserted.* For example, check that the first line of the address (&TITLE& &INIT& &LAST&) starts *immediately below* the line that begins **.RV** and that there are no extra spaces after the **.PA**. Check the flag column, as above.

   Your screen should look like this:

```
.PL 9
.PO 3
.MT 0
.MB 0
.OP
.DF MAILMRG.DTA
.RV TITLE,INIT,LAST,STR,CITY,STATE,ZIP,DESIGN,SIGNED,POSITION
&TITLE& &INIT& &LAST&
&STR&
&CITY& &STATE& &ZIP&
.PA
```

4. You may use the same label format over and over again for many different data files. It's a good idea to save the dot commands for label headers in a file, such as LBL-HDR.FMT. If you have not prepared a label file for a while, you may forget some of the vital details, such as having top and bottom margins set at zero. Include a reminder that this file is set up for the production of labels, and if any other fields are required for other purposes, then the variable references must be added where appropriate (put two dots before the text of a reminder so that it will not print). Here is an example:

```
..THIS IS THE FORMAT FOR PRODUCING LABELS - IF YOU WISH TO ADD
..EXTRA FIELDS YOU MUST PUT IN THE VARIABLE REFERENCES WHERE
..YOU WISH THE DATA TO PRINT
```

5. Since the size of labels varies so much, it is a good idea to try your first merge printing on plain paper; then you can compare the labels with the print out and check that your length and width are correct and that a page offset of 3 causes the address to start printing in the right position on the label.

6. Save the file, select **M** for MailMerge, enter the file name and press the **ESC** key to start printing. As soon as 4 or 5 addresses have printed, you can press **P** to *stop print* and then **Y** to abandon it.

7. If all is well with the format, go ahead and merge print your actual labels. If not, make the appropriate adjustments to the dot commands in your file (page length and page offset) and try again on plain paper until you are completely satisfied with the result.

Two-across Format

To print out labels in the two-across format will require precisely the same dot commands as used for the one-across. The difference is in the way you must design the format. Once you have mastered this format, you will have no problem with any of the other labels in multiple columns.

Step-by-step procedure

1. Open a new file in WordStar called LABEL-2.FMT and read in the MAIL-1.ENV file using **^KR**. These dot commands do not change:

```
.PL 9
.PO 3
.MT 0
.MB 0
.OP
.DF MAILMRG.DTA
.RV TITLE,INIT,LAST,STR,CITY,STATE,ZIP,DESIGN,SIGNED,POSITION
&TITLE& &INIT& &LAST&
&STR&
&CITY& &STATE& &ZIP&
.PA
```

They are the same as for one-across labels. Now for the new commands.

2. You have to set the file up in such a way as to cause the first name and address to be printed on the left-hand label, the second on the right-hand label, the third on the left-hand label on the next row, and so on.

   To achieve this, you enter the command **^P and press Return**, this gives you a minus sign in the flag column on the far right of your screen. This gives the *appearance* of a line feed on your screen, but when it is printed out, everything up to the *hard return* prints as one line. In sequence, then, the first line is printed on the first label, the printer makes a carriage return without a line feed, the print head tabs across to the second label and prints *its* first line, then does a carriage return *and* a line feed ready to print the second line.

3. In order to distinguish between those addresses that print on the left-hand labels and those that print on the right, you must duplicate the **.RV** and then add **1** to each variable name in the first set and **2** to each in the second.

   To duplicate **.RV**, mark the block with a **^KB** at the beginning and a **^KK** at the end, move the cursor to the next line and press **^KC** to copy the block, as shown:

```
<B>.RV TITLE,INIT,LAST,STR,CITY,STATE,ZIP,DESIGN,SIGNED,POSITION<K>
```

4. Move to the next line and press **^KC** to COPY the marked block:

```
.RV TITLE,INIT,LAST,STR,CITY,STATE,ZIP,DESIGN,SIGNED,POSITION
<K>.RV TITLE,INIT,LAST,STR,CITY,STATE,ZIP,DESIGN,SIGNED,POSITION<K>
```

5. Now turn off the highlighting by typing **^KH.**Your file will look like this:

```
.DF MAILMRG.DTA
.RV TITLE,INIT,LAST,STR,CITY,STATE,ZIP,DESIGN,SIGNED,POSITION
.RV TITLE,INIT,LAST,STR,CITY,STATE,ZIP,DESIGN,SIGNED,POSITION
&TITLE& &INIT& &LAST&
&STR&
&CITY& &STATE& &ZIP&
.PA
```

6. Now you must add the 1 and 2 to those variable names that you actually plan to use on the labels, as follows:

```
.RV TITLE1,INIT1,LAST1,STR1,CITY1,STATE1,ZIP1,DESIGN,SIGNED,POSITION
.RV TITLE2,INIT2,LAST2,STR2,CITY2,STATE2,ZIP2,DESIGN,SIGNED,POSITION
```

7. Finally, you have to position the variable names in the correct position for the addresses to print two-across on the labels.

    First cancel all tabs by pressing ^ON; then enter **A** for all. Set a new tab at column 36 by typing ^OI and entering **36** for the tab position. This marks the left margin of your second label.

8. You must then enter the variable names one line at a time, starting on the far left of the screen for the first set and tabbing to column 36 to enter the second set (see the following example).

9. After you have typed in the variables for the first line (TITLE1, INIT1 & LAST1) on the left-hand label, you must press ^**P** and **Return**, giving a minus sign in the flag column, then tab to column 36 and enter the variables for the right-hand label, as shown:

```
L---------------------------!----------------------------R
&TITLE1& &INIT1& &LAST1&                                  -

                           &TITLE2& &INIT2& &LAST2&       <
```

10. Remember, the ^**P** and **Return** tell the printer to do a carriage return *without* a line feed. If you watch the printing process you will see that after the first name is printed, the print head returns to the beginning of the same line, then moves to column 36 (as set) and prints the second name on the same line. If you have a printer that prints bi-directionally, it may be a bit more difficult to see what is happening.

11. Now continue entering the other variables for the remaining address lines as shown. Make sure your flag column (on the far right of your screen) looks just like this example:

```
L--------------------------!-----------------------------R
&TITLE1& &INIT1& &LAST1&                                -
                           &TITLE2& &INIT2& &LAST2&      <
&STR1&                                                  -
                           &STR2&                        <
&CITY1& &STATE1& &ZIP1&                                 -
                           &CITY2& &STATE2& &ZIP2&       <
```

12. Although this looks so strange on the screen, you will find that when printed out, the addresses on the two labels will look quite normal.

    As a final check, this is what your file should now look like:

```
L--------------------------!-----------------------------R
.PL 9
.PO 3
.MT 0
.MB 0
.OP
.DF MAILMRG.DTA
.RV TITLE1,INIT1,LAST1,STR1,CITY1,STATE1,ZIP1,DESIGN,SIGNED,POSITION
.RV TITLE2,INIT2,LAST2,STR2,CITY2,STATE2,ZIP2,DESIGN,SIGNED,POSITION
&TITLE1& &INIT1& &LAST1&                                -
                           &TITLE2& &INIT2& &LAST2&      <
&STR1&                                                  -
                           &STR2&                        <
&CITY1& &STATE1& &ZIP1&                                 -
                           &CITY2& &STATE2& &ZIP2&       <
.PA                                                      .
```

Make sure that you have no extra blank lines, either between each **.RV** and the variable references, or at the end of the file, after the **.PA**.

13. Try the print format on plain paper first to make sure you have everything just right. Save your LABEL- 2.FMT file and then select **M**, enter the file name and press **ESC** to start printing.

14. Check first of all to see if the merge printing is successful, and then to make sure that the spacing is correct for your two-across labels. If not, call up your format file again and adjust the tab position, page length, page offset, and so on,

until you are satisfied with the printout. Check again on plain paper and then try printing the labels.

Having watched the labels printing out and, hopefully, having achieved success, you may be able to see why you need this rather complicated format when printing two-across labels. Since the variable names between ampersands are replaced with *actual* names, which may vary enormously in length, and since you want them to print out in *set positions* on the same line, then after the first entry has printed out on the first label, you must *force a carriage return* (but without a line feed) so that the second entry starts at tab position 36 on the same line, however long or short the previous entry was.

Here is an example:

```
&STR1&                                              —

                          &STR2&                    <
```

produces the following:

```
135 New Printing House Square   1 Main Street
```

Even if these happened to be the other way round, you would still wish the *second* street name to start printing in the same position:

```
1 Main Street                   135 New Printing House Square
```

Try out the effect of simply positioning the &STR1& and &STR2& on the same line, with the tab stop at column 36 and using the same data file, and you will see how the entry of the first street name pushes the second one right across the page. It soon becomes clear why you must have the ^P with a **Return** after the first entry and before the second.

If you have variable length addresses (in terms of the number of lines of address) you will see an occasional blank line on some of your labels. This is unavoidable when using two-across (or more) labels, unless you can standardize your addresses to occupy the same number of lines.

If the occasional blank line really bothers you, but you have a stock of two-across labels, you could use the one-across label format to print all the left-hand labels first, then simply run the labels through the other way around when you reach the end of your continuous label stock (so that the right-hand labels are now on the left).

Three-across Format

I will not go through this format in such detail, since there are just a few additional points to mention. In most respects, the technique is just the same for any multicolumn format.

Step-by-step procedure

1. Open a new file in WordStar called **LABEL-3.FMT**. Read in the LABEL-2.FMT if you have just entered it.
2. This time you will need tab stops at 31 and 61 (adjust these in the light of experience gained for two-across if appropriate); the right margin should be set to **90**; and you will need to make a further copy of the **.RV** lines, ending up with three sets in all. Use the block move command as before to mark the set of **.RV** lines you need to copy with a **^KB** at the beginning and a **^KK** at the end. Then use **^KC** to copy them. The other dot commands remain the same.
3. Add a **3** to each of the third set of variable names that you plan to use on your labels and then set out the variable reference positions as before. This time you will enter a **^P** and **Return** after the second entry as well as the first and only enter a *hard return* after the third. You will end up with something like this:

```
L-------------------------!-------------------------!--------------------R
.PL 9
.PO 3
.MT 0
.MB 0
.OP
.DF MAILMRG.DTA
.RV TITLE1,INIT1,LAST1,STR1,CITY1,STATE1,ZIP1,DESIGN,SIGNED,POSITION
.RV TITLE2,INIT2,LAST2,STR2,CITY2,STATE2,ZIP2,DESIGN,SIGNED,POSITION
.RV TITLE3,INIT3,LAST3,STR3,CITY3,STATE3,ZIP3,DESIGN,SIGNED,POSITION
&TITLE1& &INIT1& &LAST1&                                              -
                    &TITLE2& &INIT2& &LAST2&                          -
                                        &TITLE3& &INIT& &LAST& <
```

```
&STR1&                                                              —
                        &STR2&                                      —
                                                &STR3&              <
&CITY1& &STATE1& &ZIP1&                                             —
                        &CITY2& &STATE2& &ZIP2&                     —
                                        &CITY3& &STATE3& &ZIP3&<
.PA
```

Your screen should be laid out more or less like this.

4. Now you can save this file and try printing it out as before, starting with plain paper until you are sure everything is satisfactory.

5. When you feel happy that you have the correct format in your file, try printing out the three-across labels.

If you have addresses in your data file with different numbers of address lines, you will find some blank lines in your labels. If this appearance really bothers you, you have the choice of using only the one-across labels or of standardizing your address format so that all addresses occupy the same number of lines.

Although label formatting may seem rather complicated to begin with, you are learning some very useful techniques that you can apply in other situations. Also, once you have achieved success with one set of addresses and labels, you can use the same format over and over again for other data files (as long as you keep the same type of labels).

FORMATTING DATA FILE OUTPUT

In the ReportStar tutorial you saw how easily your data could be selected, formatted, and turned into an attractive report. Now you will learn to produce a similar result with MailMerge and WordStar. If you only have the Wordstar and MailMerge programs, this is how you will always produce lists.

You know that if you print out your data file directly from WordStar it is a little difficult to pick out precisely the data you want. Ideally you need the data to be arranged in columns and well-spaced, so that you can run your eye down the list with ease. In ReportStar you select the data by choosing the DataStar field names as headers for columns of data. With merge printing you use a similar technique to the label formatting you have just mastered.

You will open a format file in WordStar, enter the dot commands, a data file name, and the list of variables; then decide upon the tab positions and place the variable references (the names between ampersands) where you want the data to print out.

Data Output Format File

Step-by-step procedure

1. Open a file in WordStar, such as DATA-OPT.FMT. For this list you could accept the defaults for all the page formatting dot commands (.PL, etc.), so you don't need to type any.

2. Decide which data file you wish to format and enter the file name next to a .DF and the list of variables next to a .RV. Use the QUOTES data file; to save typing in all those .RV lines again, you can read in the Q.MRG file that you used at the beginning of this chapter, when you first created the MAILMRG.DTA file.

3. When you have read in Q.MRG (or MAILMRG.DTA if you have WS and MM only) you will have to erase the lines (with ^Y) containing the dot commands, until you reach the .DF line. It is a good idea to enter the names of the data fields for those you are going to actually use (see below) in place of the F numbers.

4. Now enter a ruler line; let's say you want to make a list of clients with the date they received a quotation and the total amount quoted. You will need tab stops for three columns: the first for the name, the second for the date, and the third for the amount, as follows:

```
  . .                                                         —
L-!-------------------------!-------------!---------------R   <
```

5. Directly below the ruler line you can enter the variable references. Again, you will be printing out variable length fields, more than one on a line, so you will need to employ the same technique as you used for multiple labels.

Tab to the first position and enter the first variable

name, then press **^P** and **Return**. Notice the minus sign in the flag column.

6. Tab to the next position and enter the second variable name, and press **^P** and **Return** again. Finally, tab to the third position and enter the last variable and press the **Return** key to put in a hard return. Your file will look like this:

```
.DF B:QUOTES.DTA
.RV F1,F2,TITLE,INIT,LAST,F6,F7,F8,F9,F10,F11,F12,F13,F14,F15,F16
.RV F17,F18,F19,F20,F21,F22,F23,F24,F25,F26,F27,F28,F29,F30,F31,F32
.RV F33,F34,F35,F36,F37,F38,F39,F40,F41,F42,F43,TOTAL,DATE,F46,F47
```

Notice that this time you do not have a .PA since you don't want each name to start on a separate page. However, if you would like the list to print out *double-spaced*, simply press **Return** again to insert an extra line (as shown here).

7. Save the file with a **^KD**, select **M**, and enter the file name for merge printing, DATA-OPT.FMT.

8. Press the **ESC** key and printing will begin. After printing out the first record from your data file, a blank line will be left before the next record is printed (that is, it will be double-spaced).

   If you find that the date field is overwriting the last few characters in the name field, you will have to interrupt printing by pressing **P** and then **Y** to abandon it.

9. Call up your format file again and move the tab stops to make enough space for even your longest name. Save the edited file and proceed as before.

10. You may find it more convenient to list the names last name first, if you are making a reference list in alphabetical order. For example:

&LAST&, &TITLE& &INIT&,

If you wanted the title and initials to start in a set position, to make for easy reading, you would have to use ^P and **Return** after the last name, and start &TITLE& at an appropriate tab setting.

You will probably find it very useful to be able to format your data file output in this way, and you will soon think of other applications for this handy procedure.

Restructuring Data Files with MailMerge

If you have version 1.0 of InfoStar you will not have the database restructuring software, so here is a MailMerge technique to achieve a similar result. This is an advanced technique, so don't try it until you are familiar with handling data files in FormGen, DataStar, FormSort, WordStar, and MailMerge. To complete this maneuver you need expertise in all of these programs.

After using any particular data file for a time, you may find that there are some fields you never use or, more likely, that you would like to add some additional fields. You can use MailMerge to restructure an existing data file, using a similar method to the one you used for the Q.MRG file at the beginning of this chapter.

Step-by-step procedure

1. First make a copy of your existing form, naming the copy (with a name like NEW). Then carefully redesign the new form in FormGen until it is the way you would like it to be, by adding, deleting, and renaming fields as required. Don't be too ambitious or make the changes too complicated.

2. Make a list (by hand, on paper) of all the fields in your original form, calling them F1 to F-whatever, then list them in the new order you have created, leaving out any F-numbers (fields) you have excluded from the new form design. Insert commas to allow spaces for any new fields.
   Make sure your list exactly matches the NEW form design in terms of field names and field order.

3. Now you can open a WordStar file called NEW.MRG and enter the dot commands, precisely as in Q.MRG, including the name of your original data file next to the .DF and the full list of existing fields (using the F-numbers) next to the

.RV lines. Don't forget the .PF OFF command, which prevents print time line forming, and ensures that your new file looks just like a DataStar file.

You can read in the Q.MRG file you created earlier in this chapter, to give you a format to follow, and then delete the sections you don't want.

4. Follow the format in Q.MRG and, below the .RV lines, enter the variable references (the list of the F-numbers enclosed in ampersands) of the fields you wish to keep, in the order you want them. Separate each one with a comma. Insert a comma for each new field in the appropriate position in the list.

5. Now save the WordStar file, select MailMerge, and merge print to a disk file, giving it the name of your new data file (such as NEW.DTA). If you have a large data file, this process will take several minutes to complete.

6. Have a look at the new file as a non-document file (select **N** at the OPENING MENU); it should look just like a DataStar file.

7. Finally you should use FormSort to create an index file to match (just type FORMSORT/N NEW); try calling it up in DataStar (DATASTAR NEW) and make sure everything works correctly.

If it doesn't work the first time, don't worry—you still have your original data file. Just check for errors and try again. Once you get it right, you will find this a very useful technique.

CONDITIONAL PRINTING

Now that you have had some practice with general merge printing, you can try the facility termed *conditional printing*. As the name suggests, this allows you to specify the conditions under which merge printing of certain text will either occur—or not—according to the way you set up your file. This means you can send out a whole series of letters to various clients, in a single merge printing run, selecting and excluding appropriate paragraphs of the text of your letter, according to the client you are addressing.

There are some new dot commands to learn and some concepts about the logic of conditional printing that you must understand fully.

Dot Commands

There are three dot commands for conditional printing: the .IF command, the .EX command, and the .EF command. The IF command says "*IF* this command line is so, then GO TO the end command (the .EF) and print what follows." The .EX command says "*EX*cept when this command line is so, GO TO the end command and print what follows." The .EF command defines the position in your letter or document where printing will be resumed if the conditions you have specified next to your IF or EX statements are met.

Preparing the Matrix Document

You will start with something very straightforward, using the QUOTES data file as before.

Step-by-step procedure

1. Call up WordStar and change logged drives to B.
2. Select **D** and open a file called **CONPRIN.MRG**. Type **^KR** and read in the file called **Q.MRG** which you used at the beginning of the chapter. This will give you the data file name to use, and the list of variables:

```
.OP
.MT 0
.MB 0
.PO 0
.PF OFF
.DF B:QUOTES.DTA
.RV F1,F2,F3,F4,F5,F6,F7,F8,F9,F10,F11,F12,F13,F14,F15,F16,F17
.RV F18,F19,F20,F21,F22,F23,F24,F25,F26,F27,F28,F29,F30,F31,F32
.RV F33,F34,F35,F36,F37,F38,F39,F40,F41,F42,F43,F44,F45,F46,F47
&F3&,&F4&,&F5&,&F6&,&F7&,&F8&,&F9&,&F12&,&F46&,&F47&
```

3. You can modify this by deleting the line **.PF OFF** with **^Y**, and removing **&F46** and **&F47&** from your line of data to merge. Then replace the variable numbers, **F3, F4, F5, F12** and **F44**, with TITLE,INIT,LAST,DESIGN and TOTAL, as shown:

```
.OP
.MT 0
.MB 0
.PO 0
.DF B:QUOTES.DTA
.RV
F1,F2,TITLE,INIT,LAST,F6,F7,F8,F9,F10,F11,DESIGN,F13,F14,F15,F16
.RV F17,F18,F19,F20,F21,F22,F23,F24,F25,F26,F27,F28,F29,F30,F31,F32
.RV F33,F34,F35,F36,F37,F38,F39,F40,F41,F42,F43,TOTAL,F45,F46,F47
&TITLE&,&INIT&,&LAST&,&DESIGN&,&TOTAL&
```

Now you have a manageable data file and can test the various formats of conditional printing. Go through the two examples, and then I will explain afterward how they worked.

Conditional Commands

There are two basic conditional command lines of the form:

```
Dot command-&variable&-comparison-''expression''-GOTO-end command
```

Step-by-step procedure

1. Enter the commands:

```
.IF      &DESIGN&      =      ''SUPREME''    GOTO   .EF
.EX      &TOTAL&       >      ''$1250.00''   GOTO   .EF
```

The **.IF** or **.EX** commands must be placed in the line below the last .RV line and above the text line they refer to. The end command, **.EF**, must go after the text line. This is how it should look:

```
.OP
.MT 0
.MB 0
.PO 0
.DF B:QUOTES.DTA
.RV F1,F2,TITLE,INIT,LAST,F6,F7,F8,F9,F10,F11,DESIGN,F13,F14,F15,F16
.RV F17,F18,F19,F20,F21,F22,F23,F24,F25,F26,F27,F28,F29,F30,F31,F32
.RV F33,F34,F35,F36,F37,F38,F39,F40,F41,F42,F43,TOTAL,F45,F46,F47
```

```
.IF &DESIGN& = ''SUPREME'' GOTO
&TITLE&,&INIT&,&LAST&,&DESIGN&,&TOTAL&
.EF
```

2. Now save the file with **^KD** and select **M** to merge print CONPRIN.MRG. Make sure your printer is online and press **ESC**.

3. When you look at the printout you will see that only Finesse and Ultima records have been printed—the design you specified in your command line, Supreme, has been *excluded*.

4. Now try the **.EX** command in the CONPRIN.MRG file (I will just show the lines from the last .RV line onward):

```
.RV F33,F34,F35,F36,F37,F38,F39,F40,F41,F42,F43,TOTAL,F45,F46,F47
.EX &DESIGN& = ''SUPREME'' GOTO
&TITLE&,&INIT&,&LAST&,&DESIGN&,&TOTAL&
.EF
```

5. Save the file and merge print it. This time when you look at the printout you will see that only the Supreme records have printed. This time Supreme has been *included*.

The explanation of these two examples is as follows: The **.IF** command says, IF a record matches the specified DESIGN then **GOTO** the **.EF** end statement—in other words, bypass the text line completely.

The **.EX** command says, EXCEPT when a record matches the specified DESIGN **GOTO** the **.EF** end statement—in other words, print the text line.

In effect, .IF means EXCLUDE (*don't* print) the records that match; .EX means INCLUDE (*do* print) the records that match.

This kind of logic takes a bit of getting used to; try some more examples. This time specify that DESIGN may be Supreme *or* Finesse, using a special kind of OR, written **.OR.** (You must use uppercase letters and a period either side, exactly as shown.) It looks like this:

```
.RV F33,F34,F35,F36,F37,F38,F39,F40,F41,F42,F43,TOTAL,F45,F46,F47
.IF &DESIGN& = ''SUPREME'' .OR. &DESIGN& = ''FINESSE'' GOTO
&TITLE&,&INIT&,&LAST&,&DESIGN&,&TOTAL&
.EF
```

Based upon the logic worked out here, the **IF** command should exclude the designs that match, so when you save your file and merge print it, you should have Ultima records only. Try it now. You will see that the logic worked.

The way the computer processes these commands is very simple (and positively Spock-like in its logic!): it takes each record in turn and compares it with the **IF** or **EX** command. In the example above, the computer is asking each record:

```
IF &DESIGN& = ''SUPREME'' .OR. &DESIGN& = ''FINESSE'' GOTO EF
```

For example, looking at one data record where the DESIGN is FINESSE:

```
Does FINESSE equal ''SUPREME'' OR does FINESSE equal ''FINESSE''
```

In this case the answer is YES—FINESSE does equal FINESSE—so the command **GOTO END STATEMENT** is followed, bypassing the text line, and hence the record is excluded and does not print.

The design field in the next record is Ultima; the computer compares this with the designs specified in the command, saying:

```
Does ULTIMA equal ''SUPREME'' OR does ULTIMA equal ''FINESSE''
```

Clearly the answer is no—so the **GOTO END STATEMENT** is *not* followed, the text line is *not* bypassed, and hence the record is included and prints.

Now try some numeric values. With this first numeric example you can try out the special AND statement—written **.AND.**—and the "greater than" and "less than" signs; call up your file again and modify it as shown:

```
.RV F33,F34,F35,F36,F37,F38,F39,F40,F41,F42,F43,TOTAL,F45,F46,F47
.IF &TOTAL& > ''$1650.00'' .AND. &TOTAL& < ''$2000.00'' GOTO
&TITLE&,&INIT&,&LAST&,&DESIGN&,&TOTAL&
.EF
```

While your file is merge printing, work out the logic of this IF command. Remember that IF means "exclude matches."

Examine the printout to see that the **IF** command caused every record that had a TOTAL lying between the amounts specified to be excluded.

Go back into your file and just change the **IF** to **.EX** You know how that will work out, but go ahead and run it anyway, for more practice. Finally, you should try some *combinations* of **IF** and **.EX** commands: Call up your file and make the changes shown:

```
.RV F33,F34,F35,F36,F37,F38,F39,F40,F41,F42,F43,TOTAL,F45,F46,F47
.EX &TOTAL& > ''$1650.00'' .AND. &TOTAL& < ''$2000.00'' GOTO
.IF &DESIGN& = ''SUPREME'' .OR. &DESIGN& = ''ULTIMA'' GOTO
&TITLE&,&INIT&,&LAST&,&DESIGN&,&TOTAL&
.EF
```

Again, try to work out the result while your file is merge printing; just use the printout to confirm your logic.

You now have a list of Finesse records with totals lying between $1650 and $2000.

Is it obvious to you that you cannot have a line like this:

```
.IF &DESIGN& = ''SUPREME'' .AND. &DESIGN& = ''ULTIMA''
```

At first glance, it may seem that it should produce precisely the same result as the **.OR.** command—but it won't work, will it? There is no way that the computer program can find a record whose DESIGN field matches Supreme *and* Ultima (remember, it had no trouble finding records that matched Supreme *or* Ultima.

There are other comparison characters available for comparing the variable name against the data:

=	Equal
<>	Not equal
<	Less than
>	Greater than
<=	Less than or equal to
>=	Greater than or equal to

If you have had any difficulty in grasping these examples, run through them several times until the logic is clear, then make up some of your own, perhaps using a different data file.

If you try the ADDRESS.DTA file, you can select clients who live in various states or telephone area codes, and select only those clients for your next mailing. You will be learning some different conditional print commands in the next section on file insertion techniques, which will allow you to select certain paragraphs of text.

FILE INSERTION

One of the most useful functions in word processing is the ability to store units of information in files on disk, which can be read into the document you are entering as required. For example, a lawyer (or secretary) may prepare the same kind of contract over and over again, with just the occasional sentence or paragraph specific to one client. The standard paragraphs could be kept separately in disk files, perhaps named PARA-1, PARA-2, PARA-3, and so on.

Up to now, you have read files into documents "by hand," using the **^KR** command. Now you will learn a new automatic technique using MailMerge instead, and a new dot command, **.FI** file insert.

The technique is to prepare a document in the usual way, entering the basic background text that is required for that particular document, then at points in the text where you wish to read in a standard paragraph, you simply enter a **.FI** followed by the file name (such as .FI PARA-1.TXT).

You could have almost the whole document made up of standard paragraphs, so that the file would look like a list of **.FI** commands and file names, with the odd word or two of text interspersed where necessary. With practice you could prepare a 10 page document in five minutes!

These paragraph files, known in WordStar jargon as "boilerplate" text (because they are kept "simmering on the stove" ready for immediate use when required), can be updated easily whenever necessary, so you know that the documents that incorporate them always have access to the latest version of the text.

Step-by-step procedure

1. Start by opening a file in WordStar called PARA-1.TXT. Enter a few lines of standard information which you may need in every day letter writing. For example, you may have some standard terms and conditions of sale that are added to every invoice or quotation you send out. You could enter these into the file.

2. You must make sure that there is a final *hard return* at the end of the file.

3. Save this file and then open another called **PARA-2.TXT** and type in some other useful text.

4. Now open a third file called **DOC-1.TXT** and enter some text that will be able to incorporate the paragraphs you have on file. This is the kind of format you should create:

```
.FI STD-HDR.TXT
.SV DATE 17 October, 1985
                                        &DATE&

Dear Sirs,


We are in receipt of your order dated 10/15/85.


.FI PARA-1.TXT
.FI PARA-2.TXT


Yours faithfully,


M Jones
Accountant
```

You must have wondered about the new dot command, **.SV DATE**, and the &DATE& in the letter text. This *set variable* can be very useful when you are regularly merge printing form letters.

5. Before you save your file, type in today's date next to the **.SV DATE** command, and you will find that the date will print out correctly on each of your merge printed letters. Next time you merge print the same file, you just have to enter the new date next to the **.SV**.

6. When the month name changes length (say from July to August) you will have to adjust the position of &DATE& so that it is still justified with your text when the letter prints out.

7. Now save DOC-1.TXT with **^KD** then press **M** for merge print and enter the file name.

8. When printed out, the letter will include the paragraphs from PARA-1.TXT and PARA-2.TXT, something like this:

17 October, 1985

Dear Sirs,

We are in receipt of your order dated 10/15/85.

Please note that as you do not have an account with us, I must ask you to reorder these goods enclosing a check made out for the full amount.

If you would like to open an account with the company, please arrange for two trade references and a bank reference to be sent to me.

Yours faithfully,

M Jones
Accountant

Note that you can even use file insertion to read in the standard dot commands and ruler lines (STD-HDR.TXT), which will then be implemented when the letter or document is merge printed.

Conditional Printing with .FI

Earlier you tried conditional printing commands to select and exclude clients name from a mailing list. You can use similar commands to select or exclude various paragraphs of text in your form letters.

Try a really simple example, where you, as a Connecticut-based company, want to include a line of text that asks your local customers to add sales tax to their orders, and to ask out-of-state customers to add an amount for shipping.

Step-by-step procedure

This time we will use the Clients.Dta file, for a change:

1. Call up **WS** and open a file called **SALES.LET**.

2. Enter the following:

```
.OP
.PO 10
.DF CLIENTS.DTA
.RV CNUM,TITL,INIT,LAST,STR,CITY,STAT,ZIP,TELA,TELN
.SV DATE 1 November, 1985
&TITL& &INIT& &LAST&
&STR&
&CITY& &STAT& &ZIP&


                                        &DATE&


Dear &TITL& &LAST&,


This Fall we are offering all our regular customers the chance
to take part in a Grand Prize Drawing.  Just take some time to
browse through our new catalog and make a minimum purchase  of
$1000  - and  you could  win  a  fabulous  world   cruise!


Don't delay - order today.
```

3. At this point you want to remind your customers about sales tax or shipping.

   After that last line, add the following:

```
Don't delay - order today.


.EX &STAT& = ''CT'' GOTO SALESTAX.PAR
.FI SALESTAX.PAR
.EF SALESTAX.PAR
.IF &STAT& = ''CT'' GOTO SHIPPING.PAR
.FI SHIPPING.PAR
.EF SHIPPING.PAR


I look forward to hearing from you soon.


Sincerely,
```

```
J Bragg                                                        <
Manager                                                        <
.PA                                                            .
```

4. Now save your file with ^**KD**.

   Cast your mind back to the earlier exercise in conditional printing, so you can work out the logic of these commands.

   The **.EX** command is saying, except when the State is CT, **GOTO** the **END** command (**.EF SALESTAX.PAR**), bypassing the sales tax paragraph (and going straight to the shipping paragraph). This means that Connecticut customers will have the paragraph on Sales tax included; customers from other states will bypass this paragraph and go on to the next.

   The **.IF** command says, **IF** the State is CT, **GOTO** the **END** command (**.EF SHIPPING.PAR**) thus bypassing the shipping paragraph. This means that only the local customers will *not* include the shipping paragraph—all the rest will.

5. Next you have to make the two files that will be read in by the file insertion command. Open a file in WordStar called SALESTAX.PAR and type in a line such as:

```
Mail order customers - don't forget to add 5.5% Sales Tax.    <
                                                              <
```

   You must type this directly below the WS ruler line, with no dot commands above.

6. At the end of the line press **Return** to go to the next line, and then another **Return** to add one blank line to the file. This format is important, as you will see when you print your letters. Any extra lines or spaces you include will be read into your letter.

7. Now do the same for SHIPPING.PAR, something like this:

```
Mail order customers, please add $10 toward shipping.         <
                                                              <
```

   Note the two "hard returns" indicated in the flag column.

8. Now save your file and merge print it. Check the printout to make sure the commands worked out as expected.

9. Try out some different combinations with some of your own data files if possible, so that you really understand the way these commands work.

Look back over the earlier exercise on conditional printing and work through the logic again.

Printing Files in Succession with .FI

You can use the file insertion command, **.FI**, to print files one after the other (queue printing).

This could be used to print out the chapter files for a book in succession, for example. If the book chapters are on more than one disk, you can use the command CHANGE after the chapter number that is on another disk. You will want each chapter to start on a fresh page, so you have to make sure that each chapter ends with a .PA. Using this technique will also number the pages in succession for you.

If you would like to try this example but do not have book chapters to print, use a series of letters, or create some "dummy" files to use.

Step-by-step procedure

1. You need a file containing the dot commands for formatting the output (BOOK.HDR) and the list of **.FI** files names, such as:

```
.FI BOOK.HDR
.FI CHAPTER.1
.FI CHAPTER.2
.FI CHAPTER.3
.FI CHAPTER.4   CHANGE
.FI CHAPTER.5
.FI CHAPTER.6
```

This would cause Chapter 1 to be printed, then a new page would start for Chapter 2 (because of a **.PA** at the end of the actual chapter) and so on until all were complete. You would change disks for Chapters 4, 5, and 6. The individual chapters would still be accessible for updating and editing.

2. If you would like the page numbering of each chapter to start at **1** you could use yet another dot command, **.PN 1**. You would put this at the head of each chapter, along with any other dot commands to do with the format of your printout (page offset, top margin, and so on).

3. You can also specify the column at which you wish the page number to appear—the default is column 33 (the center of the page). If you type **.PC 70**, the page number will appear on the right of the page, as in most books.

4. Sometimes when you print a document, you may wish the first page to have no page number; if so, type **.OP** at the head of the file. If you wished the subsequent pages to be numbered from 2 onward, you would put **.PN 2** at the head of page 2.

MERGE PRINTING REPORTS

You can use the file insertion technique to incorporate data from other files, such as tables from CalcStar, DataStar or ReportStar, and produce reports that are well laid out. For example, you could include some of the data you entered in the CalcStar tutorial in a report about the success, or otherwise, of new furniture designs.

Entering the Matrix Document

The following pages show **.FI** commands; see how you would use them to lay out the actual report itself, using **.FI** to call up the data files in the appropriate places in the text.

You must first prepare the tables to be used by editing the CalcStar output files in WordStar. Look ahead at the text and data listed then produce something similar for yourself, by creating files (TABLE.1 and TABLE.2) in WordStar, and reading in the appropriate .PRN files from your CalcStar data disk.

Then open a file called TABLE.HDR and enter the appropriate dot commands and ruler line to give you the final format for your report. You can try it out on the first draft, and if necessary, change some commands if the result is not quite what you had planned. You can then use **.FI** to read in the suitable header and ruler line, as shown.

```
.FI TABLE.HDR
        INTERIM REPORT ON NEW BEDROOM RANGES  -  NOVEMBER 1985
```

INTRODUCTION

Following the decision last year to find a new design of bedroom
furniture to add to the top end of our current range, Ultima was
chosen and made available from stock in January this year.

Market research showed that there was a significant demand for a
more sophisticated product, quality being very much more
important than price at this top end of the market.

Target figures for sales and profit margin were based on the
other designs in our range and were as follows for the first six
months of this year:

```
------------------------------------------------------------------
.FI TABLE.1
------------------------------------------------------------------
```

PROGRESS REPORT

Sales went extremely well for the first three months, slightly
exceeding the target we had set. Although the second three
months were not quite so convincing, this was not because of any
great fall-off in sales.   Our rapidly increasing costs accounted
for the moderate overall achievement.   However, the showroom
managers are delighted with the product and its appeal to the
customer and are inclined to be optimistic about its future.

Here are the figures for the first six months of this year:

```
------------------------------------------------------------------
.FI TABLE.2
------------------------------------------------------------------
```

It is difficult to plan the page layout precisely when you are
calling in tables using **.FI**. The easiest way is to go ahead and
merge print a draft of the report and then make any adjustments
required to get page breaks where you want them, consistent margins, etc.

Note the use of lines of hyphens above and below the **.FI** 's. When the tables print out this sets them off nicely from the surrounding text, as you will see in Figure 13–1.

Well, that gives you a good idea of how to lay out your report. The finished result can be superior to the output direct from ReportStar, CalcStar or SuperSort.

MISCELLANEOUS COMMANDS AND USEFUL TIPS

Miscellaneous Commands

Although you have covered most of the everyday uses of MailMerge, there are some other functions that might prove useful.

Ask for variable

There is yet another dot command—**.AV**—that asks for a variable to be entered by the operator, there and then. This can be useful, for example, for entering the date.

When you set up your file, you would have the usual formatting dot commands, then you could have a **.AV**:

.AV ''Enter today's date'', DATE

The words in quotes (the prompt) will appear on the screen, the operator types in the date, and then the date will be entered in the text wherever the variable reference for date (&DATE&) is found. Notice there is a space after the date and before the second quotes (date ''); This improves the appearance on the screen when the prompt appears and you have to type in the response.

Other uses of the **.AV** are to force the operator to enter data in a particular way and to set a maximum length on the data that can be entered for one specific variable:

.AV ''Enter date in form MM/DD/YY '',DATE

or:

.AV ''Enter today's date in the form 7th October,1985 '',DATE

You can probably think of other uses for this command appropriate to your particular requirements.

FIGURE 13-1 Report Using File Insertion Technique

```
.FI TABLE.HDR
          INTERIM REPORT ON NEW BEDROOM RANGES  -  NOVEMBER 1985
```

INTRODUCTION

Following the decision last year to find a new design of bedroom
furniture to add to the top end of our current range, Ultima was
chosen and made available from stock in January this year.

Market research showed that there was a significant demand for a
more sophisticated product, quality being very much   more
important than price at this top end of the market.

Target figures for sales and profit margin were based on the
other designs in our range and were as follows for the first six
months of this year:

```
-------------------------------------------------------------------

               ULTIMA:  TARGET SALES & % PROFIT


          JAN      FEB      MAR      APR      MAY      JUN

           $        $        $        $        $        $
SALES     1050     1138     1238     1313     1488     1638
PROFIT    20%      20%      20%      20%      20%      20%


-------------------------------------------------------------------
```

PROGRESS REPORT

Sales went extremely well for the first three months, slightly
exceeding the target we had set. Although the second three
months were not quite so convincing, this was not because of any
great fall-off in sales. Our rapidly increasing costs accounted
for the moderate overall achievement. However, the showroom
managers are delighted with the product and its appeal to the
customer and are inclined to be optimistic about its future.

Here are the figures for the first six months of this year:

```
-------------------------------------------------------------------

            ULTIMA:  ACTUAL SALES, COSTS & % PROFIT


          JAN      FEB      MAR      APR      MAY      JUN

           $        $        $        $        $        $
SALES     1100     1150     1250     1310     1450     1590
COSTS     840      910      990      1050     1190     1310
PROFIT    24%      21%      21%      20%      18%      18%


-------------------------------------------------------------------
```

Print time line-forming

The **.PF** command is useful if you have a wide-carriage printer. You can prepare your document with the convenience of the 80-column screen, then you can specify that *at print time* the line length will be 120, using the **.RM** command.

For example:

```
.PF ON
.RM 120
```

Normally, you would use this command to print the whole file with a right margin of 120. If you wish to print out just a portion of the text in the wider format, you must insert these dot commands at the appropriate place in the text, and then you have to remember to restore the normal margins and turn print time line forming to the default value at the end of the specially formatted section:

```
.PF DIS
.RM DIS
```

This returns control of line forming and right margin setting to MailMerge.

Some Useful Tips

Unless you use MailMerge constantly, or at least until you have had a lot of practice, you may find it a little tricky to operate. I hope you did not have too much trouble working through the examples in this chapter. When you start setting up your own specific merge printing operations, you may encounter some unexpected problems.

Restarting in the middle of a file

One problem nearly everyone has at some time is how to restart MailMerge when it stops in the middle of printing form letters to a hundred or more different people. The problem can arise in various ways—the paper jams in the printer mechanism, the ribbon tape runs out, the computer "goes down" for some unknown reason—now what do you do?

If you press **P** to interrupt printing and **Y** to abandon the run, you will want to restart the merge printing at the letter after the last successful one printed. To achieve this, call up the data file in WordStar, mark the beginning of the file with a ^**KB**, find the last record that printed successfully with ^**QF**, move the cursor to the beginning of the *next* line, and press ^**KK**.

Now that you have marked off the block of text, you can write it to a temporary file using ^**KW** and then, while the block is still marked, press ^**KY** to delete it in the current data file. Now when you restart MailMerge, the rest of the letters will print out.

When you have finished the merge printing, call up your original data file again and read in the temporary file, using ^**KR**, and you are back to where you started. Then you can delete the temporary file.

Editing and reprinting

If you find errors on just two or three letters after a long merge printing run, you can use a similar technique to find the records you need to edit and reprint, delete the rest. Open a temporary non-document file called **ODDS** and read in your original data file using ^**KR**. Mark the beginning of the file with a ^**KB**, then use ^**QF** to find the first record you want to edit and reprint.

With INSERT ON and the cursor on the first character of your record, press ^**KK** and then ^**KY** to delete all the records above the one you want. When you have edited the record, mark the beginning of the next with a ^**KB** and use ^**QF** to find the next one for editing.

Continue until you are left with a file called ODDS containing just the records you wish to reprint. Now call up your file for merge printing and change the name of the data file (.DF) to ODDS. Save the file, select **M** and merge print the letters.

Remember, if you plan to use the original MailMerge file again, go back and change the file name next to the .DF to the original name. Don't forget to edit the same records in the original data file.

If the original data was entered in a DataStar file, the changes must be made in DataStar, not in WordStar.

CONCLUSION

That completes the tutorials and exercises demonstrating a truly integrated approach to MicroPro software. I hope you have enjoyed working through the book and that you feel you have gained a reasonable insight into the workings of the programs, both individually and in the way they interact when linked together.

Keep practicing!

Appendix A

Form listings and field attribute definitions
for QUOTES, CLIENTS, and PRICELST forms

QUOTES FORM LISTING AND FIELD ATTRIBUTE DEFINITIONS

FIELD NUMBERS

QUOTE NUMBER: ____1   CLIENT NUMBER: ___2

CLIENT DETAILS:
TITLE (Mr/Mrs/Ms): ____3   INITIALS: ____4 LAST NAME: _____5

STREET: _____6 CITY: _____7
STATE: _8   ZIP: ____9   TEL AREA CODE: ___10 TEL NUMBER: _____11

DESIGN: _____12 PRICE CODE: *
=======================================

QTY	CODE	DESCRIPTION	SIZE (cm)	UNIT PRICE	TOTAL PRICE
*	_____15	_____16	__17	____18	____19
*	_____21	_____22	__23	____24	____25
*	_____27	_____28	__29	____30	____31
*	_____33	_____34	__35	____36	____37
*	_____39	_____40	__41	____42	____43

TOTAL FOR FURNITURE   _____44
=======================================

This quotation is valid for 30 days from:

DATE: _____45

SIGNED: _____46
POSITION: _____47

QUOTES FORM LISTING AND FIELD ATTRIBUTE DEFINITIONS

ENTRY CONTROL MASK

QUOTE NUMBER : _____   CLIENT NUMBER : ___!

CLIENT DETAILS:
TITLE (Mr/Mrs/Ms) _____   INITIALS _____   LAST NAME _____

STREET   _____ CITY _____
STATE   __   ZIP _____   TEL AREA CODE ____   TEL NUMBER _____

DESIGN _____   PRICE CODE !
=====================================

QTY	CODE	DESCRIPTION	SIZE (cm)	UNIT PRICE	TOTAL PRICE
!	_____	_____	____	_____	____.__
!	_____	_____	____	_____	____.__
!	_____	_____	____	_____	____.__
!	_____	_____	____	_____	____.__
!	_____	_____	____	_____	____.__

TOTAL FOR FURNITURE   _____.__
==================================

This quotation is valid for 30 days from:

DATE   __''_''_
        _____

SIGNED   YYYYYYYYYYYYYYYYYY
POSITION YYYYYYYYYYYYYYYYYY

QUOTES FORM LISTING AND FIELD ATTRIBUTE DEFINITIONS

CONTENT CONTROL MASK

QUOTE NUMBER : _____   CLIENT NUMBER : 9999

CLIENT DETAILS:
TITLE (Mr/Mrs/Ms) _____ INITIALS _____ LAST NAME _____

STREET _____ CITY _____
STATE __ ZIP _____ TEL AREA CODE _____ TEL NUMBER _____

DESIGN DDDDDDDDDDDDDDD PRICE CODE 9
======================================

QTY	CODE	DESCRIPTION	SIZE (cm)	UNIT PRICE	TOTAL PRICE
9	H_____	_____	____	_____	999.99
9	H_____	_____	____	_____	999.99
9	H_____	_____	____	_____	999.99
9	H_____	_____	____	_____	999.99
9	H_____	_____	____	_____	999.99

TOTAL FOR FURNITURE   9999.99
====================================

This quotation is valid for 30 days from:

DATE   99/99/99

SIGNED _____
POSITION _____

QUOTES FORM LISTING AND FIELD ATTRIBUTE DEFINITIONS

FIELD ATTRIBUTE DEFINITIONS

```
                         :Req/Unused      :  Derived Fields  :  Verified
                         :right Just      :                  :  Fields
                         :Write ed c      :                  :
                         :Oper entry      :I  FILE:    CALC: :
                         :Check dgt       :n  Index  Item    :  FILE VERIFY
FIELD NUM/NAME           :Range chk : PAD/:t  Field  Num  N/S:  File Name
    LEN LIN COL ORDER KEY:Edit mask : FLOAT :
001/QUOTE NUMBER         :          :      :                 :
    005 000 019  002     : J        : PO   :            N    :
002/CLIENT NUMBER        :          :      :                 :
    004 000 047  001     : RJ    E  : P    :                 :F  CLIENTS
003/TITLE                :          :      :                 :
    005 003 023  003     :          :      :  002   002      :
004/INITIALS             :          :      :                 :
    005 003 042  004 002 :          :      :  002   003      :
005/LAST NAME            :          :      :                 :
    015 003 060  005 001 :          :      :  002   004      :
006/STREET               :          :      :                 :
    027 005 012  006     :          :      :  002   005      :
007/CITY                 :          :      :                 :
    026 005 048  007     :          :      :  002   006      :
008/STATE                :          :      :                 :
    002 006 012  008     :          :      :  002   007      :
009/ZIP                  :          :      :                 :
    005 006 023  009     :          :      :  002   008      :
010/TEL AREA CODE        :          :      :                 :
    005 006 047  010     :          :      :  002   009      :
011/TEL NUMBER           :          :      :                 :
    008 006 066  011     :          :      :  002   010      :
012/DESIGN               :          :      :                 :
    015 010 028  012     :        E :      :                 :
013/PRICE CODE           :          :      :                 :
    001 010 057  013     : R      E :      :                 :
014/QTY 1                :          :      :                 :
    001 018 001  014     : R      E :      :                 :
015/CODE 1               :          :      :                 :
    008 018 005  015     : R      E :      :                 :F  PRICELST
016/DESCRIPTION 1        :          :      :                 :
    036 018 015  016     :          :      :  015   002      :
017/SIZE 1               :          :      :                 :
    004 018 055  017     :          :      :  015   003      :
```

```
018/UNIT PRICE 1        |         |       |
    007 018 062  018    |         |       |     015    004      |
019/TOTAL PRICE 1       |         |       |                     |
    007 018 072  019    | J    E  | P F$ |                 N  |
020/QTY 2               |         |       |                     |
    001 019 001  020    | R    E  |       |                     |
021/CODE 2              |         |       |                     |
    008 019 005  021    | R    E  |       |                    |F    PRICELST
022/DESCRIPTION 2       |         |       |                     |
    036 019 015  022    |         |       |     021    002      |
023/SIZE 2              |         |       |                     |
    004 019 055  023    |         |       |     021    003      |
024/UNIT PRICE 2        |         |       |                     |
    007 019 062  024    |         |       |     021    004      |
```

QUOTES FORM LISTING AND FIELD ATTRIBUTE DEFINITIONS

FIELD ATTRIBUTE DEFINITIONS

	Req/Unused right Just Write ed c Oper entry Check dgt		Derived Fields		Verified Fields
		I FILE: CALC:			
		n Index Item		FILE VERIFY
FIELD NUM/NAME	Range chk | PAD/	t Field	Num N/S	File Name
LEN LIN COL ORDER KEY	Edit mask | FLOAT			

```
025/TOTAL PRICE 2       |         |       |                     |
    007 019 072  025    | J    E  | P F$ |                 N  |
026/QTY 3               |         |       |                     |
    001 020 001  026    | R    E  |       |                     |
027/CODE 3              |         |       |                     |
    008 020 005  027    | R    E  |       |                    |F    PRICELST
028/DESCRIPTION 3       |         |       |                     |
    036 020 015  028    |         |       |     027    002      |
029/SIZE 3              |         |       |                     |
    004 020 055  029    |         |       |     027    003      |
030/UNIT PRICE 3        |         |       |                     |
    007 020 062  030    |         |       |     027    004      |
031/TOTAL PRICE 3       |         |       |                     |
    007 020 072  031    | J    E  | P F$ |                 N  |
032/QTY 4               |         |       |                     |
    001 021 001  032    | R    E  |       |                     |
033/CODE 4              |         |       |                     |
    008 021 005  033    | R    E  |       |                    |F    PRICELST
```

```
034/DESCRIPTION 4
     036 021 015  034                            033   002
035/SIZE 4
     004 021 055  035                            033   003
036/UNIT PRICE 4
     007 021 062  036                            033   004
037/TOTAL PRICE 4
     007 021 072  037    J    E   P F$                      N
038/QTY 5
     001 022 001  038    R    E
039/CODE 5
     008 022 005  039    R    E                             F   PRICELST
040/DESCRIPTION 5
     036 022 015  040                            039   002
041/SIZE 5
     004 022 055  041                            039   003
042/UNIT PRICE 5
     007 022 062  042                            039   004
043/TOTAL PRICE 5
     007 022 072  043    J    E   P F$                      N
044/TOTAL FOR FURNITURE
     008 029 071  044    J    E   P F$                      N
045/DATE
     008 038 006  045    R    E
046/SIGNED
     018 044 010  046    R    E
047/POSITION
     018 045 010  047    R    E
```

QUOTES FORM LISTING AND FIELD ATTRIBUTE DEFINITIONS

CALCULATIONS

```
QUOTE NUMBER=QUOTE NUMBER+1
TOTAL PRICE 1=UNIT PRICE 1*QTY 1
TOTAL PRICE 2=UNIT PRICE 2*QTY 2
TOTAL PRICE 3=UNIT PRICE 3*QTY 3
TOTAL PRICE 4=UNIT PRICE 4*QTY 4
TOTAL PRICE 5=UNIT PRICE 5*QTY 5
TOTAL FOR FURNITURE=TOTAL PRICE 1+TOTAL PRICE 2+TOTAL PRICE 3+TOTAL PRICE 4+TOTAL PRICE 5
```

CLIENTS FORM LISTING AND FIELD ATTRIBUTE DEFINITIONS

FIELD NUMBERS

CLIENT NUMBER ___1
TITLE (Mr/Mrs/Ms) ___2 INITIALS ___3 LAST NAME _____4

STREET _____5   CITY _____6
STATE _7   ZIP ___8

TEL AREA CODE ___9   TEL NUMBER _____10

CLIENTS FORM LISTING AND FIELD ATTRIBUTE DEFINITIONS

ENTRY CONTROL MASK

CLIENT NUMBER ___!
TITLE (Mr/Mrs/Ms) _____ INITIALS _____ LAST NAME _____

STREET _____   CITY _____
STATE __   ZIP _____

TEL AREA CODE `'_____'`   TEL NUMBER ___'_____

CONTENT CONTROL MASK

CLIENT NUMBER 9999
TITLE (Mr/Mrs/Ms) _____ INITIALS _____ LAST NAME _____

STREET _____   CITY _____
STATE DD   ZIP 99999

TEL AREA CODE (999)   TEL NUMBER 999_9999

CLIENTS FORM LISTING AND FIELD ATTRIBUTE DEFINITIONS

FIELD ATTRIBUTE DEFINITIONS

	Req/Unused right Just Write ed c Oper entry Check dgt		Derived Fields		Verified Fields
			I FILE: CALC:		
		n	Index Item		FILE VERIFY
FIELD NUM/NAME	Range chk	PAD/	t Field Num N/S		File Name
LEN LIN COL ORDER KEY	Edit mask	FLOAT			
001/CLIENT NUMBER					
004 001 019 001 001	RJ E	P			
002/TITLE					
005 002 019 002					
003/INITIALS					
005 002 036 003					
004/LAST NAME					
015 002 055 004					
005/STREET					
027 004 008 005					
006/CITY					
026 004 044 006					
007/STATE					
002 005 008 007	R E				
008/ZIP					
005 005 020 008	R E				
009/TEL AREA CODE					
005 005 044 009	R E				
010/TEL NUMBER					
008 005 062 010	R E				

PRICELST FORM LISTING AND FIELD ATTRIBUTE DEFINITIONS

FIELD NUMBERS

CODE _____1   DESCRIPTION _____2
SIZE ___3   PRICE _____4

PRICELST FORM LISTING AND FIELD ATTRIBUTE DEFINITIONS

ENTRY CONTROL MASK

```
CODE  _____   DESCRIPTION   _____
SIZE  ___!       PRICE         _____·___
```

CONTENT CONTROL MASK

```
CODE  _____   DESCRIPTION   _____
SIZE  9999       PRICE          _999.99
```

PRICELST FORM LISTING AND FIELD ATTRIBUTE DEFINITIONS

FIELD ATTRIBUTE DEFINITIONS

	Req/Unused right Just Write ed c Oper entry Check dgt		Derived Fields		Verified Fields
FIELD NUM/NAME LEN LIN COL ORDER KEY	Range chk Edit mask	PAD/ FLOAT	I FILE: CALC: n Index Item t Field Num N/S		FILE VERIFY File Name
001/CODE					
008 000 006 001 001	R				
002/DESCRIPTION					
036 000 030 002	R				
003/SIZE					
004 001 006 003	RJW E	P			
004/PRICE					
007 001 030 004	RJW E	P F$			

Appendix B

Form listings and field attribute definitions for POLIST, INVENTRY, STATELST, CLIENTPO, and INVDATA forms

POLIST FORM LISTING AND FIELD ATTRIBUTE DEFINITIONS

FIELD NUMBERS

PO REF: __1 ITEM NO: _2 CODE: _____3 QUANTITY: 4

DESCRIPTION: _____5

UNIT PRICE: _____6 TOTAL PRICE: _____7

CLIENT NUMBER: ___8   STATE: _9   TAX RATE % ___10

ENTRY CONTROL MASK

PO REF: ___ ITEM NO: __ CODE: _____ QUANTITY: _

DESCRIPTION: _____

UNIT PRICE: _____ TOTAL PRICE: _____.__

CLIENT NUMBER: ____   STATE: __   TAX RATE % __.__

CONTENT CONTROL MASK

PO REF: 999 ITEM NO: 99 CODE: C_____ QUANTITY: 9

DESCRIPTION: _____

UNIT PRICE: _____ TOTAL PRICE: 9999.99

CLIENT NUMBER: 9999   STATE: CC   TAX RATE % 99.99

POLIST FORM LISTING AND FIELD ATTRIBUTE DEFINITIONS

FIELD ATTRIBUTE DEFINITIONS

FIELD NUM/NAME	Req/Unused right Just Write ed c Oper entry Check dgt Range chk Edit mask	PAD/ FLOAT	Int	FILE: Index Field	Item Num	CALC: N/S	Verified Fields FILE VERIFY File Name
001/PO REF							
003 001 008 001 001	RJ E	P					
002/ITEM NO							
002 001 021 002 002	RJ E	P					
003/CODE							
008 001 030 003	R E					F	INVENTRY
004/QTY							
001 001 050 004	R E						
005/DESCRIPTION							
035 003 013 005				003	002		
006/UNIT PRICE							
007 005 012 006				003	004		
007/TOTAL PRICE							
007 005 035 007	J E	P F$				N	
008/CLIENT NO							
004 007 015 008	RJ E						
009/STATE							
002 007 035 009	R E					F	STATELST
010/TAX RATE							
005 007 054 010	E			009	002		

CALCULATIONS

TOTAL PRICE=UNIT PRICE*QTY

INVENTRY FORM LISTING AND FIELD ATTRIBUTE DEFINITIONS

FIELD NUMBERS

CODE: _____1   DESCRIPTION: _____2
SIZE: ___3   PRICE: _____4

QTY IN STOCK: __5 VALUE OF STOCK: _____6 DATE LAST UPDATED: _7 /_8 /_9

ENTRY CONTROL MASK

CODE: _____   DESCRIPTION: _____
SIZE: ___!   PRICE: ____.__

QTY IN STOCK: ___ VALUE OF STOCK: _____.__ DATE LAST UPDATED: !! /!! /!!

CONTENT CONTROL MASK

CODE: C_____   DESCRIPTION: _____
SIZE: 9999   PRICE: 9999.99

QTY IN STOCK: 999 VALUE OF STOCK: __999.99 DATE LAST UPDATED: 99 /99 /99

INVENTRY FORM LISTING AND FIELD ATTRIBUTE DEFINITIONS

FIELD ATTRIBUTE DEFINITIONS

FIELD NUM/NAME LEN LIN COL ORDER KEY	Req/Unused right Just Write ed c Oper entry Check dgt Range chk Edit mask	PAD/ FLOAT	I n t	Derived Fields FILE: Index Field	 Item Num	CALC: N/S	Verified Fields FILE VERIFY File Name
001/CODE							
008 001 006 001 001	R E						
002/DESCRIPTION							
035 001 032 002	R						
003/SIZE							
004 002 006 003	RJ E	P					
004/PRICE							
007 002 032 004	RJ E	P F$					
005/QTY IN STOCK							
003 004 014 005	J E	P					
006/VALUE OF STOCK							
008 004 035 006	J E	P F$				N	
007/INV MONTH							
002 004 064 007	E						
008/INV DAY							
002 004 068 008	E						
009/INV YEAR							
002 004 072 009	E						

CALCULATIONS

VALUE OF STOCK=PRICE*QTY IN STOCK

CLIENTPO FORM LISTING AND FIELD ATTRIBUTE DEFINITIONS

FIELD NUMBERS

CLIENT NUMBER: ___1
TITLE (Mr/Mrs/Ms): ____2 INITIALS: ____3 LAST NAME: _____4

STREET: _____5 CITY: _____6
STATE: _7   ZIP: ___8   TEL AREA CODE: ____9 TEL NUMBER: _____10

CURRENT CLIENT PON:_____11 CURRENT DATE:12/13/14

ENTRY CONTROL MASK

CLIENT NUMBER: ___!
TITLE (Mr/Mrs/Ms): _____ INITIALS: _____ LAST NAME: _____

STREET: _____ CITY: _____
STATE: __   ZIP: _____   TEL AREA CODE: ''____'' TEL NUMBER: _____''

CURRENT CLIENT PON:_____ CURRENT DATE:__/__/__

CONTENT CONTROL MASK

CLIENT NUMBER: 9999
TITLE (Mr/Mrs/Ms): _____ INITIALS: _____ LAST NAME: _____

STREET: _____ CITY: _____
STATE: CC   ZIP: 99999   TEL AREA CODE: (999) TEL NUMBER: 999-9999

CURRENT CLIENT PON:_____ CURRENT DATE:99/99/99

CLIENTPO FORM LISTING AND FIELD ATTRIBUTE DEFINITIONS

FIELD ATTRIBUTE DEFINITIONS

```
                           :Req/Unused  :  Derived Fields  :  Verified
                           :right Just  :                  :  Fields
                           :Write ed c  :                  :
                           :Oper entry  :I  FILE:    CALC: :
                           :Check dgt   :n  Index  Item    :  FILE VERIFY
FIELD NUM/NAME             :Range chk : PAD/ :t  Field  Num  N/S :  File Name
    LEN LIN COL ORDER KEY :Edit mask : FLOAT :                :
001/CLIENT NUMBER          :           :       :                :
    004 001 019  001  001: RJ    E  : P     :                :
002/TITLE                  :           :       :                :
    005 002 019  002       :           :       :                :
003/INITIALS               :           :       :                :
    005 002 036  003       :           :       :                :
004/LAST NAME              :           :       :                :
    015 002 055  004       :           :       :                :
005/STREET                 :           :       :                :
    027 004 008  005       :           :       :                :
006/CITY                   :           :       :                :
    026 004 044  006       :           :       :                :
007/STATE                  :           :       :                :
    002 005 008  007       : R    E  :       :                :
008/ZIP                    :           :       :                :
    005 005 020  008       : R    E  :       :                :
009/TEL AREA CODE          :           :       :                :
    005 005 044  009       : R    E  :       :                :
010/TEL NUMBER             :           :       :                :
    008 005 062  010       : R    E  :       :                :
011/CLIENT PON             :           :       :                :
    015 007 019  011       : J       : P     :                :
012/PO MONTH               :           :       :                :
    002 007 049  012       :      E  :       :                :
013/PO DAY                 :           :       :                :
    002 007 052  013       :      E  :       :                :
014/PO YEAR                :           :       :                :
    002 007 055  014       :      E  :       :                :
```

INVDATA FORM LISTING AND FIELD ATTRIBUTE DEFINITIONS

FIELD NUMBERS

```
DATE (MM/DD/YY) _1/_2/_3
INVOICE NO ___4
TOTAL PRICE _____5
TAX RATE _____6
```

ENTRY CONTROL MASK

```
DATE (MM/DD/YY) __/__/__
INVOICE NO ____
TOTAL PRICE _____.__
TAX RATE _____.__
```

CONTENT CONTROL MASK

```
DATE (MM/DD/YY) __/__/__
INVOICE NO ____
TOTAL PRICE _____.__
TAX RATE _____.__
```

FIELD ATTRIBUTE DEFINITIONS

FIELD NUM/NAME LEN LIN COL ORDER KEY	Req/Unused right Just Write ed c Oper entry Check dgt Range chk Edit mask	PAD/ FLOAT	I n t	Derived Fields FILE: Index Field	CALC: Item Num N/S	Verified Fields FILE VERIFY File Name
001/INVDATA MONTH						
002 001 016 001						
002/INVDATA DAY						
002 001 019 002						
003/INVDATA YEAR						
002 001 022 003						
004/INVOICE NO						
004 002 011 004 001	J	P				
005/TOTAL PRICE						
008 003 012 005	J E	P				
006/TAX RATE						
008 004 009 006	J E	P				

STATELST FORM LISTING AND FIELD ATTRIBUTE DEFINITIONS

FIELD NUMBERS

STATE: _1   TAX RATE % ____2

ENTRY CONTROL MASK

STATE: __   TAX RATE % __.__

CONTENT CONTROL MASK

STATE: CC   TAX RATE % 99.99

FIELD ATTRIBUTE DEFINITIONS

	Req/Unused		Derived Fields		Verified
	right Just				Fields
	Write ed c				
	Oper entry	I	FILE: CALC:		
	Check dgt	n	Index Item		FILE VERIFY
FIELD NUM/NAME	Range chk	PAD/	t Field Num N/S		File Name
LEN LIN COL ORDER KEY	Edit mask	FLOAT			
001/STAT					
002 001 014 001 001	R E				
002/TAX RATE					
005 001 033 002	RJ E	P			

Appendix C

The report listings with field and file attribute
definitions for Transact and Turnover Reports

TRANSACT REPORT LISTING WITH FIELD AND FILE ATTRIBUTE DEFINITIONS

FIELD NUMBERS

```
R                              INVOICE
R                              =======
R
R
RDATE _1/_2/_3
P
P                              INVOICE
P                              =======
P
PDATE _4/_5/_6
P
1                                               INVOICE NO _____7
1
1CLIENT NO ___8         NAME    __9 _10 _____11
1                       ADDRESS _____12
1                               _____13
1                             14 ___15
1
1CLIENT PON  _____16  DATED 17/18/19
1
1
1PO REF _20
1
1ITEM QTY  CODE        DESCRIPTION          UNIT   TOTAL
1 NO                                        PRICE  PRICE
 _21 22 _____23  _____24 ____25 _____26
```

```
:QTY IN STOCK _27 STOCK REM _28 VALUE OF STOCK REM _____29
1
1
1
1
1          STATE 30  TAX RATE ___31                GRAND TOTAL _____32
1                                                  SALES TAX   _____33
1
1
1                                                  AMT DUE     _____34
1                                                  ====================
1
1
1
1
1
1
1
1
1
1
R
R
PTERMS: STRICTLY 30 DAYS NET
```

TRANSACT REPORT LISTING WITH FIELD AND FILE ATTRIBUTE DEFINITIONS

CONTROL CHARACTERS

```
R                              ^BINVOICE
R                              =======^B
R
R
RDATE _1/_2/_3
P
P                              ^BINVOICE
P                              =======^B
P
PDATE  _4/_5/_6
P
1                                              INVOICE NO _____7
1
1CLIENT NO ___8        NAME    __9 _10 _____11
1                      ADDRESS _____12
1                              _____13
1                              14  ___15
1
1CLIENT PON  _____16  DATED 17/18/19
1
1
1PO REF _20
1
1ITEM QTY  CODE            DESCRIPTION            UNIT   TOTAL
1 NO                                             PRICE  PRICE
 _21 _22 _____23 _____24 _____25 _____26
```

```
:QTY IN STOCK _27 STOCK REM _28 VALUE OF STOCK REM _____29
1
1
1
1
1        STATE 30  TAX RATE ___31              GRAND TOTAL _____32
1                                              SALES TAX    _____33
1
1
1                                              ^BAMT DUE     _____34
1                                              ====================^B
1
1
1
1
1
1
1
1
1
1
1
R
R
PTERMS: STRICTLY 30 DAYS NET
```

TRANSACT REPORT LISTING WITH FIELD AND FILE ATTRIBUTE DEFINITIONS

```
                    EDIT MASK CONDITIONS

R                              INVOICE
R                              =======
R
R
RDATE __/__/__
P
P                              INVOICE
P                              =======
P
PDATE  __/__/__
P
1                                                      INVOICE NO _____
1
1CLIENT NO ____        NAME      ___ ___  _____
1                      ADDRESS _____
1                              _____
1                                     __  _____
1
1CLIENT PON  _____ DATED __/__/__
1
1
1PO REF ___
1
1ITEM QTY  CODE          DESCRIPTION          UNIT    TOTAL
1 NO                                          PRICE   PRICE
  ___  __ _____  _____ E_____.__ E_____.__
```

```
:QTY IN STOCK ___ STOCK REM ___ VALUE OF STOCK REM E____.__
1
1
1
1
1      STATE __  TAX RATE _____            GRAND TOTAL E____.__
1                                          SALES TAX   E____.__
1
1
1                                          AMT DUE     E____.__
1                                          ====================
1
1
1
1
1
1
1
1
1
1
1
1
R
R
PTERMS: STRICTLY 30 DAYS NET
```

TRANSACT REPORT LISTING WITH FIELD AND FILE ATTRIBUTE DEFINITIONS

```
                    EDIT MASK CONSTANTS

R                                INVOICE
R                                =======
R
R
RDATE __/__/__
P
P                                INVOICE
P                                =======
P
PDATE __/__/__
P
1                                          INVOICE NO _____
1
1CLIENT NO ____        NAME     ___ ___  _____
1                      ADDRESS _____
1                              _____
1                              __  _____
1
1CLIENT PON  _____  DATED __/__/__
1
1
1PO REF ___
1
1ITEM QTY  CODE         DESCRIPTION          UNIT   TOTAL
1 NO                                         PRICE  PRICE
  ___  __ _____  _____  $____.__  $_____.__
```

```
:QTY IN STOCK ___ STOCK REM ___ VALUE OF STOCK REM $____.__
1
1
1
1
1      STATE __  TAX RATE _____           GRAND TOTAL $____.__
1                                         SALES TAX   $____.__
1
1
1                                         AMT DUE     $____.__
1                                         ====================
1
1
1
1
1
1
1
1
1
1
1
R
R
PTERMS: STRICTLY 30 DAYS NET
```

TRANSACT REPORT LISTING WITH FIELD AND FILE ATTRIBUTE DEFINITIONS

FILE DEFINITIONS

001/POLIST   Access: INPUT
   No. of buffers: 016
   Volume name: POLIST.DTA

002/INVENTRY   Access: REFERENCE
   Volume name: INVENTRY.DTA

003/CLIENTPO   Access: REFERENCE
   Volume name: CLIENTPO.DTA

004/INVDATA   Access: OUTPUT
   If file exists: ADD TO
   No. of buffers: 016
   Volume name: INVDATA.DTA

TRANSACT REPORT LISTING WITH FIELD AND FILE ATTRIBUTE DEFINITIONS

001/RR MONTH
   Location: Line=004 Column=006 Length=002
   Source: OPERATOR INPUT
    Prompt: ENTER MONTH (MM)
   Load if: REPORT START
   Output: File=004/INVDATA   Field=001/INVDATA MONTH

002/RR DAY
   Location: Line=004 Column=009 Length=002
   Source: OPERATOR INPUT
    Prompt: ENTER DAY (DD)
   Load if: REPORT START
   Output: File=004/INVDATA   Field=002/INVDATA DAY

003/RR YEAR
   Location: Line=004 Column=012 Length=002
   Source: OPERATOR INPUT
    Prompt: ENTER YEAR (YY)
   Load if: REPORT START
   Output: File=004/INVDATA   Field=003/INVDATA YEAR

004/R MONTH
   Location: Line=009 Column=007 Length=002
   Source: CALCULATED
    $004 = $RR MONTH
   Output: File=002/INVENTRY   Field=007/INV MONTH
           Index=023/CODE

005/R DAY
   Location: Line=009 Column=010 Length=002
   Source: CALCULATED
    $005 = $RR DAY
   Output: File=002/INVENTRY   Field=008/INV DAY
           Index=023/CODE

006/R YEAR
   Location: Line=009 Column=013 Length=002
   Source: CALCULATED
      $006 = $RR YEAR
   Output: File=002/INVENTRY   Field=009/INV YEAR
              Index=023/CODE

007/INVOICE NO
   Location: Line=011 Column=069 Length=007
   Source: CALCULATED
      #007 = INVOICE NO+1
   Editing: RIGHT JUSTIFY
   Load if: NEW PAGE
   Output: File=004/INVDATA   Field=004/INVOICE NO

008/CLIENT NO
   Location: Line=013 Column=011 Length=004
   Source: File=001/POLIST   Field=008/CLIENT NO

009/TITLE
   Location: Line=013 Column=034 Length=003
   Source: File=003/CLIENTPO   Field=002/TITLE
              Index=008/CLIENT NO
   Load if: NEW PAGE

010/INITIALS
   Location: Line=013 Column=038 Length=003
   Source: File=003/CLIENTPO   Field=003/INITIALS
              Index=008/CLIENT NO
   Load if: NEW PAGE

011/LAST NAME
   Location: Line=013 Column=043 Length=015
   Source: File=003/CLIENTPO   Field=004/LAST NAME
              Index=008/CLIENT NO
   Load if: NEW PAGE

012/STREET
   Location: Line=014 Column=034 Length=027
   Source: File=003/CLIENTPO   Field=005/STREET
           Index=008/CLIENT NO
   Load if: NEW PAGE

013/CITY
   Location: Line=015 Column=034 Length=026
   Source: File=003/CLIENTPO   Field=006/CITY
           Index=008/CLIENT NO
   Load if: NEW PAGE

014/STATE
   Location: Line=016 Column=034 Length=002
   Source: File=003/CLIENTPO   Field=007/STATE
           Index=008/CLIENT NO
   Load if: NEW PAGE

015/ZIP
   Location: Line=016 Column=038 Length=005
   Source: File=003/CLIENTPO   Field=008/ZIP
           Index=008/CLIENT NO
   Load if: NEW PAGE

016/CLIENT PON
   Location: Line=018 Column=014 Length=015
   Source: File=003/CLIENTPO   Field=011/CLIENT PON
           Index=008/CLIENT NO
   Load if: NEW PAGE

017/PO MONTH
   Location: Line=018 Column=038 Length=002
   Source: File=003/CLIENTPO   Field=012/PO MONTH
           Index=008/CLIENT NO
   Load if: NEW PAGE

018/PO DAY
   Location: Line=018 Column=041 Length=002
   Source: File=003/CLIENTPO   Field=013/PO DAY
             Index=008/CLIENT NO
   Load if: NEW PAGE

019/PO YEAR
   Location: Line=018 Column=044 Length=002
   Source: File=003/CLIENTPO   Field=014/PO YEAR
             Index=008/CLIENT NO
   Load if: NEW PAGE

020/PO REF
   Location: Line=021 Column=008 Length=003
   Control break level: 001
   Source: File=001/POLIST   Field=001/PO REF

021/ITEM NO
   Location: Line=025 Column=001 Length=003
   Source: File=001/POLIST   Field=002/ITEM NO

022/QTY
   Location: Line=025 Column=006 Length=002
   Source: File=001/POLIST   Field=004/QTY

023/CODE
   Location: Line=025 Column=009 Length=008
   Source: File=001/POLIST   Field=003/CODE

024/DESCRIPTION
   Location: Line=025 Column=019 Length=035
   Source: File=001/POLIST   Field=005/DESCRIPTION

025/UNIT PRICE
   Location: Line=025 Column=055 Length=007
   Source: File=001/POLIST   Field=006/UNIT PRICE
   Editing: RIGHT JUSTIFY   EDIT MASK

026/TOTAL PRICE
   Location: Line=025 Column=063 Length=008
   Source: File=001/POLIST   Field=007/TOTAL PRICE
   Editing: RIGHT JUSTIFY   EDIT MASK
   Output: File=004/INVDATA   Field=005/TOTAL PRICE

027/QTY IN STOCK
   Location: Line=028 Column=014 Length=003
   Source: File=002/INVENTRY Field=005/QTY IN STOCK
             Index=023/CODE

028/STOCK REM
   Location: Line=028 Column=028 Length=003
   Source: CALCULATED
    #028 = QTY IN STOCK-QTY
   Output: File=002/INVENTRY Field=005/QTY IN STOCK
             Index=023/CODE

029/VAL OF STOCK REM
   Location: Line=028 Column=051 Length=008
   Source: CALCULATED
    #029 = STOCK REM*UNIT PRICE
   Output: File=002/INVENTRY Field=006/VALUE OF STOCK
             Index=023/CODE

030/STAT
   Location: Line=033 Column=014 Length=002
   Source: File=001/POLIST   Field=009/STATE
Clear if: CONTROL BREAK 1

031/TAX RATE
   Location: Line=033 Column=027 Length=005
   Source: File=001/POLIST   Field=010/TAX RATE
   Editing: RIGHT JUSTIFY
   Output: File=004/INVDATA   Field=006/TAX RATE
   Clear if: CONTROL BREAK 1

032/GRAND TOTAL
    Location: Line=033 Column=063 Length=008
    Source: CALCULATED
      #032 = GRAND TOTAL+TOTAL PRICE
    Editing: RIGHT JUSTIFY   EDIT MASK   Clear if: CONTROL BREAK 1

033/SALES TAX
    Location: Line=034 Column=063 Length=008
    Source: CALCULATED
      #033 = TAX RATE*GRAND TOTAL/100
    Editing: RIGHT JUSTIFY   EDIT MASK
    Clear if: CONTROL BREAK 1

034/AMT DUE
    Location: Line=037 Column=064 Length=008
    Source: CALCULATED
      #034 = GRAND TOTAL+SALES TAX
    Editing: RIGHT JUSTIFY   EDIT MASK
    Clear if: CONTROL BREAK 1

TRANSACT REPORT LISTING WITH FIELD AND FILE ATTRIBUTE DEFINITIONS

CROSS REFERENCE LISTING

034/AMT DUE

013/CITY

008/CLIENT NO
    009/TITLE   INDEX FOR 003/CLIENTPO, FIELD 002
    010/INITIALS   INDEX FOR 003/CLIENTPO, FIELD 003
    011/LAST NAME   INDEX FOR 003/CLIENTPO, FIELD 004
    012/STREET   INDEX FOR 003/CLIENTPO, FIELD 005
    013/CITY   INDEX FOR 003/CLIENTPO, FIELD 006
    014/STATE   INDEX FOR 003/CLIENTPO, FIELD 007
    015/ZIP   INDEX FOR 003/CLIENTPO, FIELD 008
    016/CLIENT PON   INDEX FOR 003/CLIENTPO, FIELD 011
    017/PO MONTH   INDEX FOR 003/CLIENTPO, FIELD 012
    018/PO DAY   INDEX FOR 003/CLIENTPO, FIELD 013
    019/PO YEAR   INDEX FOR 003/CLIENTPO, FIELD 014

016/CLIENT PON

023/CODE
  ** 004/R MONTH   INDEX FOR 002/INVENTRY, FIELD 007
    005/R DAY   INDEX FOR 002/INVENTRY, FIELD 008
    006/R YEAR   INDEX FOR 002/INVENTRY, FIELD 009
    027/QTY IN STOCK   INDEX FOR 002/INVENTRY, FIELD 005
    028/STOCK REM   INDEX FOR 002/INVENTRY, FIELD 005
    029/VAL OF STOCK REM INDEX FOR 002/INVENTRY, FIELD 006

024/DESCRIPTION

032/GRAND TOTAL
    032/GRAND TOTAL   CALCULATION
    033/SALES TAX   CALCULATION
    034/AMT DUE   CALCULATION

010/INITIALS

007/INVOICE NO
    007/INVOICE NO   CALCULATION

021/ITEM NO

011/LAST NAME

018/PO DAY

017/PO MONTH

020/PO REF

019/PO YEAR

022/QTY
    028/STOCK REM   CALCULATION

027/QTY IN STOCK
    028/STOCK REM   CALCULATION

005/R DAY

004/R MONTH

006/R YEAR

002/RR DAY
    005/R DAY   CALCULATION

001/RR MONTH
    004/R MONTH   CALCULATION

003/RR YEAR
    006/R YEAR   CALCULATION

033/SALES TAX
    034/AMT DUE   CALCULATION

030/STAT

014/STATE

028/STOCK REM
    029/VAL OF STOCK REM   CALCULATION

012/STREET

031/TAX RATE
    033/SALES TAX   CALCULATION

009/TITLE

026/TOTAL PRICE
    032/GRAND TOTAL   CALCULATION

025/UNIT PRICE
    029/VAL OF STOCK REM   CALCULATION

029/VAL OF STOCK REM

015/ZIP

TURNOVER REPORT LISTING WITH FIELD AND FILE ATTRIBUTE DEFINITIONS

FIELD NUMBERS

```
R                        TURNOVER
R                        ========
R
R TURNOVER REPORT DATE _1/_2/_3
R
. INVOICE NO ___4      TAX RATE ____5
: TOTAL PRICE _____6 SALES TAX _____7 AMT DUE _____8
R TURNOVER _____9 TOTAL SALES TAX _____10 TOTAL AMT DUE _____11
```

CONTROL CHARACTERS

```
R                        ^BTURNOVER
R                        ========^B
R
R TURNOVER REPORT DATE _1/_2/_3
R
. INVOICE NO ___4      TAX RATE ____5
: TOTAL PRICE _____6 SALES TAX _____7 AMT DUE _____8
R ^BTURNOVER _____9 TOTAL SALES TAX _____10 TOTAL AMT DUE _____11^B
```

EDIT MASK CONDITIONS

```
R                        TURNOVER
R                        ========
R
R TURNOVER REPORT DATE __/__/__
R
. INVOICE NO ____      TAX RATE _____
: TOTAL PRICE F_____._ SALES TAX F_____._ AMT DUE F_____._
R TURNOVER F_____._ TOTAL SALES TAX F_____._ TOTAL AMT DUE F_____._
```

TURNOVER REPORT LISTING WITH FIELD AND FILE ATTRIBUTE DEFINITIONS

            EDIT MASK CONSTANTS

```
R                         TURNOVER
R                         ========
R
R TURNOVER REPORT DATE __/__/__
R
. INVOICE NO ____      TAX RATE _____
: TOTAL PRICE $_____ SALES TAX $_____ AMT DUE $_____
R TURNOVER $_____ TOTAL SALES TAX $_____ TOTAL AMT DUE $_____
```

            FILE DEFINITIONS

```
001/INVDATA      Access: INPUT
   No. of buffers: 016
   Volume name: INVDATA.DTA
```

TURNOVER REPORT LISTING WITH FIELD AND FILE ATTRIBUTE DEFINITIONS

FIELD DEFINITIONS

001/REPORT MONTH
    Location: Line=003 Column=023 Length=002
    Source: OPERATOR INPUT
     Prompt: ENTER MONTH (MM)
    Load if: REPORT START

002/REPORT DAY
    Location: Line=003 Column=026 Length=002
    Source: OPERATOR INPUT
     Prompt: ENTER DAY (DD)
    Load if: REPORT START

003/REPORT YEAR
    Location: Line=003 Column=029 Length=002
    Source: OPERATOR INPUT
     Prompt: ENTER YEAR (YY)
    Load if: REPORT START

004/INVOICE NO
    Location: Line=005 Column=013 Length=004
    Control break level: 001
    Source: File=001/INVDATA   Field=004/INVOICE NO

005/TAX RATE
    Location: Line=005 Column=032 Length=005
    Source: File=001/INVDATA   Field=006/TAX RATE

006/TOTAL PRICE
    Location: Line=006 Column=014 Length=008
    Source: File=001/INVDATA   Field=005/TOTAL PRICE
    Editing: EDIT MASK

007/SALES TAX
   Location: Line=006 Column=033 Length=008
   Source: CALCULATED
      #007 = TOTAL PRICE*TAX RATE/100
   Editing: EDIT MASK

008/AMT DUE
   Location: Line=006 Column=050 Length=008
   Source: CALCULATED
      #008 = TOTAL PRICE+SALES TAX
   Editing: EDIT MASK

009/TURNOVER
   Location: Line=007 Column=012 Length=009
   Source: CALCULATED
      #009 = TURNOVER+TOTAL PRICE
   Editing: EDIT MASK

010/TOTAL SALES TAX
   Location: Line=007 Column=038 Length=008
   Source: CALCULATED
      #010 = TOTAL SALES TAX+SALES TAX
   Editing: EDIT MASK

011/TOTAL AMT DUE
   Location: Line=007 Column=061 Length=009
   Source: CALCULATED
      #011 = TOTAL AMT DUE+AMT DUE
   Editing: EDIT MASK

TURNOVER REPORT LISTING WITH FIELD AND FILE ATTRIBUTE DEFINITIONS

CROSS REFERENCE LISTING

008/AMT DUE
    011/TOTAL AMT DUE   CALCULATION

004/INVOICE NO

002/REPORT DAY

001/REPORT MONTH

003/REPORT YEAR

007/SALES TAX
    008/AMT DUE   CALCULATION
    010/TOTAL SALES TAX   CALCULATION

005/TAX RATE
    007/SALES TAX   CALCULATION

011/TOTAL AMT DUE
    011/TOTAL AMT DUE   CALCULATION

006/TOTAL PRICE
    007/SALES TAX   CALCULATION
    008/AMT DUE   CALCULATION
    009/TURNOVER   CALCULATION

010/TOTAL SALES TAX
    010/TOTAL SALES TAX   CALCULATION

009/TURNOVER
    009/TURNOVER   CALCULATION

Glossary

Words printed in capital letters in these explanatory notes have their own separate listing.

BACK SPACE KEY The Back Space key has two modes of operation: in the CP/M or MS-DOS operating system, it deletes characters as it passes backward over them; in WordStar, it moves the cursor back over entered text without deleting it.

BACKUP This is an exact duplicate of another disk. It is essential to keep backup copies of all disks with data or programs on them. This is especially important if you use a hard disk system. Making copies is called backing up.

BOOTING UP This is a term for starting up the computer. It is said to be derived from the idea that the computer is pulling itself up by its bootstraps to get started. You have to boot up with a SYSTEM DISK in the floppy disk drive (or from the system tracks on the hard disk); what the computer is actually doing when it starts up is reading the information from the system tracks, then loading the operating system into computer memory. You know that booting is successful when you see the A> prompt (or C> for a hard disk) on your screen.

BYTE This is the unit of storage on a floppy disk, hard disk, or in computer memory. Each character, for example a single letter, comma, hyphen, number, or space, occupies at least one byte.

CAPACITY Capacity of disks is measured in K (kilobytes or Kbytes) or MB (megabytes). The K is short for 1,000 and the M for 1 million. Floppy disks may store as little as 100K or as much as 2MB: hard disks on personal computers may store 10 to 20MB.

CHKDSK This is an MS-DOS function which means *check disk*—it allows you to check the statistics of any disk in use, to see how much space is occupied by how many files, and to see how much free space is left for further use. See also STAT (the equivalent CP/M command).

COLD BOOT
Performing a cold boot, as the name implies, starts the system up from cold. This happens when you first turn on or POWER UP the computer, and also when you press the RESET button. *See also* WARM BOOT.

COMMAND FILE
A command file is a program containing specific instructions to the computer—it has the filename extension .COM. In MS-DOS systems, there is a file named COMMAND.COM which contains useful UTILITIES for copying, renaming, or deleting files, for example, and for checking the statistics of your system.

CONFIGURATION
This is the specific arrangement of computer and peripheral devices—the screen, keyboard, printer, modem, and so on. You may also talk about the configuration of a single item, such as a hard disk, meaning the way the hard disk has been partitioned or sectioned off into logical drives and user areas. When applied to software, *configuration* implies the customizing of a program to suit the HARDWARE it will run on—also called the INSTALLATION.

CTRL KEY
The Ctrl key is always used in conjunction with another key, rather like a shift key on a typewriter; however, instead of producing the character or combination of characters you type, it causes some special function to be performed. It is used in the operating system and in most programs.

COPY
This is the MS-DOS command for copying files from one location to another. A typical command line would be: COPY A:FILENAME.EXT B:FILENAME.EXT (which would copy an existing file from the disk in drive A to the disk in drive B).

CORRUPT
If data on a disk is damaged, it is called *corrupt*. This corruption may occur in all sorts of ways, often due to electrical or magnetic interference. It is possible to fit a device that protects your computer against surges or spikes in the power supply, and it is good practice to turn off and unplug the computer during electrical storms.

CP/M
The initials stand for Control Program/Monitor (often said to stand for Control Program for Microprocessors). This program was developed by Digital Research back at the very beginning (1973) of the microcomputer revolution and hence, for some years, became the nearest thing the industry had to a standard OPERATING SYSTEM. See also MS- DOS, IBM DOS.

CURSOR CONTROL KEYS
There may be a set of arrow keys on your keyboard, or incorporated in the numeric keypad, which move the cursor around the screen in the direction of the arrows. They are programmed to work within most software today. If you press them when you are in the operating system (next to the A> or B> prompt) they do not function (except to type out control characters).

DEFAULT   When you call up a program such as WordStar, there are certain preset functions. You may accept these *by default* (hence defaults) or you can reset them to suit yourself with the program provided (an installation program).

DEL   This is a built in function in the MS-DOS (or IBM DOS) operating system which allows you to Delete files from floppy or hard disks when they are no longer required. The command should be used with caution since, once deleted, your files are virtually irrecoverable.

DIR   The DIR command is a built in function in the CP/M and MS-DOS operating systems. When you type DIR next to the operating system prompt, you will see a listing of all the files on your LOGGED DRIVE (or WORKING DRIVE).

DISKETTE   This is the proper name for the flexible disks you use in your computer for the storage of information; also known as FLOPPY DISKS.

DISTRIBUTION DISK   The disks supplied in your Operating System software package and MicroPro programs are the distribution disks. As soon as you have copied them, put them in a safe, cool, dry place, preferably off-site.

ENTER KEY   The key which causes the equivalent of a *carriage return* (i.e. moves the cursor to the beginning of the next line) may be marked ENTER or RETURN, or may simply have an arrow on it. On some keyboards, there is one key marked RETURN (usually within the main keyboard) and another marked ENTER in the separate numeric keypad (if present).

ERA   This is another built in CP/M function that allows you to Erase (or delete) files from your disks. Use it with caution—once your files are erased they are, to all intents and purposes, irrecoverable. You should be even more careful if you ever use the global erase command—ERA *.*. Fortunately, if you type this command, you are asked to type Y or N to confirm it.

ESCAPE KEY   The Esc key is usually positioned at the top left hand corner of your keyboard, though on some systems it may be part of the numeric keypad. You will probably use it most inside the MicroPro programs, when instructed to do so, to escape from executing an unintended command.

FILE   Every time you enter data into the computer memory and then save it, you create a file on disk. Each file needs to have a unique *file name*, which in CP/M and MS-DOS may be up to eight characters long, and may have an additional *file name extension* of up to three characters, separated from the file name by a period, for example, NEWFILE.TXT.

FLAG COLUMN   In Wordstar the far right column on the screen contains characters—called *flags*—that give you information about the character or line of text you have entered or show that you have not yet entered anything on a particular line. For example, if you press the RETURN KEY after typing in some text, you will see a *less than* sign in the flag column (<). If you allow text to WORD WRAP as you type it in, the flag column will be blank: the lines below the point where you are currently entering text for the first time (so they have not been entered or edited previously) will have a period in the flag column.

FLOPPY DISK
This is the common name for the flexible diskettes you use in the floppy disk drives of your computer for the storage of information, in the form of files.

FLOPPY DISK DRIVE
The disk drive holds your floppy disks. It consists of the slot in which you insert the disk, a cover, a latch you close after inserting the disk, a motor (which you can hear when the disk drive is active), and the head that actually reads the information from the disk surface (rather like a stylus on a record). There is a disk drive active light that shows you when the disk drive head is reading from or writing on the disk. You should not attempt to remove a disk from the drive when the light is on. *See also* HARD DISK.

FORMAT
The format of your disks describes the way that the disk surface is arranged in terms of tracks and sectors, and whether the data is stored single- or double-sided and single- or double density.

FORMATTING DISKS
Before you can use a brand new floppy disk in your computer, it has to be formatted: this is the process that organizes the disk surface in tracks and sectors so that data is stored correctly for your particular system. *Remember that when you format a disk you erase everything from its surface.*

FUNCTION KEYS
There may be a set of keys across the top of your keyboard, or perhaps in a block on the left side, that are preprogrammed to perform specific functions—both in the operating system and inside programs. They are usually a different color than the main keys and labeled f1, f2, and so on. Also, the arrow keys and the keys in the numeric keypad may have additional functions built in for controlling cursor movements, for example. The main advantage of the function keys is that they enable you to perform many of the control key functions with a single keystroke.

HARD DISK
It is quite common now for a small business computer to contain a large capacity hard disk—anything from 5 to 20 megabytes (MB) is standard, and in larger systems, up to 100MB may be installed. The primary advantage to the hard disk is its enormous storage capacity—but it also improves the performance of the system, being much faster in use than a floppy disk. For the more advanced software packages, this is essential, certainly if you are running the complete MicroPro range as an integrated system you would appreciate the extra performance.

HARD RETURN
In the word processing program, WordStar, there are two kinds of Return—the soft return (which is invisible to you, but is recognized by the program), and the hard return, which is visible as a *less than* symbol (<) on the far right column of the Wordstar screen. The soft return is a function of word processing that allows the line to be reformatted if you later decide to add or delete text: once a hard return has been entered

(simply by pressing the Return key at the end of a line) then that line cannot be reformatted automatically.

HARDWARE | Your computer hardware consists of the computer, its keyboard and screen, the printer, and any other peripheral devices you have added.

IBM DOS | The IBM PC runs its own version of MS-DOS, which is called IBM DOS: to all intents and purposes these are identical.

INSTALLATION | Installing the hardware of a system involves attaching all the bits and pieces together and ensuring that they are functioning correctly. Installing software configures the programs to match the particular hardware they are designed to run on.

JUSTIFICATION | When a block of text is aligned to a margin, it is said to be justified. You are accustomed to seeing most text left-justified, and text in newspapers and some books right-justified. It is a matter of personal preference whether you like your letters and documents to be right justified or allowed to form *ragged right* (that is, with no right justification, as in typewritten text).

KILOBYTE | One kilobyte (1K) is taken to be 1,000 bytes. In fact, more accurately, it is 1,024 bytes.

LOAD | When you place a disk containing data into the floppy disk drive of your machine and then transfer it to the computer memory, you are said to be *loading the data.*

LOGGED DRIVE | In a dual-floppy disk system, the drive you boot (start up) from is always labeled Drive A and will display the A> prompt on the screen. Whenever you see the A> prompt, you know that drive A is your current working drive—or you can say that you are logged on to drive A. If you change to drive B (by typing B: next to the A> prompt) you will now see the B> prompt on the screen, and you will be logged on to drive B. If you have a hard disk system that boots up from the hard disk, then you will normally find yourself at the C> prompt (where A and B are the floppy disk drives).

MASTER WORKING DISK | The master working disk is a copy of the original DISTRIBUTION DISK containing particular programs installed to run on your computer system. You need to make yet another copy of this—a BACKUP DISK—which you do not use except to copy a new master working disk! You should keep the backup and distribution disks in a safe place in case you ever find that you have a corrupted disk and need to make fresh copies.

MEGABYTE | The *mega* implies one million; however, to be accurate, one megabyte is actually 1,024,000 bytes (1.024 million).

MS-DOS | These letters stand for MicroSoft Disk Operating System (and are the copyright of the MicroSoft Corporation). The introduction of this new operating system in early 1980, and, in particular, its choice by IBM as the DOS for the IBM PC, means that MS-DOS has taken over as the "industry standard" for the 1980s, from the CP/M standard of the 1970s. See also IBM DOS.

OPERATING SYSTEM

The operating system may be MS-DOS (IBM DOS) or CP/M. Your computer without its operating system is analogous to a car without fuel. Until you have booted up the system and loaded CP/M or MS-DOS into the computer memory, the computer will not show any signs of life. Once loaded, the operating system software ensures that the computer and all its peripheral devices function happily together and obey the commands you type on the keyboard.

PARTITION

In some hard disk MS-DOS systems, particularly those intended for multiuser or multifunction use, it is possible to divide the large hard disk into several different partitions of predetermined size. You could have each user in a business system use their own hard disk partition, for example, or you could separate the different types of software into partitions. On the IBM PC/AT you can even have different OPERATING SYSTEMS running in each partition—MS-DOS in partition one for example, and Concurrent CP/M in partition two.

PIP

The copying program in CP/M is called PIP—Peripheral Interchange Program—an obscure name, if ever there was one. You will use it almost exclusively, probably, for copying files from one disk drive to another, or from the hard disk to floppy disks if you have a hard disk system. As the name suggests, though, the program can also transfer information between various peripheral devices. For more details about PIP you should read your CP/M operating system manual, or a good book about it, like the *Osborne CP/M Guide*, written by Thom Hogan. PIP is a CP/M function but is not built in (you will see the program listed in the directory as PIP.COM). *See also* COPY for the equivalent MS-DOS command.

POWER UP

This means turn on. For example, you must *power up* your computer before loading the operating system.

PROGRAM

A computer program is a set of commands to your computer, written in a language it understands, which when loaded cause it to function in a particular way. For example, when you load WordStar, the computer becomes a word processor, and if you change to CalcStar, it becomes a powerful calculator. CP/M and MS-DOS are special kind of programs that give the computer essential information about how to function.

PROMPT

In CP/M or MS-DOS systems, the prompt is the symbol that denotes that the computer is waiting for an instruction from you and is present whenever you are not using a software program. It will be A> if you are logged on to drive A, B> if drive B, and so on. It is so-named because it is *prompting* you to enter an instruction.

RAGGED RIGHT

This term is used in word processing to describe text that is justified to the left margin only.

RAM This is said to stand for Random Access Memory, but more accurately should be called Read And write Memory. There are various types of chips, used for different purposes, in your computer. The RAM chips allow you to load your information in to them and to transfer it to a disk when you want to save it (hence READ and WRITE). A vital point to remember about RAM is that it is volatile; once you turn off the power, any data on the chips is erased.

REBOOT *See* WARM BOOT.

REN This is another built-in CP/M or MS-DOS function. This lets you change the name of a file. In CP/M the command line is written in the form: REN FILENAME.NEW=FILENAME.OLD that is, you put the new name first and the existing name after the equals sign. In MS-DOS it is the other way around—REN FILENAME.OLD FILENAME.NEW (note the space instead of the equals sign).

REPEAT KEYS You will find that all the keys on your keyboard will repeat the character they represent if you hold them down for a moment or two: touch typists sometimes experience difficulty with this.

RESET BUTTON On most computers you will find a small button around the back of the machine. It is a kind of panic button—only to be used in dire emergencies. You may find one day that for no apparent reason the disk drive is whirring away, but absolutely nothing is happening, and you have tried hitting Esc, ^C—still nothing. You have no choice but to press RESET and accept that you have lost what was in the computer memory. If the information is truly vital to you, you could try talking to your dealer: he or she just may be able to help you to recover it as long as you don't load any other program in after the reset.

RETURN KEY See ENTER KEY.

SECTORS Sectors are pie-shaped subdivisions of the tracks on your floppy disk surface. By combinations of track and sector numbers any point on the disk surface can be accessed.

SOFT RETURN In word processing there is no need to press the RETURN KEY when you reach the end of a line; the software is programmed to do this for you. It takes account of your margin settings and performs WORD WRAP for you. All the time you allow the computer to word wrap, there will be a blank in the flag column. As soon as you press Return, at the end of a paragraph, for example, a < appears in the flag column. Soft returns are stored in the WordStar program, so that if you should later need to insert or delete text from a line ending in a soft return, you would be able to reformat the line automatically with the ^B paragraph reform command.

SOFTWARE Programs that instruct the computer how to interpret your commands from the keyboard, and to act accordingly, are called by the general term software; for example, WordStar, C-BASIC, and dBase III, are all software programs.

STAT This is another CP/M function, but like PIP it is not built-in; you will see it listed in the directory as STAT.COM. When you type STAT (short for statistics) you will be told how much space, in kilobytes, remains on the logged disk drive. You can see the space left on another drive by typing STAT B: for example; if you type STAT *.* you will see a list of files in alphabetical order with details of how many Kbytes each file occupies. *See also* CHKDSK—the MS-DOS version.

SYSGEN This CP/M program lets you add system tracks to your floppy disks so that you can boot from them. It does not destroy data on the disk when you add the tracks, so you can do this any time, even to a disk on which you have stored programs. In MS-DOS you can format a disk and add a system to it simultaneously. The command FORMAT B:/S would format the disk in drive B and add the system tracks to it. Remember that formatting the disk removes anything stored on it, so only do this to a blank disk or to a disk containing old data you wish to reuse.

SYSTEM DISK This is a disk that has an operating system loaded on its system tracks: you can only boot up your computer from a system disk.

TRACKS The floppy disk surface is divided into concentric rings or tracks when you format it. Data is stored according to the arrangement of tracks and sectors on the surface.

TYPE The TYPE command is another of the built-in CP/M and MS-DOS commands. It enables you to list on the screen the text you have entered in a file without leaving the operating system (normally you would have to call up Wordstar, for example). If you type the command: TYPE FI-LENAME.TXT and then press ^P before you press Return, you can have the listing printed out by your printer.

USER AREA The hard disk on your CP/M system may be divided into two main drives, A and B, and each of these may be further divided into 15 user areas. You can use the areas simply to separate the types of program you are using, or if more than one person is using the computer for business purposes, then it is a good idea to allot particular user areas to each person. *See also* PARTITION.

UTILITIES This term describes the built in functions in CP/M or MS-DOS that perform various housekeeping jobs around your system: Rename, Erase, and so on.

WARM BOOT When you press ^C (after changing disks in the floppy disk drive, for example), some internal parameters of your system are reset. Unlike a cold boot, it does not reload the operating system and so does not destroy the contents of memory.

WORD WRAP In word processing you do not have to press Return at the end of each line; the built in word wrap function uses the information about margins and line length and does this for you automatically.

WORKING DISK This is the disk normally containing the programs, such as Wordstar and MailMerge, that you boot up from and use every day, in drive A. You should use a separate data disk in drive B. It is good practice to keep your data and programs on different drives, even on a hard disk.

WORKING DRIVE   *See* LOGGED DRIVE.

Index